Chinese Antitrust Exceptionalism

Chinese Antitrust Exceptionalism

How the Rise of China Challenges
Global Regulation

ANGELA HUYUE ZHANG

OXFORD
UNIVERSITY PRESS

OXFORD
UNIVERSITY PRESS

Great Clarendon Street, Oxford, OX2 6DP,
United Kingdom

Oxford University Press is a department of the University of Oxford.
It furthers the University's objective of excellence in research, scholarship,
and education by publishing worldwide. Oxford is a registered trade mark of
Oxford University Press in the UK and in certain other countries

© Angela Huyue Zhang 2021

The moral rights of the author have been asserted

First Edition published in 2021

Impression: 3

Published in the United States of America by Oxford University Press
198 Madison Avenue, New York, NY 10016, United States of America

British Library Cataloguing in Publication Data

Data available

Library of Congress Control Number: 2020944062

ISBN 978–0–19–882656–9

DOI: 10.1093/oso/9780198826569.001.0001

Printed and bound by
CPI Group (UK) Ltd, Croydon, CR0 4YY

To Richard A. Posner

Preface

It had been almost three months since Hong Kong closed all its schools due to the coronavirus outbreak. And my five-year-old son was bored to tears. I decided that I needed to find something to keep him busy. An idea flashed through my mind when my publisher sent me an email asking for thoughts on my book cover.

'Alan, would you like to design the cover for my book?' I asked.

Alan looked at me with a twinkle in his eyes, 'What is your book about?'

It suddenly dawned on me that a five-year-old could not even begin to fathom the word 'antitrust'. How would I describe it? I tried by responding:

> 'Well, there were two kids on the playground, one called Europe and the other called America. Suddenly, a new kid called China came along and wanted to join the game. But this game was unfamiliar to China, and she played it according to a different set of rules. This annoyed the other two kids and they decided to square up to her.'

> 'Oh, that's easy-peasy. I can do it!' he exclaimed. Alan was very excited about his new project.

As someone who had only taken two drawing lessons, Alan appeared to have underestimated the challenge. And so had I, when I first conceived the idea of the book.

Almost four years ago, I approached Oxford University Press with the idea of writing a book detailing how China's unprecedented rise would pose challenges to the global antitrust regulatory order. Long before China adopted its Anti-Monopoly Law in 2007, the United States and the European Union had already established the global rules and norms of antitrust regulation. Despite this, China did not shy away from making decisions that were often considered to deviate from existing international standards. China resembles that new kid on the playground: not only has it developed as a new antitrust regulator but also as a foreign target for antitrust regulation. In recent years, Chinese companies' ambitious forays into Western markets have created unease among Western regulators, making them question whether their existing regulatory framework is enough to deal with Chinese firms. Clearly, legislators in the United States and the European Union did not have the Chinese state-led economy in mind when designing their antitrust regulatory frameworks.

As I embarked on this project, I realized that I was not just writing a book about antitrust law but also about Chinese politics, economic institutions, and international relations. Moreover, the fast-changing legal and political developments that have occurred over the past four years have delayed and complicated the process of writing this book. After maintaining a decade-long tripartite enforcement structure, the three former Chinese antitrust enforcement agencies were consolidated in 2018, forming a brand new agency housed under a newly created central ministry called the State Administration for Market Supervision. Since bureaucratic politics played a crucial role in driving antitrust enforcement in its first decade, I decided that it was important to elaborate on this new enforcement structure and its implications for Chinese antitrust enforcement in the foreseeable future. Meanwhile, Donald Trump's ascendency to the Presidency of the United States has had an indirect impact on Chinese antitrust policy as the Chinese government has responded in kind to US trade and legal sanctions by flexing its antitrust regulatory muscles. At present the Chinese legislature is proposing changes to the Anti-Monopoly Law to increase its sanctioning power in order to boost China's extraterritorial regulatory capacity.

Aside from these fluid legal and institutional developments, the difficulty of writing this book has been compounded by the fact that it covers antitrust enforcement across three major antitrust jurisdictions, China, the European Union, and the United States. In recent years, foreign regulators have tightened their scrutiny over Chinese firms. In 2016, the EU's antitrust regulator made a startling decision, declaring that it would treat all Chinese firms in the energy sector as a single entity for the purpose of merger assessments. This alarmed many practitioners and businesses who feared that the European Union might soon group all Chinese state-owned firms as a one 'China, Inc'. Two years later, the US Supreme Court intervened in a high-profile export cartel case concerning a group of Chinese vitamin C manufacturers who argued that they had been compelled by the Chinese government to fix prices.

Despite these complications, my original framework has remained the same, and the new developments have in effect strengthened my thesis, namely that there exists inevitable friction between China and the global antitrust regulatory order. Indeed, even though this book focuses on antitrust, it is essentially a book about globalization and the ineluctable conflicts resulting from China's rise. Not coincidentally, the reason I chose this topic was highly pertinent to my own personal background. I, myself, am a quintessential product of globalization. Born and raised in mainland China, I received my first law degree from Peking University in China. I then went on to study in America, receiving both my master and doctoral degrees from the University of Chicago. Upon graduation, I practised law for five years at several international law firms based in New York, London, and Brussels. I taught in London and am now enjoying academic life in Hong Kong. These overseas experiences and the multicultural exposure gave me the opportunity to study China from a variety of different angles. As both an insider and outsider, I hope to provide an in-depth analysis of Chinese antitrust exceptionalism that is honest, balanced, and equitable.

Throughout the writing of this book, I was fortunate to have received kind support and help from many friends and colleagues. First and foremost, I owe an immense intellectual debt to my doctoral advisor, Richard Posner, whose pragmatic legal approach has had a profound influence on my scholarship. Years after I graduated from the University of Chicago, he continued to read and comment on much of my work. It was his friendship and unwavering support that solidified my pursuit as an independent legal scholar. I am also grateful to my former professors at the University of Chicago, particularly Lisa Bernstein and Saul Levmore, who inspired me to pursue a career in academia. I owe a great debt of gratitude to Harry First, Eleanor Fox, Curtis Milhaupt, Daniel Sokol, Spencer Waller, and Wentong Zheng, all of whom have generously offered pertinent comments and criticisms regarding my work in this area. Many antitrust practitioners, scholars, and government officials in China, too many to name here, have candidly shared their insights into antitrust practice with me over the years. My interactions with them have been a source of lasting inspiration for me.

I was fortunate to start my academic career at King's College London and am grateful to my former colleagues, particularly Allison Jones, Bill Kovacic, Christopher Townley, and Richard Whish for providing me with a stimulating research environment in antitrust law. My good fortune continued at the University of Hong Kong, and I would especially like to thank my colleagues Thomas Cheng, Xin He, and Hualing Fu for their insightful comments on individual chapters of this book. My research assistants Zahra Kamaruddin, Carissa Ma, and Jonathan Yeung provided me with excellent support throughout this process. I received indispensable help from Anu Bradford, who gave me brilliant advice during the final stages of this book. My husband Alex Yang, a business school professor, read the entire manuscript with a sharp and critical eye, even though antitrust is far from his field of research. I wrote a significant portion of the book during the challenging time of COVID-19. I thank my angels

Alan and Alice for their complete cooperation, during quarantine and school closures, without which I would never have been able to finish this book.

Certain portions of this book rely on my own previous work. In particular, Chapter 3 draws on my published article 'The Antitrust Paradox of China Inc', 50 N. Y. U. J. Int'l L. & Pol. 159 (2017) to which I have made substantive revisions, and Chapter 4 is a revised version of 'Strategic Comity', 44 Yale J. Int'l L. 281 (2019). I was able to take the important step to develop this book thanks to the funding from the University Grants Committee of Hong Kong. I would like to acknowledge the support of my General Research Fund grant 'Antitrust and the Rise of China: An Institutional Analysis' (Project No 17603918).

Last but not least, I would like to thank my editor Imogen Hill at Oxford University Press, who has been extremely patient with me and has walked me tirelessly through the essentials of book publishing.

The morning after I delegated the task of designing a book cover to Alan, I saw him standing in front of our bookshelf, searching for inspiration to help his project. My son is pretty serious about keeping his commitments, I thought to myself. So I asked him:

'Alan, now the three kids are fighting with each other, do you think they will ever be friends and play together again in the future?'

'Of course!' Alan said confidently.

'Why do you think so?' I asked.

'Well, kids fight all the time. After they fight, they play together again', Alan replied.

Alan was obviously not thinking about game theory when he replied. But I think he is right, as I will show you in the following chapters. And I remain hopeful that China, Europe, and the United States will eventually reach a compromise and 'play together again'.

Hong Kong
July 2020

Contents

List of Abbreviations

AIC	Regional Office of State Administration for Industry and Commerce
ALL	Administrative Litigation Law
AMC	Anti-Monopoly Commission
AML	Anti-Monopoly Law
APE	Government Shareholding Agency (France)
API	active pharmaceutical ingredients
AQSIQ	State General Administration of Quality Supervision, Inspection, and Quarantine
AUCL	Anti-Unfair Competition Law
CEO	chief executive officer
CFIUS	Committee on Foreign Investment of the United States
CFO	chief financial officer
CGN	China General Nuclear Power Corporation
CIC	China Investment Corporation
EUMR	EU Merger Regulation
FCPA	Foreign Corruption Practice Act
FDA	Food and Drug Administration
FDI	foreign direct investment
FGC	Fujian Grand Chip
G	gigabyte
GATT	General Agreement on Tariffs and Trade
GSK	GlaxoSmithKlein
ISP	Internet service provider
ITC	International Trade Commission
MIIT	Ministry of Industry and Information Technology
MOE	mixed ownership enterprise
MOFCOM	Ministry of Commerce
NDRC	National Development and Reform Commission
NOC	national oil company
OECD	Organisation for Economic Co-operation and Development
OFAC	Office of Foreign Assets Control
P&G	Proctor & Gamble
POE	privately owned enterprise
PPE	personal protective equipment
PPTN	People's Post and Telecommunication News
REN	Redes Energeticas Nacionais
RPM	resale price maintenance

SAIC	State Administration for Industry and Commerce
SAIC-GM	Shanghai Automotive Industry Company and General Motors
SAMR	State Administration and Market Supervision
SASAC	State-owned Assets Supervision and Administration
SEC	Securities Exchange Commission
SEP	standard essential patents
SOE	state-owned enterprises
SPC	State Planning Commission
SPC	Supreme People's Court
SQSIQ	Administration of Quality Supervision, Inspection and Quarantine
SWF	Sovereign Wealth Fund
TFEU	Treaty on the Functioning of the European Union
TVEs	township and village enterprises
VER	voluntary export restraints
VIE	variable interest entity
WTO	World Trade Organization

Chinese Antitrust Exceptionalism

In early 2020, the outbreak of COVID-19 brought the Chinese economy to a standstill. Most Asian economies took an immediate hit from the drastic fall in Chinese demand, and global supply chains rooted in China were also disrupted. The world was quickly learning just how much it depended on China. As one economist put it: 'When China sneezes, the rest of the world catches a cold.'[1] China's emergence as a global superpower is often perceived in the West as a threat to the liberal world order, with Western democracies debating whether to engage further with or contain the country. Parallel to its surging political and economic influence, China is quietly posing a fundamental challenge to the normative fabric of the global legal order. As China and its trading partners become embroiled in a growing number of disputes across various fronts, the consequences of China's rise and its accession to the global trade rules have become the subject of vast commentary.[2] Despite the increasing interest, there has yet to be a comprehensive and in-depth study of China's impact on global antitrust policy, an area of law that could become a source of friction in trade. This book is designed to fill this gap.

Around the world, antitrust laws refer to rules and regulations that have been designed to promote vigorous competition and protect consumers from anticompetitive business practices. For multinational companies, antitrust has become part and parcel of their global compliance routine. A typical merger between two large companies requires approval from not just the countries where they are headquartered but also a whole host of other jurisdictions in which the merger has triggered the notification thresholds. A cartel formed by a group of leading suppliers would not only be investigated in their home jurisdictions, but also in the numerous countries to which these firms have supplied their products. Similarly, abusive conduct of a dominant firm can affect customers or suppliers overseas and prompt investigations by foreign antitrust

---

[1] Stephen S. Roach, *When China Sneezes*, PROJECT SYNDICATE (24 Feb. 2020). Many of the footnote references in this book are online materials and they can be easily accessible online.

[2] Many trade law scholars have explored this question in the context of global trade orders. *See* e.g., Mark Wu, *The 'China, Inc.' Challenge to Global Trade Governance*, 57 HAR. INT'L L. J. 284 (2016); Wentong Zheng, *Trade Law's Responses to the Rise of China*, 34 BERKELEY J. INT'L L. 109 (2016).

Chinese Antitrust Exceptionalism. Angela Huyue Zhang, Oxford University Press (2021). © Angela Huyue Zhang.
DOI: 10.1093/oso/9780198826569.003.0001

authorities. With the proliferation of antitrust laws in emerging and developing economies over the last two decades, large multinational companies are facing an uphill battle in terms of navigating an increasingly complex regulatory maze, constantly tweaking or modifying products and services to suit the requirements of different antitrust regimes.

This is invariably the case as no centralized antitrust governance exists at the global level. International lawyers once proposed the construction of a global antitrust regime with a supranational enforcement agency or framework, but their proposals were ultimately aborted.[3] Despite a lack of central governance, many of the regimes that latterly adopted antitrust laws have taken their cues from the United States or the European Union (EU), the world's two most advanced antitrust regimes. With their long-standing history of antitrust legislation and vast experience in enforcement, the two jurisdictions have generously offered legislative and enforcement advice as well as assistance to other nations striving to adopt their own antitrust laws,[4] and in doing so, these veteran regimes have managed to shape the enforcement approach of the nations they assisted. Most antitrust lawyers are accustomed to the fact that the United States and the European Union are setting the antitrust enforcement trends that other jurisdictions simply seem to emulate.

And then there is China. After fourteen years of wrangling and debate, China began implementing its Anti-Monopoly Law (AML) in 2008. Among the world's greatest economic powers, China brings up the rear in adopting modern antitrust law. Although Chinese antitrust law closely resembles that of the European Union, a reflection upon China's track record in antitrust enforcement over the past decade reveals many of its idiosyncrasies. Despite being a relatively new antitrust regime, China has not hesitated to impose harsh antitrust remedies on offshore merger transactions and intervene aggressively in business practices, departing from the usual approach of Western antitrust authorities. This is especially true after 2013, when China ramped up

---

[3] *See* Eleanor M. Fox, *Toward World Antitrust and Market Access*, 91 AM. J. INT'L L. 1 (1997); Andrew T. Guzman, *Antitrust and International Regulatory Federalism*, 76 N. Y. U. L. REV. 1142 (2001); Anu Bradford, *International Antitrust Negotiations and the False Hope of the WTO*, 48 HAR. INT'L L. J. 383 (2007).

[4] William E. Kovacic, *Merger Enforcement in Transitions: Antitrust Controls on Acquisitions in Emerging Economies*, 66 U. CINCINNATI L. REV. 1071 (1998); David Gerber, *Constructing Competition Law in China: The Potential Value of European and U.S. Experience*, 3 WASHINGTON UNIV. GLOBAL STUD. L. REV. 315 (2004); MARK WILLIAMS, COMPETITION LAW IN CHINA, HONG KONG AND TAIWAN (2005); Michael S. Gal, *The 'Cut and Paste' of Article 82 of the EC Treaty in Israel: Conditions for A Successful Transplant*, 9 EUROPEAN J. L. REFORM 467 (2007); William E. Kovacic, *The United States and Its Future Influence on Global Competition Policy*, 22 GEORGE MASON L. REV. 1157 (2015); Anu Bradford et al., *The Global Dominance of European Competition Law Over American Antitrust Law*, J. EMPIRICAL LEGAL STU. 731 (2019).

enforcement on anticompetitive conduct. Businesses, sometimes confounded and rattled by the Chinese government's pervasive intervention, complained of protectionism, unequal treatment, and the lack of due process. Yet China seems confident in straying from the beaten path. With a vast and dynamic market, China is a jurisdiction that few multinational companies can afford to ignore. This is why even though foreign firms have made mounting complaints to their respective chambers of commerce and governments, few have sought to launch a formal complaint against Chinese antitrust agencies in court. In most cases, disgruntled businesses paid their fines, made the necessary adjustments to their business strategy in China, and moved on.

But this is only part of the story. China is not only exceptional as an antitrust regulator but also as a target of antitrust regulation. In addition to being the second largest recipient of foreign direct investment (FDI) and a principal importer, China is the world's largest exporter and one of the leading outward investors. Since the Great Recession in 2008, the growing prowess of Chinese firms and their rapid expansion into overseas markets has sparked global fears that China is taking over the world.[5] These fears have been amplified by the fact that state-owned enterprises (SOEs) account for the lion's share of FDI from China. In recent years, Chinese SOEs' swift expansion into Europe has raised the eyebrows of antitrust regulators. SOEs are not new to Europe, but the sheer scale of Chinese state ownership and the Chinese government's pervasive control of its economy have got on the nerves of European policy-makers. EU competition enforcers, who had never before encountered SOEs with such intricate yet opaque ties to their government, have delved deeply into the SOEs' ownership structures and are contemplating to treat all Chinese SOEs as part of a 'China, Inc.' However, following such an approach will have enormous implications for future antitrust cases. In fact, it may even jeopardize the Commission's jurisdiction over cases involving the mergers and cartels between Chinese firms.

Across the Atlantic, Chinese companies have suffered the same fate. A number of Chinese manufacturers, coordinated by government-sponsored trade associations, have had to grapple with successive private lawsuits and hefty fines for operating export cartels in the United States. Unbeknownst to many Americans, the United States relies heavily on China for the supply of pharmaceutical drugs as well as the critical ingredients and raw materials

---

[5] Angela Huyue Zhang, *Foreign Direct Investment from China: Sense and Sensibility*, 34 Nw J. Int'l L. & Bus. 395 (2014).

needed to make them.[6] The latest figures estimate that almost 97 per cent of the antibiotics and 90 per cent of the vitamin C used in America are now made in China.[7] Meanwhile, 80 per cent of the active pharmaceutical ingredients, the basic components used to manufacture drugs in America, rely on imports from China and India.[8] Experts have warned that as Chinese manufacturers gain greater control over the US supply of drugs, they might collude to raise prices to exploit American consumers.[9] The vitamin C cartel formed in the early 2000s is a case in point where Chinese manufacturers were found to have hiked up their prices of vitamin C products almost six-fold during this period.[10] Chinese exporters did not deny the allegations of price coordination, instead defended themselves on the grounds that they had been compelled by the Chinese government to do so in order to avoid potential anti-dumping charges. In a similar fashion to European regulators, US judges, including those on the Supreme Court bench, have struggled to determine the extent to which the Chinese government intervenes in Chinese exports, especially when confronted with somewhat conflicting and inconsistent factual circumstances. When a Chinese central government ministry came to the rescue of these Chinese firms by submitting an amicus brief boldly insisting that it had forced price-fixing practices among exporters, further controversy arose as to how much deference a US court should give to statements presented by a foreign government. The resolution of such cases, therefore, hinges not only on the logic of law, but also on politics.

In parallel, as Western countries become increasingly alarmed of China's rise, there is a looming danger that such conflict might morph into antagonism and political catastrophe. Take, for example, the trade war that erupted between the United States and China in 2018. In addition to the imposition of high tariffs on Chinese goods, the Trump Administration has been aggressively prosecuting and sanctioning leading Chinese technology firms and their executives. However, by leveraging the administration's almost unbridled prosecutorial discretion in sanctions law as bargaining chips in trade negotiations, President Trump is setting a bad example for China to follow. In retaliation, China is wielding its antitrust law strategically to demonstrate its

---

[6] ROSEMARY GIBSON & JANARDAN PRASAD SINGH, CHINA RX: EXPOSING THE RISKS OF AMERICA'S DEPENDENCE ON CHINA FOR MEDICINE (2018).

[7] Yanzhong Huang, *The Coronavirus Outbreak Could Disrupt the U.S. Drug Supply*, COUNCIL ON FOREIGN RELATIONS (5 Mar. 2020).

[8] Id.

[9] U.S.–China Economic & Security Review Commission, Hearing on Exploring the Growing U.S. Reliance on China's Biotech and Pharmaceutical Products, Written Testimony of Rosemary Gilson (31 July 2019).

[10] Id.

own extraterritorial regulatory capacity. The two sides are now locked in a dangerous race of regulatory competition, leaving a disastrous outcome to chance.

In this book, I focus on how Chinese exceptionalism, as shown in both the way China regulates and the way China is regulated, poses challenges to the existing global antitrust regulatory order, one that is dominated by the pre-existing standards and norms set by the advanced regimes such as the United States and the European Union. It is well-known that much of the Western world has long been chafed by China's distinctness in the global political economy. Politically, China is an authoritarian country with a one-party system. Ideologically, China is committed to communism, which has traditionally perceived law as an instrument of the 'Party-state'. Economically, China embraces a form of state capitalism that allows the state to play a central role in the economy despites decades of market reform. Institutionally, China lacks checks and balances, and its judiciary is too weak to counteract abusive administrative power. Concurrently, the Chinese state is so vast and complex that it is often difficult to obtain a coherent and accurate account of the country. As will be illustrated, Chinese antitrust exceptionalism in fact stems from the inherent contradictions present in the Chinese regime, an observation that runs throughout this book.

To begin, political power is highly concentrated in the hands of the Chinese Communist Party (the Party), which has further tightened its grip over various aspects of the Chinese society under the leadership of President Xi Jinping. But China is no longer ideological except in the pro forma way.[11] And the Party's renewed emphasis on Party control and discipline reveals more of its insecurity than its strength. Moreover, despite its appearances, the China state is hardly a monolith. Instead, power is fragmented within the Chinese bureaucracy. At the central level, different ministries with overlapping functions and divergent missions are relentlessly competing with each other for power, influence, and prestige, as demonstrated in Chapters 1 and 2. At the regional level, local governments engage in intense rivalry to achieve higher GDP growth, resulting in perennial local protectionism, as elaborated in Chapters 1, 3, and 4.

Second, large Chinese companies with ambitious expansion programmes overseas are often deemed part of a massive 'China Inc.' that is belligerently advancing the Party's objectives. But in reality, the Party is constantly struggling to strike a balance between political control and market efficiency. After all, the Party's legitimacy depends on its ability to deliver consistent economic

[11] Bilahari Kausikan, *China's Zealous 'Wolf Warrior' Diplomacy Highlights Both Beijing's Power and Insecurity*, SOUTH CHINA MORNING POST (4 June 2020).

growth. In order to achieve this, the Party needs to delegate significant autonomy to Chinese SOEs to incentivize them to become efficient competitors,
as elaborated in Chapter 3. This delegation, though, comes at a cost as agency
problems become rampant among these corporate behemoths, as observed in
the same chapter. And contrary to the popular belief that Chinese SOEs are
managed under one roof, they in fact belong to different levels of the Chinese
government in different regions. With each local government vying to prop up
its own champions to increase local employment and tax revenue, this results
in intense competition among domestic firms and chronic overcapacity problems, as will be illustrated in Chapters 3 and 4.

As such, it would require the careful consideration of extra-legal and institutional factors beyond antitrust law itself for businesses and lawyers to understand the Chinese regulatory outcome, and for foreign policy-makers to
formulate an optimal regulatory response to Chinese companies' overseas
conduct. This is not to trivialize law, rather it is to acknowledge the limits of
the law. No law, however refined, can anticipate all contingencies and metic-
ulously spell out the rules and procedures to be followed in every conceivable
circumstance.[12]

Recognizing the law's incompleteness first requires us to take a closer look
at the actors responsible for enforcing and interpreting the law. In the case of
Chinese antitrust enforcement, the main actors are administrative agencies
who enforce the law but are subject to few challenges from the judiciary. To
understand why these agencies do what they do, we need to understand their
incentives and the constraints they face. China's vast bureaucratic machine,
ranging from the central government to local authorities, handles different
regulatory aspects of a company from the cradle to the grave. Despite its importance, much of the inner workings of the Chinese bureaucracy largely remain a mystery to outsiders. This book therefore represents an intensive effort
to unpack the black box of the Chinese regulatory process and the incentives
of the different actors involved. By closely examining the roles of bureaucratic
politics, administrative discretion, and use of reputational sanctions exercised during Chinese antitrust enforcement, I hope to provide readers with a
window into the private ordering of Chinese antitrust compliance. Antitrust is
certainly just a small part of a firm's regulatory compliance practice. However,
this book is not simply about the law per se but rather the incentives of Chinese

---

[12] AVINASH K. DIXIT, THE MAKING OF ECONOMIC POLICY: A TRANSACTION-COST POLITICS
PERSPECTIVE 20 (1998).

law enforcers and the underlying institutional factors shaping the enforcement of the many facets of business regulation in China.

Recognizing the law's incompleteness would also require us to discern new contingencies not foreseen by those who drafted the law. Indeed, antitrust law, originally formulated to tackle abusive monopolies in the market economy, was not constructed with the nature of Chinese SOEs in mind. But one of the most distinctive features of Chinese state capitalism is precisely the central role played by the SOEs, many of whom are deemed national champions and are increasingly active in the global markets.[13] In fact, to survive and thrive in the Chinese institutional environment, Chinese firms, regardless of their ownership structure, need to 'capture' the state.[14] In doing so, they gain special advantages from the authorities and return such favours by aligning themselves with the interests, goals, and priorities of the government.[15] For instance, while Chinese SOEs have special privileges and enjoy generous subsidies, they are also subject to varying degrees of political control and supervision by the Party.[16] Although successful private businesses such as Huawei, Alibaba, and Tencent have emerged in new technological and innovation markets without strong SOE incumbents, they too are not immune from political influence. As there are many grey areas of doing business in China, the Chinese government, through its expansive and powerful bureaucratic departments, can take any business hostage through various legal or extra-legal means. Successful private entrepreneurs in China are well aware of the importance of forging close links with the government through institutional or informal channels.[17] Such intricate connections between businesses and the government therefore make it extremely difficult to assess the independence of Chinese firms. But at the same time, China's highly decentralized economic structure and ensuing local protectionism have led to chronic problems of overcapacity, resulting in fierce competition among Chinese exporters and extremely low prices in overseas markets. This paradoxical feature of the Chinese economy presents a serious predicament for antitrust regulation, which often requires a clear delineation

---

[13] Li-Wen Lin & Curtis J. Milhaupt, *We Are The (National) Champions: Understanding The Mechanisms of State Capitalism in China*, 65 STAN. L. REV. 697 (2013); YASHENG HUANG, CAPITALISM WITH CHINESE CHARACTERISTICS: ENTREPRENEURSHIP AND THE STATE (2008).

[14] Curtis J. Milhaupt & Wentong Zheng, *Beyond Ownership: State Capitalism and Chinese Firm*, 103 GEO. L. J. (2015).

[15] Id. at 688.

[16] Zhuang Liu & Angela Huyue Zhang, *Ownership and Political Control: Evidence from Charter Amendments*, 60 INT'L REV. L. & ECON. (2019).

[17] BRUCE J. DICKSON, READ CAPITALISTS IN CHINA: THE PARTY, PRIVATE ENTREPRENEURS, AND PROSPECTS FOR POLITICAL CHANGE (2003); BRUCE J. DICKSON, WEALTH INTO POWER: THE COMMUNIST PARTY'S EMBRACE OF CHINA'S PRIVATE SECTOR (2008); SCOTT KENNEDY, THE BUSINESS OF LOBBYING IN CHINA (2005).

of a firm's boundaries at the outset. It also puts Chinese firms in a vulnerable position: if they sell at a highly competitive price, they could be subject to antidumping duties in importing countries; if they coordinate to raise prices, they could be challenged for antitrust violations.

Viewed in this light, globalization has not only brought about economic prosperity for China and its trading partners but it has also engendered inevitable conflicts between China and the rest of the world. As economist Dani Rodrik has presciently warned us, we need to face the uncomfortable truth that we cannot simultaneously pursue democracy, national determination, and economic globalization.[18] At the time of writing, Sino-US relations are encountering the most daunting challenges since the two countries first established formal diplomatic ties almost forty years ago. After Trump's ascendency to US Presidency, the US government launched a series of attacks targeting Chinese trade policies, accusing China of using opaque administrative approvals to force the transfer of technology to Chinese businesses.[19] Some of the cases elaborated in this book may lend support to these allegations. As Chinese antirust agencies belligerently press forward with antitrust enforcement, these actions have also often brought about outcomes that benefit domestic industries at the expense of foreign firms. But this interpretation of my findings obscures a more fundamental issue with Chinese law enforcement. As I will elucidate in this book, instead of a top-down process where the central government sets out clear goals and priorities of enforcement, Chinese antitrust enforcement is largely a bottom-up process driven by bureaucratic departments with divergent missions, cultures, and structures. As such, the incentives and constraints faced by Chinese antitrust agencies have significantly affected the type of cases that are brought, the manner in which the agencies coordinate with each other, the approach that is taken to tackle the cases, and, most importantly, the final regulatory outcome.

Understanding this point is crucial before one starts to ponder solutions to ease the current Sino-US conflict. Since the flare-up of the trade war, the Trump Administration has been placing pressure on China to amend many of its national laws to enhance legal protection for US businesses in its jurisdiction. But such a legalistic approach misses the point and does little to resolve the issue.[20] The biggest challenge facing US businesses is not the law itself.

---

[18] DANI RODRIK, THE GLOBALIZATION PARADOX: WHY GLOBAL MARKETS, STATES, AND DEMOCRACY CAN'T COEXIST xviii (2011).

[19] White House, *How China's Economic Aggression Threatens the Technologies and Intellectual Property of the United States and the World*, June 2018.

[20] Angela Huyue Zhang, *The U.S.–China Trade Negotiation: A Contract Theory Perspective*, 51 GEO. J. INT'L L.809 (2020).

As we see in the case of Chinese antitrust, even sound substantive rules that China has borrowed from advanced regimes such as the European Union and the United States can be easily undercut when the wrong legal institutions and procedures are being used to enforce them. In reality, the institutional environment and bureaucratic incentives are often the key factors resulting in biased enforcement outcomes that puts foreign businesses at a disadvantage. Instead of forcing China to rewrite its national laws, the US' top priority should be to help China promote structural reform of its bureaucracy and enhance due process in administrative enforcement.[21]

The delegation of antitrust enforcement to the National Development and Reform Commission (NDRC), one of the three former Chinese antirust agencies, is a prime example. The predecessor of the NDRC was the State Planning Commission, a supra-ministry that was very powerful during the days China was centrally planned. Over the years, the NDRC, particularly its price control departments, has seen a significant reduction in power. Hence, the agency deemed the development of antitrust as a golden opportunity to step back into the policy-making limelight. It is not surprising then, that the antitrust bureau at the NDRC prioritized its enforcement efforts in strategic industries and daily consumer goods with the goal of stabilizing prices, and also applied the same pre-emptive enforcement measures used in price supervision to coerce companies to lower prices. As such, the odd enforcement outcome we observe in Chinese antitrust enforcement is actually the product of ubiquitous interagency competition in China. Indubitably, the path dependency of institutions would imply that it is very difficult to overcome the bureaucratic inertia. But the first step of conflict resolution between China and the United States is, at the very least, to understand the root cause of the problem rather than speculating and accepting what we see on the surface.

And among all the major US complaints about Chinese trade policy, perhaps the hardest one to resolve is China's subsidies for SOEs which help these firms gain an unfair competitive advantage. The United States is not the only country to have raised its concerns over China's state-led capitalism. EU countries, led by Germany and France, are calling on Brussels to do more to level the playing field for European firms when competing with Chinese firms. In June 2020, the European Commission unveiled its proposal to revamp EU competition rules in order to tackle state-backed acquisitions from China. Evidently, the Chinese state's active intervention in the domestic economy has had a lasting impact on the ability of Chinese firms, state- or privately owned, to adapt to the

---

[21] Id. at 864-65.

regulatory requirements overseas. This will also present continuing challenges for Western policy-makers who are beginning to realize that their existing regulatory frameworks are inadequate to deal with the distinctive features of Chinese firms.

This begs the question: how can we address the conflict between China's rise and the global antitrust order? There is no quick and easy fix, as such tensions, as laid out extensively in this book, are deeply rooted in the incompatibility between the Chinese political economy and the Western liberal order. At the same time, there has been no sign that China will converge with or adapt to Western values and standards. However, I remain hopeful about the prospect of China's integration into the global antitrust regime. My optimism stems precisely from the dual challenges arising from the two dimensions of Chinese antitrust exceptionalism. As Chinese antitrust agencies hold foreign businesses hostage through the aggressive enforcement of antitrust law, foreign regulators can do the same by holding Chinese firms hostage, not necessarily through antitrust but also via other regulatory rules such as investment and trade. As I will illustrate, both the European Union and the United States are already heading in that direction. It is this reciprocal exchange of hostages that gives me hope for a peaceful resolution of the conflict. Of course, there is much uncertainty about how the situation will develop and whether the conflict might worsen in the future. However, as game theorists have long discovered about the magic of repeated interactions, in the absence of central governance, repetition can act as an enforcement mechanism enabling the emergence of a cooperative outcome.[22] Thus, if we are patient and far-sighted enough, peace will be possible, and the world will eventually find the solution for a live-and-let-live approach to accommodate China's rise.[23]

To help readers navigate the different parts of the book, the following is a summary of the principal findings of each chapter laid out in the book.

Part I: How China Regulates

Part I explores one dimension of Chinese antitrust exceptionalism by delving deeply into the political and legal institutions that have created the many idiosyncrasies of the current Chinese antitrust regulatory regime. Using a bottom-up perspective, I will show how bureaucratic incentives and constraints shaped

---

[22] Robert J. Aumann, *War And Peace*, NOBEL PRIZE LECTURE, 8 Dec. 2015.
[23] ROBERT AXELROD, THE EVOLUTION OF COOPERATION (2016).

Chinese antitrust enforcement outcomes during the first decade of its implementation. As foreign firms were frequent targets of antitrust investigations in China, many of them struggled to adapt to the requirements in the Chinese regime.

Chapter 1: Bureaucratic Politics behind the Rise of Antitrust

This chapter presents the first intrinsic facet of Chinese antitrust exceptionalism by showing how Chinese antitrust enforcement is driven by bureaucratic incentives while being constrained by the formal and the tacit rules of the bureaucracy. Bureaucratic politics, though ubiquitous to any government, warrants special attention in the Chinese context. Chinese antitrust agencies are seldom subject to judicial scrutiny, and as a result, have monopolized the administrative enforcement of the AML. Similar to their European counterparts, Chinese antitrust officials from the central government are policy entrepreneurs who have promoted the rapid expansion of antitrust enforcement. The severe sanctions that can be imposed under the AML give high-powered incentives to both government enforcers who want to expand their policy control and businesses who wish to use the law strategically to sabotage rivals. Furthermore, the three former Chinese antitrust agencies were not assembled from scratch but were pre-existing departments within large central ministries. Naturally, the bureaucratic mission, culture, and structure of each of these agencies had shaped their enforcement agendas. Much of the discussion revolves around the NDRC as the agency stood out as the most aggressive institution among the three former agencies. Its rich record of enforcement also allows us to assess the link between these institutional factors and enforcement pattern in depth. In 2018, the three agencies were merged into a single bureau under a newly created central ministry. Looking ahead, I will elaborate on the continuing challenges faced by this new agency, including the bureaucratic hierarchy, the power fragmentation, and the regional inertia.

Chapter 2: Regulatory Hostage-taking and Shaming

This chapter presents the second intrinsic facet of Chinese antitrust exceptionalism by illustrating how resourceful Chinese antitrust agencies can leverage their regulatory discretion as well as the media to overcome their bureaucratic and capacity constraints to advance difficult cases. Despite mounting complaints against Chinese antitrust authorities for the lack of transparency and due processes as expounded upon in Chapter 1, few companies have appealed the enforcement decisions. Instead, many businesses under investigation have quickly admitted guilt and voluntarily reduced prices, displaying an unusual level of cooperation. As it turns out, the primary reason holding firms back from defying the administrative authorities is not necessarily the perceived low probability of success in a Chinese court but rather the high transaction costs associated with such an appeal. Chinese antitrust authorities possess wide discretion over enforcement and can apply it proactively to entire firms to settle the cases. Moreover, each of the three former Chinese antitrust agencies and the incumbent agency is nested within a large central ministry that oversees various aspects of market regulation. Firms operating in China, whether foreign or domestic, are likely to continue to interact with these agencies and their host ministries in the future. Businesses therefore avoid taking an aggressive and adversarial approach for fear of future retribution. In addition, Chinese government agencies are adept at using media strategies during enforcement. In several high-profile cases, the antitrust bureau at the NDRC deftly mobilized public sentiments through the state media, strategically shaming firms to prevent defiance of their orders, and relentlessly suppressing experts from voicing opinions that might threaten the legitimacy of its measures. In so doing, the NDRC was able to overcome its capacity and bureaucratic constraints, thereby quickly cementing its reputation as an astute and forceful regulator.

Part II: How China Is Regulated

Part II examines the other dimension of the Chinese antitrust exceptionalism by detailing the antitrust challenges that Chinese firms experience overseas. In this Part, I will discuss the ways in which foreign regulators have been investigating Chinese firms' ambitious overseas forays and the latter's struggles adapting to Western regulatory compliance. And while the Chinese political and legal institutions are the primary root causes of Chinese exceptionalism as elaborated in Part I, the conflicts we observe in Part II stem from the distinct structure of the Chinese political economy where, even though economic governance is highly decentralized, the government plays a pervasive role in directing economic activities of Chinese firms.

Chapter 3: The EU Merger Probe into China, Inc.

This chapter examines a third facet of Chinese antitrust exceptionalism: when EU antitrust regulators apply a legalistic approach to scrutinize Chinese firms' acquisitions, they are faced with a dilemma as this method could lead to the paradoxical outcome of being over- and under-inclusive at the same time. Confronted with a massive flow of Chinese capital into Europe, the European Commission has subjected Chinese SOEs to increased scrutiny in recent years. In merger cases involving Chinese SOEs, the Commission has often pondered the question of how to define the boundaries of the China, Inc. Antitrust laws as developed in mature jurisdictions such as the European Union are accustomed to applying a bright-line test in assessing the independence of a SOE. But deciphering the degree of independence of Chinese SOEs is far from a black-and-white issue. Although the Chinese state has the voting power to influence SOEs, it may lack both the incentive and the ability to coordinate competition between them. As a consequence, formal corporate control by the Chinese state may only be weakly correlated with the anticompetitive effects its control could cause. Paradoxically, while the Commission's use of a bright-line test in determining company independence can cast too wide of a net, it could also allow some firms to get away with anticompetitive behaviour. The EU merger review only acts on acquisitions of controlling interest. This means that Chinese SOEs can bypass the EU antitrust scrutiny by making minority acquisitions in Europe. However, minority shareholding in rivals can still create anticompetitive effects, as abundant economic literature has demonstrated. In fact, there is a blurred line between SOEs and privately owned enterprises in China, and a Chinese SOE could escape antitrust scrutiny entirely by employing a non-controlling subsidiary as a vehicle to acquire European assets. Given this regulatory dilemma, I argue that a thoughtful response to acquisitions by Chinese SOEs necessitates a shift in regulatory focus from defining what constitutes an undertaking to understanding the effects of Chinese state ownership. I also caution against deploying competition policy too broadly when reviewing Chinese SOE acquisitions. As the EU's existing antitrust regulatory framework is not fully equipped to handle Chinese investments, it is not surprising to see that both the European Union and some of its Member States are tightening their foreign investment review to scrutinize Chinese takeovers.

Chapter 4: US Scrutiny over China's Trade Dominance

This chapter analyses a fourth facet of Chinese antitrust exceptionalism by demonstrating how China's unique economic institutions have placed Chinese exporters in a quandary: if they sell at low prices, they might violate trade law against antidumping; if they coordinate with each other to raise prices, they might violate antitrust rules against cartels. For many Americans, the COVID-19 pandemic is a wake-up call to their heavy reliance on China for essential medical supplies. In fact, Chinese dominance in some pharmaceutical markets has created conducive conditions for the formation of export cartels. The most well-known case, involving a number of Chinese vitamin C producers reached the US Supreme Court. Contrary to the Chinese SOEs' adamant claims in Europe that they are completely independent from the state, Chinese exporters said they held little price-setting power and had been compelled by the Chinese government to fix prices in order to avoid potential antidumping duties. Indeed, the persistent issue of excess capacity, which is deeply rooted in China's highly decentralized economic structure and its state-led governance model, has been the main impetus for the government to organize export cartels. Similar to the European regulators, US courts have struggled to determine the degree of independence that Chinese firms actually had. In an unprecedented move, China's Ministry of Commerce submitted an amicus brief to the US courts acknowledging its use of compulsion. This raised further issues about when to defer to a foreign government's interpretation of its own law and the proper application of the comity doctrine. The US Supreme Court ruled that even though US courts should give respectful consideration to submissions made by foreign governments, they are not bound to it. To make sense of the Supreme Court's ruling, I draw upon insights from game theory to unravel the complicated dynamics between the importing and exporting country in export cartel cases. I argue that the optimal strategy for the United States is contingent on the strategy of the exporting country, whose strategy is in turn dependent on the US' strategy as well as its own domestic politics and trade policy. The optimal regulatory response thus hinges not only on antitrust law but also politics. Viewed in this light, the US Supreme Court resolved the Vitamin C case pragmatically by according a high level of deference to the executive branch. And as America's trade interests can be highly fluid, this could expose Chinese exporters to more antitrust and trade challenges in the years to come.

Part III: Regulatory Interdependence

In a departure from previous chapters, which mainly focus on Chinese antitrust exceptionalism as manifested in domestic antitrust policy, this Part will demonstrate that a close interdependence exists between the regulatory moves of the United States and those of China in terms of leveraging their extraterritorial regulatory capacity.

Chapter 5: Weaponizing Antitrust During Sino-US Tech War

This chapter examines the last facet of Chinese antitrust exceptionalism by assessing how Chinese antitrust law can be employed as a countermeasure against foreign trade sanctions. Against the backdrop of the bitter Sino-US technology war, this chapter applies game theory analysis of cooperation and conflict to examine the role of antitrust in China's tit-for-tat strategy against the aggressive US sanctions. The US executive branch has wide discretion in prosecuting foreign businesses and individuals, and has used such legal discretion strategically as an instrument of trade and foreign policy against China. China has retaliated in kind by invoking a number of regulatory measures. In particular, the Chinese antitrust authority has flexed its muscles by holding up large mergers between foreign multinationals, amending its antitrust law to allow for high monetary fines and potential criminal liabilities, and threatening to impose heavy sanctions on firms that boycott or refuse to supply key components to Chinese technology companies. As a result, the line between national security and antitrust policy, once belonging to separate spheres, has become increasingly blurred amid the growing Sino-US tensions. However, similar to other countries that have applied countermeasures against US sanctions law, China faces significant economic constraints in weaponizing its antitrust law against US businesses. Using antitrust law for geopolitical purposes will hurt China's reputation and undermine its long-term strategy of attracting foreign investors. I therefore predict that China will at most deploy its antitrust laws to fight a limited war with the United States, rather than using these laws as a weapon of mass retaliation.

For transactional lawyers who have been trained in Western antitrust standards and norms, Chinese exceptionalism in antitrust presents unprecedented challenges. China is sui generis; lawyers and policy-makers who deal with issues germane to China can no longer be complacent with the understanding of the law itself. The examples illustrated in this book show that antitrust law is never applied in a vacuum; its enforcement is deeply embedded in the institutional environments and its outcome is entangled with the underlying economic and political factors. And while this book focuses on antitrust law, it tells a far more comprehensive story about the conflicts that arise from China's integration into the global economy. It also offers a cautionary tale of the challenges that globalization presents for law and global economic order.

PART I

HOW CHINA REGULATES

This Part explores the first major dimension of Chinese antitrust exceptionalism by delving into Chinese political and legal institutions that have posed significant challenges for foreign firms operating in China. This Part consists of two chapters. In Chapter 1, I will explain the rise of Chinese antitrust regulation by analysing the incentives of the antitrust enforcers, as well as the path dependent nature of the bureaucratic performance. In Chapter 2, I will try to unravel the myth behind the paucity of appeals against antitrust agencies in China. I specifically focus on the immense administrative discretion possessed by antitrust authorities and the media strategies that they could use to advance difficult cases.

PART I
HOW CHINA REGULATES

This Part explores the first major dimension of Chinese antitrust exceptionalism: the diverging core Chinese political and legal institutions that have posed core distinctive challenges for foreign firms operating in China. This Part considers them in gross. In Chapter 1, I will explain the overall logic underlying important aspects of...

1

Bureaucratic Politics behind the Rise of Antitrust

It was Monday 4 August 2014. A bustling Mercedes-Benz sales office near the Shanghai Hongqiao International Airport was open as usual.[1] Its staff were just returning from their lunch break. Without any warning, ten stern-looking men dressed in business suits barged in. They claimed to be antitrust officials from the National Development and Reform Commission (NDRC). For the next ten hours, they scoured every inch of every room and cubicle, interrogated senior managers, proceeded to search desk drawers and files, gathered documents, and downloaded proprietary data from computers. 'Those investigators didn't take any breaks. They didn't drink tea or eat snacks or dinner', said an employee at the scene. 'It was a very serious affair.'[2]

Mercedes-Benz was not alone in its predicament. In the preceding months, several luxury car manufacturers in China were also searched. Unannounced inspections like this one, known as 'dawn raids' in the United States and Europe, form part of a common investigation tactic employed by competition authorities to investigate and probe suspected antitrust infringements. Chinese antitrust lawyers have been scrambling to educate their clients on how to cope with these unannounced visits. Every employee that could potentially be present during such a raid would require coaching on how to handle potential difficult situations. This might include anyone from the security guard to technicians on the information technology team.

The year 2014 turned out to be quite hectic and stressful for many antitrust lawyers in the country. Antitrust was a relatively new practice in China at that time, and the Anti-Monopoly Law (AML) had only been in effect for six years. In 2009, the Ministry of Commerce (MOFCOM) made global headlines after it blocked Coca-Cola's proposed acquisition of Huiyuan, a local Chinese juice manufacturer.[3] However, investigations into anti-competitive conduct, a core

---

[1] This incident was reported in newspaper. *See* Michelle Price & Norihiko Shirouzu, *Food and Flirting; How Firms Learn to Live with China Antitrust Raids*, REUTERS (11 Aug 2014).
[2] Id.
[3] Angela Huyue Zhang, *Problems in Following E.U. Competition Law: A Case Study of Coca-Cola/ Huiyuan*, 3 PEKING U. J. L. STU. 96 (2011).

Chinese Antitrust Exceptionalism. Angela Huyue Zhang, Oxford University Press (2021). © Angela Huyue Zhang. DOI: 10.1093/oso/9780198826569.003.0002

area of antitrust practice, did not gain much momentum until 2013. That year saw the Price Supervision and Anti-Monopoly Bureau, the antitrust unit of the NDRC, come to the fore of the global stage with a series of high-profile investigations into foreign multinational companies. The State Administration for Industry and Commerce (SAIC), the second agency which was responsible for conduct-related antitrust enforcement, simultaneously ramped up enforcement efforts by starting a probe into Microsoft's allegedly anticompetitive practices in China.

But the rise of Chinese antitrust regulation presents us with an apparent enigma. China is notorious for having weak legal institutions and poor law enforcement.[4] For years, the country has been heavily criticized at home and abroad for its lax and ineffective regulation in areas such as intellectual property, food safety, and the environment.[5] So what accounts for the sudden rise of active antitrust enforcement in China? In his seminal article, 'The Theory of Economic Regulation', George Stigler explains patterns of industry regulation by situating them in the context of supply and demand.[6] He proposes a 'capture theory', demonstrating how regulation is acquired from the government and employed by an industry for its own benefits. Stigler's theory offers significant insights into the emergence of rampant industry regulation, which he believes inhibits new rivals, suppresses substitutive or complementary businesses, and imposes price controls.

However, unlike general industry regulation in which a particular industry can expect to reap the lion's share of benefits from regulation, the benefits of antitrust regulation are diffused and widely distributed, making it difficult for any interest group to 'capture' the regulator. Although the capture theory cannot be directly applied to antitrust regulation, Stigler's approach 'forces a fundamental change' to the way regulation is studied.[7] Instead of treating regulation as a free good, Stigler treats regulation as 'the outcome of the forces of demand and supply'.[8] In this sense, this particular economic framework for studying regulation helps shed light on the rise of Chinese antitrust regulation.

---

[4] *See generally* STANLEY LUBMAN, BIRD IN A CAGE: LEGAL REFORM IN CHINA AFTER MAO (1999); ALBERT H. Y. CHEN, AN INTRODUCTION TO THE LEGAL SYSTEM OF PEOPLE'S REPUBLIC OF CHINA (2011); RANDALL PEERENBOOM, CHINA'S LONG MARCH TOWARD RULE OF LAW (2002).

[5] *See generally* ANDREW C. MERTHA, THE POLITICS OF PIRACY: INTELLECTUAL PROPERTY IN CONTEMPORARY CHINA (2005); John Kojiro Yasuda, *Meeting China's Food Safety Challenge*, Paulson Policy Memorandum (April 2017); XIAOYING MA & LEONARD ORTOLANO, ENVIRONMENTAL REGULATION IN CHINA: INSTITUTIONS, ENFORCEMENT AND COMPLIANCE (2000); Alex Wang, *The Search for Sustainable Legitimacy: Environmental Law and Bureaucracy in China*, 37 HAR. ENVTL. L. REV. 365 (2013).

[6] George J. Stigler, *The Theory of Economic Regulation*, 2 BELL J. ECON. & MGMT. SCI. 3 (1971).

[7] Sam Peltzman, *Toward A More General Theory of Regulation*, 19 J. L. & ECON. 211, 211 (1976).

[8] Richard A. Posner, *Theories of Economic Regulation*, 5 BELL J. ECON. & MGMT. SCI. 335, 344 (1974).

Thus far, most of the literature on China's antitrust laws has taken a 'demand perspective', adopting a 'top-down' approach which focuses on understanding the motivations behind the Chinese government's promotion of antitrust regulation. For example, Huang Yong, a prominent Chinese antitrust scholar, rationalized China's adoption of the AML by suggesting that four 'desires' were to be found in the country: 'the desire to establish a market economy, the desire to contain excessive state power, the desire to protect national interest and the desire to narrow income disparity'.[9] While Wang did not elaborate on the relative weight of each factor, he observed that 'the desire to protect national interest' seemed to have attracted staunch domestic support from both the Chinese public and government.[10] Prior to the implementation of the AML, academics and policy-makers were already aware of the cases in which foreign companies had acquired significant stakes in state-owned enterprises (SOEs) and domestic firms with well-known brands or technology firms operating in sensitive and strategic industries.[11] Fearing that foreign companies would come to control China's key industries, some policy-makers advocated using antitrust laws as a tool to protect national interests, especially in light of the 'hostility' Chinese companies faced when establishing overseas ventures.[12]

In addition to fears about national economic security, there was widespread domestic concern that foreign companies were dominating Chinese markets with superior financial and technical capabilities, especially after China's accession to the World Trade Organization (WTO) in 2001.[13] As observed by Wentong Zheng, protectionism was the crucial driving force behind the ultimate adoption of the AML.[14] He noted a sudden acceleration of the AML's drafting process after the SAIC published a report entitled 'Competition-restricting Conduct of Multinational Companies in China and Countermeasures'. In this report, the SAIC accused multinational companies such as Microsoft and Tetra Pak of anticompetitive conduct in China

---

[9] Yong Huang, *Pursuing the Second Best: The History, Momentum, and Remaining Issues of China's Anti-Monopoly Law*, 75 ANTITRUST L. J. 117, 120 (2008).

[10] Id. at 123.

[11] *See e.g.*, R. Hewitt Pate, *What I Heard in the Great Hall of the People—Realistic Expectations of Chinese Antitrust*, 75 ANTITRUST L. J. 195, 205 (2008); Thomas R. Howell et al., *China's New Anti-Monopoly Law: A Perspective from the United States*, 18 PACIFIC RIM L. & POLICY J. 53, 91–92 (2009).

[12] *See e.g.*, Huang, *supra* note 9, at 123; *see also* Pate, *supra* note 11, at 100.

[13] Yong Huang & Richean Zhiyan Li, *An Overview of Chinese Competition Policy: Between Fragmentation and Consolidation*, in CHINA'S ANTI-MONOPOLY LAW: THE FIRST FIVE YEARS 5 (Adrian Emch & David Stallibrass eds., 2013).

[14] Wentong Zheng, *Transplanting Antitrust in China: Economic Transition, Market Structure, and State Control*, 32 U. PA. J. INT'L L. 643, 718–19 (2010).

and forewarned the danger of foreign companies monopolizing parts of the Chinese market.[15]

Given this legislative background and environment, foreign firms unsurprisingly are viewing Chinese antitrust regulation with cautious suspicion. Their concern is hardly unwarranted. David Vogel has long argued that liberal trade policies provide incentives for other countries to tighten their regulatory standards.[16] He has identified the so-called California effect in areas of environmental and consumer regulation, where trade liberalization became the impetus for countries to promote more stringent regulatory standards. Vogel has argued that stricter standards give domestic producers a competitive advantage because it is easier for them to comply with the laws in their own country. As most of China's private domestic businesses are relatively small and uncompetitive, antitrust laws are largely not applicable to them. Moreover, due to their superior political status, SOEs can enjoy de facto immunity from the AML. Viewed in this light, the AML does seem to confer a competitive advantage on domestic industries as it increases the regulatory burden for their foreign rivals operating in China.

Andrew Cuzman, another renowned scholar on trade and regulation, proposed that governments have the incentive to externalize the cost of antitrust policies.[17] He explained that in effecting an antitrust policy, the government may not take into consideration the harm inflicted on foreign firms. As such, the government's antitrust policy would gravitate towards protecting the welfare of domestic businesses, even at the expense of foreign ones. Cuzman therefore foresaw the discrimination against foreigners during antitrust enforcement as a predicted and rational response of governments.[18] Consistent with the analysis of these influential scholars, many commentators have speculated that the costs of AML compliance would, for the most part, be borne by foreign multinational companies undertaking business in China. A demand perspective would therefore assume little scope for the application of antitrust regulation to Chinese domestic companies.

In the following discussion and in the next Chapter, I will argue for a divergent approach to studying Chinese antitrust law. Instead of employing a

---

[15] SAIC, Zaihua Kuaguo Gongsi Xianzhi Jingzheng Xingwei Biaoxian Ji Duice (在华跨国公司限制竞争行为表现及对策) [*Competition-Restricting Conduct of Multinational Companies in China and Countermeasures*], 5 Gongshang Xingzheng Guanli (工商行政管理) [Biweekly of Industry and Commerce Administration] 42 (2004).

[16] *See generally* DAVID VOGEL, TRADING UP: CONSUMER AND ENVIRONMENTAL REGULATION IN A GLOBAL ECONOMY (1995).

[17] Andrew T. Guzman, *International Antitrust and the WTO: The Lesson from Intellectual Property*, 43 VA. J. INT'L L. 933, 938 (2003).

[18] Id. at 939.

'top-down' model that solely accounts for the demand-side determinates of the AML, I will delineate a 'bottom-up' approach that emphasizes the 'supply perspective'.[19] By viewing Chinese regulators as rational actors who are utility maximizers, the supply approach stresses the motivations of and the constraints under which Chinese regulators act as the chief driving force behind antitrust regulation. My approach is inspired by the seminal work of Kenneth Lieberthal and Michel Oksenberg, two political scientists who were pioneers in illuminating how bureaucratic structures, policy processes, and outcomes are all interrelated in contemporary China.[20]

The supply perspective yields rich insights and warrants special attention for a number of reasons. First, Chinese administrative enforcement agencies, particularly those in Beijing, have played a dominant role in enforcing the AML. As is the case in the European Union, China relies primarily on public rather than private enforcement of the AML. As a result, the main architects of antitrust regulation have so far been Chinese administrative agencies. Because antitrust is an area of legal practice that relies heavily on technical and economic assessments, much of the policy implementation and agenda-making work has been delegated to the specialist antitrust agencies themselves. Moreover, as the targets of antitrust enforcement are often large and successful companies with nationwide influence, the central authorities in Beijing naturally hold the reins of enforcement. Unlike local enforcers, who face significant political and economic constraints from the local government, central enforcers are policy entrepreneurs who have been able to commit themselves credibly to tough antitrust regulations and who have quickly established their legal authority via a number of high-profile cases. Furthermore, the severe sanctions possible under the AML can incentivize agencies to over-enforce in order to gain reputation and political clout. Rival businesses and plaintiffs' lawyers have also played an active intermediary role in helping the agencies push forward with their aggressive enforcement.

Second, Chinese administrative agencies possess immense discretionary power in enforcing the AML. This, in part, has to do with the nature of antitrust law, which is fundamentally tasked with assessing the economic effects of the behaviours in question. Black letter law is ill-suited for such a task as it risks

---

[19] Wendy Ng applied a supply-and-demand approach to understand both the Anti-Monopoly Law (AML) and its social context. While her work has described the role of the different stakeholders involved in the drafting of the AML, it has yet to delve deeply into the incentives and constraints faced by regulators in tackling concrete cases. *See generally* WENDY NG, THE POLITICAL ECONOMY OF COMPETITION LAW IN CHINA (2017).

[20] *See* KENNETH LIEBERTHAL & MICHEL OKSENBERG, POLICY MAKING IN CHINA: LEADERS, STRUCTURES, AND PROCESSES 3 (1988).

basing antitrust law on the conduct rather than the ensuing economic effects. Moreover, ambiguities present in the AML and the absence of detailed guidelines for implementation provide further latitude to the enforcement agencies. Some of the goals set out in the AML are vague and potentially conflicting; it is not entirely clear which goal would prevail should conflicts arise.[21] The responsibility of assessing behaviours thus falls on the shoulders of law enforcers who enjoy wide discretion in assessing economic effects. Additionally, unlike their counterparts in the United States and Europe, Chinese authorities have rarely been challenged in court. Chinese antitrust agencies therefore wield enormous power, and little judicial check exists to guard against the abuse of this power. As a consequence, the Chinese antitrust agencies vertically integrate the functions of investigation, prosecution, and adjudication.

Third, the output of administrative agencies is more difficult to observe and measure than that of private entities.[22] Business managers, for example, are rewarded on the basis of objective indicators such as the firm's earnings. An agency head, on the other hand, is judged and rewarded on the basis of the appearance of success, which could mean reputation, influence, absence of criticism, and other less objective achievements.[23] For example, Chinese antitrust regulators often tout the number of cases they have investigated and the fines imposed on companies as evidence of their achievements. But the success of antitrust enforcement lies not only in the quantity of enforcement but also in its quality, which is especially tricky to evaluate in the Chinese context. Furthermore, as these antitrust agencies are rarely challenged in court, this gives antitrust bureau chiefs the incentive to over-enforce, since they gain advantage by initiating more cases which can expand their own influence and reputation.

Fourth, despite the absence of judicial scrutiny, Chinese administrative enforcement agencies operate under severe constraints. One such constraint stems from their limited capacity. As China only adopted the AML in 2007, the antitrust authorities have encountered steep learning curves every step of the way, from rule-making to prosecution and adjudicating cases. To make matters worse, Chinese agencies are extremely understaffed. Across the three former

---

[21] In addition to protecting consumer welfare, Article 1 of the AML also aims to safeguard 'social public interest" and "promote the healthy development of the socialist market economy'. Similarly, Articles 4 and 27 of the AML suggest that both competitive and non-competitive factors should be considered during enforcement, such as influence on the socialist market economy and the macroeconomic market, influence on technological progress, and influence on consumers and other competitors.

[22] RICHARD A. POSNER, ECONOMIC ANALYSIS OF LAW 339 (9th ed. 2014).

[23] JAMES Q. WILSON, BUREAUCRACY: WHAT GOVERNMENT AGENCIES DO AND WHY THEY DO IT 197 (1991).

Chinese antitrust agencies, there were fewer than 100 officials dedicated to antitrust enforcement in Beijing, many of whom were in charge of other policy matters as well.[24] And even shortly after the consolidation of the three agencies in 2018, there were fewer than fifty officials working at the central antitrust bureau in Beijing, although the bureau also technically has the ability to tap into its local network of enforcers.[25] The bureaucracy is another significant constraint agencies face. Unlike antitrust agencies in many other countries, none of the three former Chinese antitrust agencies were independent bodies. Rather, they were housed within large ministries and were subject to the formal and informal rules within their own departments as well as the extensive bureaucratic network across China. Given these two constraints, selective enforcement was inevitable as Chinese antitrust agencies prioritized cases that were likely to yield the most net benefit—not just for their own department but also the larger ministries to which they belonged.

Last but not least, there is path dependence in agency enforcement. Chinese antitrust agencies were not assembled from scratch but rather from preexisting departments of the central ministries. During the first decade of the enforcement of the AML, the responsibility to enforce the legislation was shared among three agencies. MOFCOM was responsible for merger enforcement and the NDRC and SAIC were jointly responsible for conduct investigations. The three agencies were only amalgamated into a single antitrust bureau in 2018 and placed under the newly created State Administration and Market Supervision (SAMR) ministry. Depending on their bureaucratic mission, culture, and structure, these former antitrust agencies had different incentives and goals when it came to enforcing the AML, and they took divergent approaches in prosecuting cases. Moreover, these agencies were ultimately led by individuals whose personal objectives and career ambitions could also play a paramount role in influencing enforcement outcomes. As such, the incentives and constraints they faced significantly affected the type of cases they brought, the manner in which the agencies coordinated with each other, the approach they took to tackle the cases, and, above all, the final regulatory outcomes.

This chapter is organized as follows. I will begin by explaining the rise of antitrust regulation in China and elaborate on important contributing factors.

---

[24] NG, *supra* note 19, at 175–76. As China is a very large country, these agencies also have their corresponding offices at the local level. For instance, the NDRC added 150 staff members to its various local offices to help enforce the AML in 2013. But these officials were not solely in charge of antitrust matters, they were also in charge of price supervision matters. Similarly, the SAIC could also tap into its vast network of local agencies.

[25] Id. at 176.

I will then move on to explain the phenomenon of path dependence in Chinese antitrust enforcement. Based on the enforcement record of the three former antitrust agencies, particularly that of the NDRC, I will explicate how bureaucratic mission, culture, and structure have been important determinants in antitrust enforcement. Looking ahead, I will highlight the bureaucratic constraints that will continue to challenge Chinese antitrust enforcement in the years to come.

1. The Rise of Antitrust Regulation in China

From a supply perspective, there are two major factors contributing to the rise of antitrust regulation in China. The first is the emergence of central policy entrepreneurs who can credibly commit themselves to tough antitrust enforcement in China. The second is the nature of antitrust sanctions, which gives both the regulators and plaintiffs' lawyers strong incentives to push forward enforcement.

1.1 Central Policy Entrepreneurs

Chinese antitrust enforcement is distinguishable from other areas of market regulation in one important aspect: it tackles mostly monopolies. As a consequence, the regulatory targets of the AML are often firms with leading positions in the national market. This naturally places the central enforcement agencies at the helm when it comes to directing the policy agenda and implementing the law. For instance, the power to review mergers was consolidated in the hands of MOFCOM with no involvement from local authorities. Similarly, although both the NDRC and the SAIC could in theory tap into their large local networks to carry out enforcement measures, they mostly launched high-profile cases from Beijing.[26] Even though it appears that some high-profile cases were brought by local agencies, the central agencies were in fact working actively behind the scenes, giving detailed instructions and supervision to the

---

[26] Both the NDRC and the SAIC promulgated rules on the AML enforcement procedure, dividing the jurisdictions between the central agencies and provincial agencies. For instance, the SAIC's Rules on the AML Enforcement Procedure stipulated that the central agency in Beijing was responsible for the investigation of cases of nationwide impact whereas the provincial agencies were responsible for cases that occur or primarily occur in their respective provinces. Similarly, the NDRC's Anti-Price Monopoly Administrative Enforcement Rules stipulated that it shall investigate 'big and important cases', whereas the provincial offices were in charge of local cases.

local authorities.[27] Viewed in this light, antitrust enforcement plays an imperative role in consolidating the power of the central government in market supervision.

In this respect, the Chinese experience with antitrust enforcement is akin to that of the European Union. Giandomenico Majone contends that an important contributing factor to the success of EU antitrust regulation has been its promotion by Commission officials who are well qualified to be policy entrepreneurs.[28] In Majone's view, Commission officials are more credible enforcers of the EU law than those from the Member States:

> [s]uccessful policy entrepreneurs possess three basic qualities. First, they must be taken seriously either as experts or as leaders of powerful interest groups, or as authoritative decision-makers. Second, they must be known for their negotiating skills. And third, and probably most importantly, they must be persistent. Because of the way they are recruited, the structure of their career incentives, their long-term horizon, and their strategic advantage in policy initiation, Commission officials often display the qualities of a successful policy entrepreneur to a degree unmatched by national civil servants or even politicians.[29]

Similar to Commission officials, antitrust officials working in Beijing are well-positioned to take the lead in antitrust enforcement. Unlike local agencies, whose budgets and personnel are subject to the whims of local governments, central antitrust authorities face fewer constraints in bringing cases against firms that are local champions. Housed within large powerful central ministries that have amassed vast regulatory control over businesses, few companies have dared to ignore their regulatory requests. Central antitrust enforcers therefore have strong incentives to promote antitrust enforcement, which is deemed an exciting new venture for the expansion of their policy control. As technocrats with long-term career perspectives, these central enforcers can be persistent in their pursuit as their career prospects are directly tied to that of antitrust regulation in China. The rise of antitrust regulation affords them both prestige and power, which could be translated into political patronage for growing their faction networks or rent-seeking. As weak enforcement would undermine their authority, central enforcers are adamant about maintaining their image as

---

[27] Angela Huyue Zhang, *Bureaucratic Politics and China's Anti-Monopoly Law*, 47 CORNELL INT'L L. J. 671, 700 (2014).

[28] GIANDOMENICO MAJONE, REGULATING EUROPE 71 (1989).

[29] Id.

tough regulators. Their commitment to tough enforcement renders stringent antitrust regulation more credible in the eyes of firms all over China.

Xu Kunlin, the former Director General of the Price Supervision and Anti-Monopoly Bureau, the antitrust unit at the NDRC, is a quintessential example of a central policy entrepreneur. Before working on antitrust matters, Xu had been a central technocrat in charge of price supervision and control for more than two decades. Xu joined the State Price Bureau in 1984. The bureau was subsequently merged with the State Planning Commission, a powerful central ministry that was the predecessor to the NDRC. As China embarked on marketization, this area of regulatory control had been shrinking rapidly as prices were gradually liberalized. Xu's price supervision department then saw antitrust as an opportunity to revive the declining influence of the agency and help expand its policy control. Conveniently, Xu's appointment was in line with the agency's ambitions. Xu was forty-four years old when he was appointed as Director General of the antitrust unit in 2009. Young and ambitious, Xu opened a number of investigations into many high-profile targets during his tenure, including, but not limited to, the telecom giants China Telecom and China Unicom (2011); state-owned white liquor companies Maotai and Wuliangye (2013), large gold retailers in Shanghai (2013), premium infant formula manufacturers (2013); US patent assertion entity Interdigital (2013); luxury car manufacturers and dealers (2014–2015); and US chip maker Qualcomm (2015). As I will elucidate in this chapter and the next, Xu's personal ambition and tough enforcement style played a significant role in shaping Chinese antitrust enforcement during its early years.

Contrary to the popular perception that Chinese antitrust agencies have no incentive to pursue domestic companies, especially those owned by the government, the NDRC made remarkable efforts in tackling incumbent or formerly state-owned monopolies. The investigation of China Telecom and China Unicom, two state-owned giants in the telecommunication sector in 2011 offers a prime example. The NDRC certainly had its own agenda in tackling this case. By intervening in these two companies, the NDRC could expand its policy control in the telecom sector, as will be elaborated in detail when I discuss bureaucratic hierarchy in this chapter. Nonetheless, the case itself exemplified a bold attempt by the agency, even though the investigation was ultimately suspended due to significant political opposition. In reality, the NDRC had investigated many more cases involving SOEs than was publicly disclosed.[30] For

---

[30] Angela Huyue Zhang, *Strategic Public Shaming: Evidence from Chinese Antitrust Investigations*, 237 CHINA Q. 174 (2019).

instance, in 2009 the NDRC investigated a number of state-owned airlines for alleged price-fixing behaviours. However, no punishments were publicly imposed because their cases had been 'harmonized', that is they had been resolved inside the bureaucracy. Clearly, the NDRC had met with much political opposition from within the bureaucracy for targeting large central monopolies, just as it did when it attempted to rein in China Telecom and China Unicom.

However, when it comes to local monopolies, the central agency faces considerably fewer constraints as it is not bound by the authority of the local governments. This explains why in 2013 the NDRC was able to impose a hefty fine of RMB 449 million on Maotai and Wuliangye, two premium white liquor manufacturers who are local champions in their respective provinces. In fact, the fines imposed on these two liquor companies represented the largest fine ever imposed by the Chinese antitrust authority at that time. In that same year, the NDRC investigated five Shanghai gold retailers, three of which were owned by the Shanghai government. Notably, although in both cases the decisions were issued by regional offices of the NDRC, the central office in Beijing was inconspicuously directing them from behind the scenes.

As a matter of fact, Chinese antitrust authorities face even fewer bureaucratic constraints when they chase after foreign firms. As one senior antitrust lawyer once said to me: 'foreign firms are soft persimmons that are much easier to squeeze than the SOEs'.[31] It thus comes as no surprise that many of the prominent targets of Chinese antitrust enforcement are foreign multinational companies. As I will further discuss in Chapter 2, foreign firms are generally reluctant to confront Chinese administrative agencies directly. As there are many grey areas of doing business in China, businesses are vulnerable to regulatory pounces from Chinese government agencies. They are at the mercy of these authorities, to the extent that their activities have been taken hostage by the Chinese government. Thus, despite voicing grievances, foreign firms have more often than not taken a cooperative and conciliatory approach in dealing with the government.

But one company epitomizes the rare exception to the rule: Qualcomm. The NDRC began its investigation into Qualcomm in 2009 after receiving complaints from both American and Chinese companies. Chinese cell phone manufacturers argued that Qualcomm's licencing practices gave the company an unfair advantage in the domestic market as the American chip company was charging its royalty fee based on the price of the whole handset rather than the smallest saleable patent-practising unit. This means that, if licensees uses

---

[31] Telephone interview with a senior antitrust lawyer, Beijing, Nov. 2017.

Qualcomm's patent in producing the chip for a cell phone, Qualcomm could calculate the royalty on the basis of the wholesale price of the entire phone rather than the chip itself. This legal challenge directly threatened the core of Qualcomm's business as the firm derived more than half of its annual revenue from China. Qualcomm was aware of the high stakes involved and expended numerous hours and resources to defend its case. From 2013 to 2014, Qualcomm representatives reportedly met with the NDRC more than twenty-eight times. Its Chief Executive Officer (CEO), Derek Aberle, personally flew to Beijing to meet with Xu Kunlin eight times.

In 2014, Qualcomm tried to hire leading Chinese antitrust experts to defend its case and approached Zhang Xinzhu, a renowned antitrust expert who also served on the expert consultation committee of the Anti-Monopoly Commission under the State Council. Zhang, along with other fellow economists from an economic consulting group, submitted a report to the NDRC, vigorously defending Qualcomm's pricing practices. In addition to engaging experts, Qualcomm spent a great deal of resources lobbying the US government, and the case was elevated to the highest levels of both the US and Chinese governments. China's regulatory actions were denounced by then-White House spokesperson Patrick Ventrell: 'The United States government is concerned that China is using numerous mechanisms, including anti-monopoly law, to lower the value of foreign-owned patents and benefit Chinese firms employing foreign technology.'[32] When President Xi Jinping and former President Barack Obama met in Beijing in 2014, the US President raised these concerns again.[33] Chinese premier Li Keqiang defended the case and even met with Qualcomm's executive chairman, Paul Jacobs.[34] The political pressures that Xu was confronted with at that time were unprecedented.

Concurrent with the Qualcomm investigation, the NDRC saw a growing number of complaints and allegations about due process violations and discriminatory treatments from chambers of commerce in the United States and Europe. Although the NDRC had brought many cases scrutinizing high-profile targets, none of these cases directly threatened the survival of their targets. But the Qualcomm case was different; if the NDRC decided to impose a condition requiring Qualcomm to modify its licencing practices, the firm would have no longer found it viable to operate in China, its most important

---

[32] Michael Martina & Matthew Miller, *As Qualcomm Decision Looms, US Presses China on Antitrust Policy*, REUTERS (16 Dec. 2014).

[33] Id.

[34] Matthew Miller, *China Antitrust Regulators says Qualcomm Case to be Settled Soon*, REUTERS (26 Dec. 2014).

revenue-generating market. Faced with a matter of life or death, Qualcomm was prepared to go to court if the NDRC's ultimate decision was not favourable towards the firm.[35]

Despite its aggressive and forceful approach, the NDRC was averse to being challenged in court. Intensive court intervention would have increased the time and resources needed for the NDRC to reach a decision.[36] An appeal would have sent a signal to the public that the defendant was not satisfied with the administrative decision and that it held a sceptical view of their procedures. A trial might also have exposed many weaknesses of the agency in managing the inquiry, collecting evidence, and adjudicating the case. In the event of an unfavourable court judgment, agency heads could have been held accountable for mishandling the case.

This explains why the NDRC was willing to offer concessions to Qualcomm to avoid being challenged in a Chinese court. The final decision, reached after a prolonged negotiation, appears to have been a live-and-let-live compromise between the two. The NDRC did not contest Qualcomm's business model as it had done earlier, nor did it confiscate its illegal gains, which was legally permissible under the AML. Instead, the NDRC levied a record fine of RMB 975 million on Qualcomm, helping the agency gain significant media attention at home and abroad and earn its title as China's most powerful and forceful antitrust regulator. In return, Qualcomm volunteered to offer a discount on its royalty rates and charged its customers on the basis of 65 per cent rather than 100 per cent of the wholesale price of the handsets sold in China.[37] As the NDRC initially urged Qualcomm to change its pricing model based on the smallest saleable patent-practising unit, Qualcomm's offer was a much watered down version of the agency's original request. This commitment, arguably the most important among all the remedies offered by Qualcomm, was curiously omitted in the final decision released by the NDRC. Qualcomm therefore accepted the NDRC's penalty decision and agreed not to appeal. As such, the outcome in the Qualcomm case appears to have been a win-win solution for both the agency and the company.

The Qualcomm case successfully helped the NDRC establish its legal authority and solidify its image as a harsh antitrust regulator. It also earned Xu Kunlin a great deal of political eminence. Xu was quickly promoted after the conclusion of the case. After a few brief stints, he became the General Secretary

---

[35] Interview with two senior lawyers involved in the case, Beijing, July 2016.

[36] WILSON, *supra* note 23, at 282.

[37] Susan Ning et al., *Qualcomm Investigation Finally Closed: Some Changes in Business Model in Addition to an RMB 6.0888 Billion Fine*, CHINA LAW INSIGHT (Feb. 12, 2015).

of the NDRC in 2016 and was subsequently appointed as the Deputy Mayor of Shanghai in 2017. In Chinese politics, it is quite rare for a central technocrat to ascend into provincial leadership positions. This sent a clear signal that the upper echelons of the Chinese government had recognized Xu's leadership in antitrust enforcement and were satisfied with the accomplishments achieved by the agency in a short period of time.

1.2 The High-Powered Antitrust Sanctions

Chinese government officials have generally viewed antitrust enforcement as a promising new venture that can significantly facilitate and expand their policy control.[38] This partly has to do with the inherent nature of antitrust laws, which empower regulators to impose heavy sanctions on infringing firms. Under the AML, administrative authorities can confiscate illegal gains and impose fines of between 1 per cent and 10 per cent of a company's turnover (revenue) from the previous financial year.[39] There is no ceiling for imposing antitrust fines; the fine is calculated based on the harm inflicted and is proportional to the revenue of the firm. As the enforcement targets are often large and successful multinational companies with deep pockets, the cost incurred from antitrust fines can often be astronomical and judgment proof issues rarely occur. Antitrust sanctions therefore have potent deterrent effects.

Notably, the elastic ceiling of antitrust fines stands in stark contrast to the inelastic ceilings of fines for other types of economic regulation. Take the example of the Anti-Unfair Competition Law (AUCL). The law, first promulgated in 1993, saw a major amendment in 2017.[40] The 1993 version of the law has a number of overlaps with the AML, covering the abuse of monopoly power over public utilities, administrative monopolies, predatory pricing, tying, and bid rigging. However, unlike the AML, there is no requirement of proof of dominant position for predatory pricing and tying, thus the burden of proof is much lighter under the AUCL. The sanctions prior to its revision though were quite feeble. For instance, a firm liable for tying or bundling was responsible for the damage caused to its competitors but no penalty was imposed.[41] For other violations (e.g. abuse of monopoly by public utilities and bid rigging),

---

[38] Zhang, *supra* note 27, at 704.

[39] Arts. 46 and 47, the AML.

[40] The Anti-Unfair Competition Law (promulgated by the Standing Comm. Nat'l People's Cong., 2 Sep. 1993, effective Dec. 1, 1993, amended on 14 Nov. 2017).

[41] Art. 23, Anti-Unfair Competition Law (1993 version).

the maximum fine was only RMB 200,000.[42] The 2017 version of the AUCL removed all the competition-related provisions and increased the quantity of sanctions and fines. In comparison to the AML, the penalties are low, with the maximum fine, even under the 2017 version, standing at only RMB 3 million.[43]

Of course, high sanctions do not always bring direct monetary profits for antitrust officials working in central ministries. The fines collected by the agencies from the companies are moved to the treasury and have no effect on their personal salary or the budget of their departments. But, all things being equal, imposing a high fine is positively correlated with a law enforcement agency's policy control, which can be translated into power, prestige, or opportunities for rent-seeking. In a thought-provoking essay on optimal law enforcement published in 1974, Gary Becker and George Stigler pointed out that one of the most important distinguishing factors of public enforcement versus private enforcement lies in the structure of compensation.[44] While private enforcers derive profit directly from enforcement, public enforcers are normally paid a flat salary. In other words, their monetary compensation remains the same irrespective of the fines they set in their role. At the same time, firms violating the laws, or that are subject to investigation, will attempt to avoid punishment by expending resources to defend themselves. In the most extreme cases, they are willing to pay the law enforcers up to the price of the fines in order to receive immunity. As the public enforcers' expected gains from enforcement are lower than the violators' expected losses, Becker and Stigler argue that public enforcers are susceptible to rent seeking. For example, officials may commit malfeasance by dropping a case in exchange for monetary benefits. This implies that public enforcers may be more likely to under-enforce than private enforcers.

Malfeasance has been observed in Chinese antitrust enforcement before. A few months prior to the implementation of the AML, news broke out that Sun Jingyi, an ex-MOFCOM official in charge of approving foreign acquisitions of domestic assets under the pre-AML merger control regime, had been arrested on corruption charges. Sun had reportedly colluded with his friends and former classmates who worked at a Chinese law firm and accepted bribes in exchange for approving foreign acquisitions of domestic assets. Since the enactment of the AML, however, there have been no antitrust-related corruption scandals and malfeasance cases. This may be because many of those targeted under the AML are foreign multinational companies. While corruption

---

[42] Arts. 23 & 27, Anti-Unfair Competition Law (1993 version).

[43] Arts. 19–24, Anti-Unfair Competition Law (2017 version).

[44] Gary S. Becker & George J. Stigler, *Law Enforcement, Malfeasance, and Compensation of Enforcers*, 3 J. LEGAL STUD. 1, 14 (1974).

is rampant in China, it is not as common within foreign firms. Foreign anti-corruption enforcement by US and European authorities has spiked in recent years, thus foreign firms operating in China are subject to tight regulatory scrutiny from overseas. President Xi Jinping's aggressive anti-corruption campaign may have also played a role in deterring antitrust officials from pursuing rent-seeking opportunities.

On the other hand, public enforcers can over-enforce. Government agencies could have self-interested motives to maximize financial recoveries, even if their compensation and salary are not linked to the financial awards won.[45] High fines, in particular, put the antitrust agencies in the media spotlight at home and abroad, increasing their profile and visibility as well as helping them accumulate greater political merit. As Margaret Lemos and Max Minzer wrote in their thought-provoking article, 'For Profit Public Enforcement',

> Money has two significant advantages over other forms of relief: it is easy to understand and easy to quantify and compare. An agency can easily trumpet a 'record' financial judgment. It is far more difficult for public enforcers to convey the importance or the scale of injunctive remedies. The difficulty is compounded when the public policy payoff of nonmonetary relief is uncertain and will be realized, if at all, in future years.[46]

The authors cautioned that these financial and reputational incentives for public enforcers could motivate agencies to initiate more enforcement actions, detract their attention from nonmonetary remedies, and compete with each other for a higher amount recovered from enforcement.[47]

High fines are not the only ammunition at the disposal of the antitrust regulators. What also worries businesses are the behavioural or structural remedies that the antitrust authority forces upon them. The AML allows Chinese regulators to exert extraterritorial jurisdiction over a foreign business on the basis of the firm's sales in the Chinese market. Thus, the Chinese antitrust agency can intervene in transactions or conduct that have little to do with China as long as those companies involved have sufficient sales in China. For example, Chinese antitrust agencies can impose stringent remedies on a proposed takeover transaction or block it entirely.[48] During the tie-up between Western Digital

---

[45] Margaret H. Lemos & Max Minzner, *For-Profit Public Enforcement*, 127 HAR. L. REV. 853, 856 (2014).
[46] Id. at 857.
[47] Id.
[48] Art. 48, the AML.

and Hitachi along with the merger between Samsung and Seagate, MOFCOM applied a conflicting and detrimental condition. The merging parties were instructed to hold their subsidiaries separate and maintain them as competitors after the merger, thus undermining the original goal of the deal.

In some cases, the power of the authority is subtler. In merger transactions, even a delay in granting clearance to a merger deal is sufficient to contribute to its collapse. For example, due to the dim prospect of winning merger approval from the Chinese antitrust authority amid growing US–China trade tensions in 2018, senior executives at Toshiba Corporation once considered giving up a USD 18 billion sale of the company's NAND flash-memory unit to a consortium led by Bain Capital.[49] Fortunately, the deal was ultimately approved. Qualcomm's USD 44 billion bid for NXP Semiconductors offers another case in point. The transaction had gathered clearance from eight antitrust regulators worldwide. China was the only and last jurisdiction holding up the deal.[50] These cases saw the Chinese antitrust agency flex its regulatory muscles without imposing any punishments, as the agency can wield tremendous power by merely holding up global transactions.

Indeed, the tougher the antitrust sanctions, the more reputational reward Chinese antitrust regulators are able to reap.[51] These actions assist in building the agency's reputation as a vigorous and aggressive regulator. It further benefits its employees, including both career and non-career regulators. From the standpoint of a career official, especially the agency head of an antitrust unit, austere sanctions attract media attention and enable the agency to win public endorsement and recognition from superior agencies, paving the way for the agency head's advancement in the bureaucratic system. An agency head who is in his forties or fifties, therefore, tends to take an assertive approach, as he can anticipate more opportunities for career advancement than those nearing retirement. The swift ascension of Xu Kunlin, the former head of the antitrust bureau of the NDRC is a good example. After Xu's departure, the NDRC appeared less aggressive when launching new investigations. This partly had to do with the different leadership style of the new agency head. Zhang Handong, Xu's successor, was approaching his retirement age and hence saw little to be gained for his own career prospects from aggressive enforcement.

Meanwhile, for 'non-career' regulators who do not see their governmental positions as permanent, the power and prestige of the agency that employs

---

[49] Takashi Mochizuki & Kosaku Narioka, *Toshiba Pessimistic about Prospects for $18 Billion Chip Deal*, WALL ST. J. (9 May 2018).

[50] *Antitrust with Chinese Characteristics: Command and Control*, THE ECONOMIST (16 Apr. 2018).

[51] Lemos & Minzner, *supra* note 45, at 856–57.

them can also be highly valuable for their own career progression outside the bureaucratic network. Wentong Zheng observed that regulators have 'market expansion' incentives; that is, they are interested in expanding the market demand for services they would be providing upon their departure from the government.[52] This seems to be the case in China as antitrust lawyers with antitrust agency experience and connections are highly sought after by the private bar. Since the commencement of the AML enforcement, several former antitrust officials have moved into private practice and taken lucrative senior positions within law firms. The trend of leaving the public sector for the private sector became especially common after President Xi launched his anti-corruption campaign, which made it much riskier and less profitable to work for the government. With the consolidation of the three former agencies into a single antitrust bureau with a more limited number of senior posts, many officials currently see few prospects for further advancement in the antitrust department. Since 2018, some officials have left the new antitrust bureau and moved to large domestic technology giants such as Alibaba and Tencent as well as to foreign multinationals that have a strong demand for antitrust compliance in order to shield themselves from potential antitrust charges. Therefore, uncompromising enforcement can increase exit options for non-career officials.

Meanwhile, the lack of procedural safeguards and judicial oversight of agency actions makes the antitrust bar less effective in constraining the actions of the administrative authorities. As will be illustrated in Chapter 2, challenging antitrust decisions in court is not a realistic option in most cases; firms under inspection would rather pay the fines and move on. Lawyers are therefore careful and avoid taking an antagonistic approach in defending their clients as they do not wish to offend the agencies and risk being boycotted by them. At the same time, antitrust has become one of the fastest developing legal practices in the country and there is a growing demand for regulatory compliance work in the country. A symbiotic relationship has been formed between lawyers and regulators in China. As a senior Chinese antitrust lawyer I met in Beijing said: 'Without these regulators, we wouldn't have any business. They are really the parents that feed and clothe us.'[53]

While a vigorous defence may not be as rewarding in China as in other jurisdictions, Chinese lawyers have found that antitrust complaints can be a potential source of revenue. Daniel Sokol has long observed the phenomenon of private firms strategically using government-brought antitrust cases to raise

---

[52] Wentong Zheng, *The Revolving Door*, 90 NOTRE DAME L. REV. 1265, 1269 (2015).
[53] Interview with a senior lawyer, Beijing, July 2016.

costs for their rivals.[54] He suggested that such strategic leveraging of public enforcement is often regarded a less costly and more effective complement to private action.[55] Google, for instance, was once one of the few vocal complainants against Microsoft and had filed complaints with the US Department of Justice and the European Commission (Commission) in order to make life difficult for Microsoft.[56] Microsoft turned the tables in 2011, filing a complaint to the Commission against Google, arguing that the same rules formerly arrayed against it should now be applied to Google.

Now, the complaint business has expanded into China. Chinese agencies have mostly relied on a reactive rather than proactive approach to starting investigations. On one public occasion, Xu Kunlin, the former head of the NDRC's antitrust division, acknowledged that almost all actions initiated by Chinese administrative agencies had been due to complaints from either domestic or foreign companies.[57] These complaints provide important tip-offs to administrative agencies and empower them to go after targeted firms. Thus, Chinese antitrust authorities welcome complaints wholeheartedly. As one experienced Chinese antitrust lawyer put it: 'complaints make the regulators' life easier and reduce their workload'.[58] These plaintiffs' antitrust lawyers therefore become important intermediaries who assist regulators in insistently pushing forward enforcement.

Complaints are most prevalent in the high-technology sector, where industry titans are at loggerheads over patent licencing issues.[59] In the past few years, many of China's most high-profile investigations were opened based on complaints from rivals, including both domestic and foreign firms. For instance, the SAIC's 2014 investigation into Microsoft was sparked by a complaint from Kingsoft, a Beijing-based software company which sells a Microsoft Office alternative called WPS.[60] Kingsoft alleged that the applications it developed were not compatible with Windows or Microsoft Office in some cases. Another unnamed company also raised the complaint in 2013 that Microsoft had failed to disclose in full information relating to its operating system and its Office suites, generating problems of interoperability and tie-in sales.[61]

---

[54] Daniel Sokol, *The Strategic Use of Public and Private Litigation in Antitrust and Business Strategy*, 85 S. Cal. L. Rev. 689 (2012).

[55] Id. at 690.

[56] Id. at 722.

[57] *Whistle Blowers Spur Vast Majority of Chinese Investigations*, PaRR (22 May 2014).

[58] Interview with a senior Chinese antitrust lawyer, Beijing, June, 2016.

[59] Michael A. Carrier, *A Roadmap to the Patent Smart Phone Wars and FRAND Licensing*, 2 Competition Policy Int'l Antitrust Chronicle (2012).

[60] Richard Adhikari, *China Levels Antitrust Allegations against Microsoft*, Commercial Times (6 Jan. 2016).

[61] Id.

Similarly, the well-known Qualcomm case was launched after multiple complaints were filed against the company, starting in 2009.[62] The Mobile Phone China Alliance, an industry lobby group publicly stated that it had filed a complaint to the NDRC against Qualcomm's anti-competitive practices, which was apparently an important trigger for the Qualcomm probe.[63] Chinese Internet giants have also been accused of exclusionary practices by their domestic rivals. In recent years, competition between large online retailing platforms have intensified, with some major platforms demanding their merchants to 'choose one from the other' during large online promoting events such as the popular Singles' Day. The company receiving the most criticism has been Alibaba, the owner of Taobao and Tmall, two of the most successful online retailing platforms in China. Since 2017, JD.com, another hefty online retailer in China, has joined forces with a cyberspace think tank to lobby the Chinese antitrust regulator to begin investigations into Alibaba for its exclusionary practices. The aggressive lobbying campaign appears to be effective, as the Chinese antitrust authority began to review the exclusionary practices of Chinese Internet platforms in 2019.

In short, antitrust officials from the central ministries in Beijing are policy entrepreneurs who can commit themselves credibly to tough antitrust enforcement in China. The severe sanctions that agencies can impose under the AML also give high-powered incentives to both the regulators and plaintiffs' lawyers to advance antitrust enforcement.

2. The Path Dependence of Enforcement

Every bureaucratic organization has its own history and memories. As a consequence, they have the tendency of being inertial.[64] Political scientists have characterized such inertia as a phenomenon of path dependence.[65] As Margaret Levi once described it: 'Path dependence has to mean, if it is to mean anything, that once a country or region has started down a track, the costs of reversal are very high. There will be other choice points, but the entrenchments of certain

---

[62] Joe Zhang, *China's Antitrust Crackdown Hits Qualcomm with US$975 Million Fine: What Can Other Host States Learn from the Story*, IISD (21 May 2015).

[63] Charles Clover, *China: Monopoly Position*, FIN. TIMES (26 Jan. 2015).

[64] Scott E. Robinson & Kenneth J. Meier, *Path Dependence and Organizational Behaviour: Bureaucracy and Social Promotion*, 36 AM. REV. PUBLIC ADMINISTRATION 241, 242 (2006).

[65] *See* Paul Pierson, *Increasing Returns, Path Dependence, and the Study of Politics*, 94 AM. POLIT. SCI. REV. 251, 252 (June 2000).

institutional arrangements obstruct an easy reversal of the initial choice.[66] To put it plainly, history matters. Taking steps in one direction will induce further movement in the same direction. Taking each step down the path will increase the probability of continuing along the same path, where the costs of switching directions becomes increasingly high further down the line.

Chinese antitrust enforcement in its first decade is a perfect illustration of such a path dependence phenomenon. During this period, the primary enforcement responsibilities of the AML were split among three administrative agencies: the MOFCOM, the NDRC, and the SAIC. Although the three former agencies were established in 2008, none of them were new, instead they were born out of pre-existing departments of various central ministries. Even though the three agencies were consolidated in 2018, the employees of the new antitrust bureau came from the three former agencies. As I will elaborate below, bureaucratic mission, culture, and structure have all impacted AML enforcement. My discussion focuses particularly on the NDRC, the most assertive agency among the three former enforcers. Its rich record of enforcement offers us an opportunity to closely examine the link between these institutional factors and its enforcement pattern.

2.1 Bureaucratic Mission

Officials working at central ministries are often regarded as technocrats as they have specialized knowledge and training in a specific government function. This government function is key to the bureaucratic position held by the central technocrats, as it can be summed up by the familiar Chinese phrase 'where you stand [on an issue] depends on where you sit [in the bureaucracy]'.[67] From the perspective of central technocrats, maintaining their organizations means more than just ensuring their survival; it involves acquisition of both autonomy and resources.[68] Indeed, each of China's central ministries has its own particular missions that are pursued with zeal. They endeavour and work assiduously to make the top leaders understand as well as appreciate their ministry's expertise and contribution.[69] Unsurprisingly, antitrust officials working at large

---

[66] Margaret Levi, *A Model, A Method, and A Map: Rational Choice in Comparative and Historical Analysis*, in COMPARATIVE POLITICS: RATIONALITY, CULTURE, AND STRUCTURE 28 (Mark I. Lichbach and Alan S. Zuckerman eds., 1997).

[67] *See* LIEBERTHAL & OKSENBERG, *supra* note 20, at 28.

[68] WILSON, *supra* note 23, at 196.

[69] Id. at 29.

central ministries view antitrust as another means of fulfilling their original mission and to gain greater policy control within the scope of their designated responsibilities.

While all three former agencies had competing interests in antitrust policy control, antitrust was not their only competitive arena. The NDRC was mainly in charge of macroeconomic management and industrial planning with its predecessor being the State Planning Commission (SPC). The SPC, founded in 1952, played a crucial role during the period when the Chinese economy was entirely centrally planned. The MOFCOM, on the other hand, was primarily responsible for formulating and implementing both inbound and outbound policies of trade and investment. It played a key role in representing China in trade deal negotiations with foreign countries; China's accession to the WTO has been considered one of its crowning achievements. As might be expected, the MOFCOM was generally seen as more liberal and pro-market compared to other agencies, such as the NDRC, with respect to its views on economic affairs. In contrast to the MOFCOM and NDRC, the SAIC was smaller in size and stipulated a narrower mandate, with tasks that included the administration of enterprise registration, the regulation of unfair competition behaviour, and consumer protection.

The NDRC stood out among these three agencies because its mission as a social-industrial planner was clearly at odds with the mandates of antitrust regulation. Indeed, while antitrust law intervenes only when there is a market failure, the NDRC leveraged the law as a tool to fulfil its original mission to maintain market stability and price control. And the agency did not shy away from asserting this as its priority. For instance, Lu Yanchun, Deputy Director General of the antitrust unit at the NDRC, announced in 2013 that the department would continue to prioritize its enforcement efforts against price-related monopolies in six major industries: aviation, household chemicals, automobiles, telecoms, pharmaceuticals, and home appliances. From 2011 to 2018, the NDRC launched significant actions against major economic interests including telecommunications, infant formula powder, white liquor, automobiles, high technology companies, and consumer electronics.

The NDRC's insistent interventions in the economy have deep roots in its bureaucratic memory. While the three former enforcement agencies possessed the same ministerial rank, the NDRC was in practice far more authoritative and interventionist due to its historical and political background. Its predecessor, the SPC, was known as the 'little State Council', in charge of the organization of both production and distribution of major commodities together with the construction of significant projects. The SPC underwent several restructurings and reorganizations over the years. The most sizeable restructuring took place in 2003, two years after China joined the WTO. The SPC merged with part of the State Economic and Trade Commission, another supra-ministerial organization that was predominantly tasked with coordinating government agencies to implement the SPC's economic plans. In line with the agreements and in order to appear more compatible with China's new goal of building a market economy, the State Council removed 'planning' from the SPC's title and replaced it with 'development and reform'.

Despite the change in name, the NDRC continued to rely on direct government intervention to solve many of its economic problems; this is not surprising since promoting government intervention was precisely related to the NDRC's own bureaucratic interests.[70] In particular, the responsibilities of price control fell on the shoulders of two departments within the NDRC—the Price Bureau and the Price Supervision and Anti-Monopoly Bureau (i.e. the antitrust unit). The Price Bureau was in charge of regulating the prices of certain basic commodities in a number of sectors including natural gas, diesel, electricity, some medicines, and basic telecom rates. The Price Supervision and Anti-Monopoly Bureau was tasked with preventing price instability and controlling inflation, in addition to antitrust enforcement. In fact, among its forty-six staff members, only one-third of them administered antitrust legislation, while the rest looked after price supervision.

Since the 1980s, the NDRC—including its price control departments—has seen a significant decrease in power.[71] Prices of commodities were increasingly liberalized and the power of the state to mandate prices has been drastically weakened since China's entry into the WTO. But experts have observed that, since the financial crisis in 2008, the NDRC has clawed its way back to the forefront in large part due to the Hu Jingtao-Wen Jiabao administration, which chose to concentrate on redistributive welfare policies at the expense of further market reform.[72] As the government redirected its efforts towards social policy, the NDRC saw an opportunity to put itself back on top. By winning strong support from top Chinese leaders, it spearheaded a series of important government interventionist measures such as battling rising inflation.[73]

---

[70] Barry Naughton, *Since the National People's Congress: Personnel and Programs of Economic Reform Begin to Emerge*, 41 CHINA LEADERSHIP MONITOR 1 (2013).

[71] Barry Naughton, *Strengthening the Center, and Premier Wen Jiabao*, 21 CHINA LEADERSHIP MONITOR 1 (2007).

[72] Barry Naughton, *Inflation, Welfare and the Political Business Cycle*, 35 CHINA LEADERSHIP MONITOR 1 (2011).

[73] Id. *See also* Barry Naughton, *The Inflation Battle: Juggling Three Swords*, 25 CHINA LEADERSHIP MONITOR 1 (2008).

Given China's substantial economic liberalization over the decades, one might question why the government continues to resort to direct price control rather than monetary policy to suppress inflation. However, for the Chinese leadership, inflation is not a purely economic matter; it is a highly sensitive political matter that has been repeatedly associated with political failures as well as turmoil in recent Chinese history.[74] Therefore, when inflation went out of control in 2010, Chinese policy-makers made combatting inflation its highest priority. This provided the NDRC with an opportunity to catapult itself back into the policy-making limelight. From December 2010 onwards, the NDRC closely monitored the daily prices of primary food products and put pressure on merchants not to increase prices. In 2011, it launched a massive campaign to mobilize merchants, chambers of commerce, and the public into whipping inflation.

In April that same year, the NDRC convened a meeting with a number of private chambers of commerce and pressured them to restrain prices. In response, twenty-four out of twenty-eight Federation chambers of commerce signed an undertaking to stabilize prices. In May, the Shanghai Price Bureau, a regional office of the NDRC, fined Unilever RMB 2 million for publicly declaring its intention to raise prices and thus violate the Price Law.[75] The hefty penalty came after the NDRC's 'informal chat' with Unilever and other leading household goods manufacturers, during which the NDRC suggested that the manufacturers refrain from price hikes. Nevertheless, the NDRC's sanctioning proved ineffective as Unilever reportedly raised prices shortly afterwards. This time, however, there was nothing that the NDRC could do as Unilever had unilaterally raised prices without making a public announcement.

From 2011, the NDRC began to appreciate the use of the AML as a powerful tool for fulfilling its original mission of 'price control' without appearing as though it was undermining market forces. It initiated a large number of cases involving wholesale manufacturers who were conducting minimum resale price maintenance (RPM), that is, fixing the retail prices of their products. Notably, RPM cases are highly controversial as manufacturers often have perfectly procompetitive reasons to impose price restraints, while there are only limited circumstances under which RPM

[74] Id.

[75] NDRC, *Lian He Li Hua Sanbu Zhangjia Xinxi Raoluan Shichang Zhixu Shoudao Yanli Chufa* (联合利华散布涨价信息扰乱市场秩序受到严厉处罚) [*Unilever Received Harsh Penalty for Disseminating Price Increase Information and Disrupting Market Order*], NDRC PRESS RELEASE (6 May 2011).

would lead to anticompetitive effects. In reality, RPM is no longer an en-forcement priority in major antitrust jurisdictions such as the United States and the European Union. Despite such controversy, the NDRC has priori-tized RPM enforcement.

One practical reason to account for the agency's strong preference is that it was easier for the agency to prove and prosecute RPM cases compared to other types of cases such as cartel or abuse of dominance cases. Cartels are often formed discretely, and it is difficult for an enforcement agency to obtain direct evidence of collusion. Nowadays, competition authorities generally rely on leniency programmes to entice cartelists to break down the cartels. As such, most of the large cartel cases investigated by the NDRC were global cartels where the cartels had failed and had filed leniency applications in other juris-dictions. Similarly, abuse of dominance cases requires a high burden of proof as the agency must first establish the company's dominant market position and then show that the anticompetitive effects of the alleged abusive conduct out-weigh its pro-competitive effects.

By contrast, it was much easier for the NDRC to prove that price restraints were implemented in RPM cases. The imposition of price restrictions was often accompanied by written evidence and the complainants were also able to assist with the gathering of important evidence. After obtaining proof, the NDRC then proceeded to rule such practices as anticompetitive without con-ducting a comprehensive effects analysis. At the same time, there has been heated debate among Chinese academics over whether an enforcement agency is required to demonstrate the anticompetitive effects of RPM agree-ments under the AML. The Chinese courts had previously requested plaintiffs to carry such a burden of proof, the agency on the other hand insisted on a per se illegality approach, which meant that vertical agreements were strictly banned. In this way, the NDRC was able to prosecute cases very quickly and efficiently.

The relative ease of launching RPM cases then gave the NDRC the ability to leverage harsh antitrust measures forcing manufacturers to reduce prices for consumer goods. The Infant Formula case offers a prime example. As an im-portant consumer product, the prices of milk powder were closely monitored by the NDRC. When inflation spiralled out of control, milk powder was one of the commodities subject to the NDRC's temporary price controls. At the time of the financial recession, the agency sent an emergency notice to all local provincial authorities to ensure compliance with its procedures. In 2011, on separate occasions, the NDRC invited manufacturers of infant formula milk powder to convene for 'informal chats' and compelled them to prevent price increases. However, these companies continued to raise prices despite repeated warnings from the NDRC. Complaints about these companies' RPM practices therefore provided the NDRC with the perfect excuse to rein in prices. A few days after the NDRC's announcement of its antitrust investigation into the infant milk powder industry, Wyeth announced that it would cooperate with the NDRC's investigation, rectify its behaviour immediately, and lower its wholesale prices by an average of 11 per cent. Other milk powder manufacturers quickly followed suit. In the end, Wyeth and two other infant formula manufacturers were rewarded with total immunity for their proactive cooperation with the NDRC, while three other manufacturers received a fine totalling RMB 668 million.

From an antitrust law perspective, however, it is very unusual for an antitrust authority to ask manufacturers to lower their prices as part of the remedies for an RPM case. But such an uncommon remedy is perfectly consistent with the NDRC's goal of controlling prices. In addition to price control, the NDRC had another important mission at the time: formulating industrial policy and coordinating industry planning. It delegated this responsibility to the Industry Coordination Bureau, a sister bureau of the Price Supervision and Anti-Monopoly Bureau, as well as to the Price Bureau. One deputy director simultaneously oversaw and managed these three bureaus. Given the clear incompatibility between the objectives of the three bureaus, there were speculations that antitrust simply served as a convenient method of facilitating industrial policy goals. It was widely speculated that the NDRC's investigation into Qualcomm and Interdigital had been driven by industrial policy. In both cases, Chinese manufacturers had relied heavily on standard essential patents (SEPs) provided by American firms, thus antitrust investigation could have conferred these Chinese manufacturers with greater bargaining power during negotiations for the licence of SEPs.

By comparison, the SAIC kept a lower profile while taking antitrust enforcement action. The majority of the SAIC's investigations were conducted by local offices and involved small, local companies with insignificant fines and remedies. It was not until 2013 that the SAIC announced that it had launched an enquiry into Tetra Pak and Microsoft. The SAIC's relatively conservative style could be attributed in part to the bureaucratic mission of the agency. Unlike the NDRC, which saw itself as a macroeconomic planner, the SAIC had a long bureaucratic history of being a market regulator. The divergent objectives of the two agencies therefore led to vastly different regulatory outcomes.

2.2 Bureaucratic Culture

Every organization has its own culture. James Wilson, a distinguished expert on bureaucracies, defines organizational culture as a 'persistent, patterned way of thinking about the central tasks of and human relationships within an organization'.[76] 'Culture is to an organization what personality is to an individual', Wilson observes. 'It changes slowly, if at all'.[77] As Lieberthal and Oksenberg highlight, past experiences of officials may lead them to conclude certain basic assumptions about risk assessments, the reliability of information gathered, and efficacy of various initiatives, which can play a critical role in shaping their perceptions about the matters on hand.[78] Indeed, the bureaucratic culture in which antitrust enforcers have been immersed significantly affects how they operate and carry out their tasks.

While both the NDRC and the SAIC were jointly responsible for conduct-related antitrust enforcement, the NDRC emerged into the more aggressive though less professional enforcer of the two. To understand the difference in the enforcement styles of these two agencies, it is useful to look at the organizational culture of each of these agencies. The SAIC had a long tradition of enforcing various commercial laws and regulations, including the Consumer Protection Law, the Anti-Unfair Competition Law (AUCL), and the Trademark Law. Previous research indicates that the SAIC had an extensive network of officials responsible for handling the investigation and enforcement of commercial laws and regulations.[79] The author noted that up to a quarter of the local office of SAIC in Shanghai (roughly between 230 and 250 employees) were engaged in both economic inspection and enforcement.[80]

In particular, the antitrust unit of the SAIC was made up of enforcement officials at both the central and various local levels overseeing the enforcement of the AUCL since 1993. The AUCL prohibits a wide range of 'unfair trade practices', such as counterfeiting, trademark confusion, commercial bribery, false advertising, infringement of commercial secrets, and fabrication of news to damage business reputation. It also contains some antitrust provisions like the prohibition against bid rigging and abuse of dominant market positions by public utility companies, and the prohibition of tying and predatory pricing to squeeze out competitors. In fact, the main responsibility of the staff members

---

[76] WILSON, *supra* note 23, at 91.
[77] Id.
[78] *See* LIEBERTHAL & OKSENBERG, *supra* note 20, at 28.
[79] MERTHA, *supra* note 5, at 178.
[80] Id.

at the SAIC was to investigate unfair trade practices and antitrust was only a fraction of what they did. According to the statistics disclosed by the agency, the SAIC and its local branches investigated eighty-two antitrust violations during the first decade of its enforcement of the AML.[81] However, the figure is vastly overshadowed by the number of anti-unfair competition cases brought by the agency. In the first half of 2017 alone, the SAIC and its local branches investigated 11,812 unfair competition cases.[82] The prior experiences of these administrative officers in handling the AUCL cases therefore influenced how they approached and tackled antitrust cases.

Capitalizing on their vast experience in unfair competition enforcement, the SAIC officials viewed antitrust as another instrument of administrative law enforcement. Senior leaders at the SAIC emphasized the importance of following rules and procedures in administrative enforcement, which set the boundaries of their enforcement activities.[83] When compared to the highly belligerent and prolific NDRC, one SAIC official commented grudgingly: 'Of course they [the NDRC] can bring more cases. Many of their enforcement activities have not complied with due process requirements and indeed have violated the requirements of administrative law'.[84] She mentioned that the NDRC did not have the requisite experience of a law enforcement agency.[85] She further claimed that some of the NDRC's staff members were not well equipped with knowledge in administrative law and had not been trained properly to carry out administrative enforcement.[86] The statements of the SAIC officials echoed the observations of lawyers.

The antitrust unit of the NDRC was the only bureau within the ministry that was in charge of law enforcement as it was originally the Price Supervision Bureau assigned to monitor prices and control inflation. Not surprisingly, few officials working at the antitrust unit of NDRC had a background in law and its staff had put a greater emphasis on economic outcome rather than due process during enforcement. Xu Kunlin, the former Director General, once indicated that only two staff members were dedicated to antitrust investigation while the rest were working on price supervision when he first joined the antitrust unit in 2009. After the bureau assumed the duty of antitrust enforcement, the

---

[81] *Fanlongduan Fa Shishi Shinian Yilai Gongshang He Shichang Jiandu Bumen Chachu Longduan Anjian 82 Jian* （反垄断法实施10年以来工商和市场监管部门查处垄断案件82件）[*State Administration and Market Supervision Departments Investigated 82 Antitrust Cases during the First Decade of the Enforcement of the Anti-Monopoly Law*], Xinhua Net (7 Sep. 2017).

[82] Id.

[83] Interview with two senior SAIC officials, Beijing June, 2016.

[84] Id.

[85] Id.

[86] Id.

bureau acquired twenty more members of staff and the team was reshuffled. However, even after this change, only a third of its employees were in charge of antitrust enforcement while the others continued to work on price supervision. As might be expected, the institutional memory of the Price Supervision Bureau persisted.

In the early stages of an antitrust investigation, the NDRC frequently invited companies suspected of antitrust violations for a discussion, also known as an administrative interview. The NDRC's preference for pre-emptive interventions has much to do with the agency's prior experiences. After multiple phases of market reform, most prices in China had been liberalized. Therefore, the NDRC no longer had the power to impact prices directly in most areas. As such, one of the means of controlling inflation for the agency was to hold administrative interviews with merchants and attempt to coerce them not to raise prices. During these administrative interviews, the NDRC usually obtained information from the companies or individuals that would allow them to improve their understanding of the situation. They also reminded the interviewees of the importance of regulatory compliance and warned them of the consequences of failing to follow through with them. If the NDRC had obtained some evidence of legal violations, it would urge the parties to confess their wrongdoings and rectify their conduct. As such, receiving an invitation for an administrative interview was viewed as an ominous sign.

Because the interview was largely an informal procedure, the agency could send out invitations to companies at its discretion. Moreover, the administrative interview was generally not actionable under Chinese administrative law, thereby shielding the NDRC from judicial scrutiny. Administrative interviews were also deemed efficient as they required little effort on the part of the administrative agency. The NDRC did not need to spend time or effort in terms of gathering evidence nor did it need to shoulder any responsibility if the investigation had failed. This saved the agency significant transaction costs, especially if the individual or the company readily conformed to the actions suggested by the agency.

As the antitrust unit of the NDRC was simultaneously in charge of price supervision and antitrust enforcement, it is not a coincidence that the practice of conducting administrative interviews during price supervision was carried over to antitrust investigations. In fact, the administrative interview became an indispensable, even dominant, part of the NDRC's antitrust investigation and prosecution process. In July 2013, the NDRC invited representatives from over thirty companies to a training event on compliance with the Chinese AML.[87]

---

[87] Michael Martina, *Tough Talking China Pricing Regulator Sought Confessions from Foreign Firms*, REUTERS (21 Aug. 2013).

A long list of multinationals participated, including but not limited to GE, Siemens, Samsung Electronics, Microsoft, Volvo, IBM Corp, Michelin, Tetra Pak, Intel Corp, Qualcomm, Dumex, and Arris Group Inc. During this closed-door meeting, one NDRC official hinted that over half of the companies present were currently under scrutiny. He then taught companies how to write self-criticism reports and showed letters from companies admitting guilt in past antitrust cases. He warned the companies present not to employ lawyers to challenge their investigations, threatening a doubling or tripling of penalties. As one senior antitrust lawyer once lamented: 'They [the NDRC] don't analyze. They just conduct an interview and ask for an admission [of guilt].'[88]

Another contentious case was the NDRC's investigation into InterDigital in December 2013. The enquiry was provoked by complaints from Chinese firms, alleging that InterDigital had abused its monopoly power over SEPs by filing a complaint against Chinese firms in the United States for patent infringement. The NDRC had reportedly requested InterDigital's CEO, William Merritt, to speak with officials and cooperate with the investigation by informing Interdigital's Chinese legal counsel that 'it cannot guarantee the safety of Interdigital's executives'.[89] Fearing arrest, Interdigital's executives responded by saying that they would not be able to attend such meetings. In the end, they met face to face as Interdigital issued a press release apologizing for their misunderstanding of Chinese laws and the NDRC's statements.

In September 2014, Reuters published a sensational news story entitled " 'Mr Confession" and His Boss Drive China's Antitrust Crusade'.[90] Based on interviews with two dozen lawyers, business executives, and experts, the report detailed ample criticism from many Chinese antitrust lawyers and the overseas business community about regulatory irregularities and a lack of due process in Chinese antitrust enforcement. According to the article, 'lawyers and executives describe meetings with the NDRC as "interrogations", where raised voices, flaring tempers, and verbal reprimands are commonplace'. Some lawyers also noted that the antitrust bureau had used 'widespread behind-the-scenes tactics—from personal threats to forced apologies and brow beatings' to coerce firms to cooperate with the agency's investigation. One NDRC official was supposedly putting pressure on firms under investigation not to hire external lawyers to defend themselves. Meanwhile, a persistent defence lawyer

[88] Id.

[89] Sakthi Prasad, *InterDigital Execs Fear Arrest, Won't Meet China Antitrust Agency*, REUTERS (16 Dec. 2013).

[90] Michael Martina & Matthew Miller, *'Mr. Confession' and His Boss Drive China's Antitrust Crusade*, REUTERS (15 Sep. 2014).

was threatened with a ban from future meetings with the regulator. A Chinese lawyer who represented a foreign firm in an NDRC probe described the bureau's action as 'reminiscent of the Red Guard tactics' during the Cultural Revolution. The NDRC's antagonistic pre-emptive intervention in early cases was highly controversial and led to much criticism about its abuse of administrative power and violation of due process.

2.3 Bureaucratic Structure

Experts on bureaucracies have long recognized the correlation between a bureaucratic structure and regulatory outcomes.[91] The institutional design affects the power distribution among regulatory agencies from the manner in which data and information is collected, the way policy choices that are prioritized, and, above all, how final decisions are made.[92] From the outset, the division of labour among the three former antitrust agencies had been subject to a great deal of criticism from both domestic and foreign commentators. Many believed that it was inefficient and costly to distribute the work and resources across three divergent ministries, especially given that China was a new regime in need of both human resources and knowledge in antitrust enforcement.[93] Moreover, even though MOFCOM's responsibility was relatively distinct from that of the other two agencies, the division of labour between the NDRC and the SAIC had been rather bewildering. For example, using the benchmark of whether or not a behaviour is related to the issue of price led to much confusion and many potential conflicts between the SAIC and the NDRC.[94] Although the Anti-Monopoly Commission (AMC) was created as a commission underneath the State Council to manage the coordination between the three agencies, in practice the AMC rarely met and thus its existence seemed to be merely symbolic.

A brief overview of the history of these three former antitrust agencies will help to explain the rather unusual division of labour among these agencies. Before the AML was implemented, each of these agencies had already been responsible for enforcing some competition-related rules and regulations.

---

[91] Jennifer Nou, *Intra-Agency Coordination*, 129 HAR. L. REV. 421, 422 (2015).

[92] ROBERT A. KATZMANN, REGULATORY BUREAUCRACY 7 (1980).

[93] Nathan Bush, *Constraints on Convergence in Chinese Antitrust*, 54 ANTITRUST BULL. 87 (2009); Salil K. Mehra & Yanbei Meng, *Against Antitrust Functionalism: Reconsidering China's Antimonopoly Law*, 49 VIR. J. INT'L L. 379, 408 (2008).

[94] Angela Huyue Zhang, *The Enforcement of the Anti-Monopoly Law in China: An Institutional Design Perspective*, 56 ANTITRUST BULLETIN 631 (2011).

Prior to the adoption of the AML, MOFCOM had reviewed hundreds of foreign acquisitions of domestic firms under the Provision on the Acquisitions of Domestic Companies by Foreign Investors since 2003. The NDRC had been acting as a price regulator in its enforcement of the Price Law, which was enacted in 1998 with provisions against price fixing and price-related unfair trade practices. Meanwhile, the SAIC had been responsible for the enforcement of the AUCL since its enactment in 1993. Although the AUCL prohibits a wide range of 'unfair trade practices', it also contains a few antitrust provisions such as the prohibition against bid rigging and abuse of dominant market positions by public utility companies. As revealed in the legislative history, the SAIC and MOFCOM both vied to be the main antitrust enforcer as they had been most closely involved with the drafting of the AML, whereas the NDRC was reluctant to surrender its power in overseeing price regulation and supervision.[95] A compromise was then reached so that each of the three agencies could have some authority. Predictably, the division of labour among them under the AML mirrors that of the pre-existing regime.

On 11 March 2018, the State Council proposed a plan to overhaul China's central ministries. The plan, subsequently confirmed by the 13th National People's Congress on 17 March 2018, recommended the reduction of the number of central ministries by eight, while also eliminating seven vice-ministerial agencies. The plan would create seven new ministries, including the State Administration for Market Supervision (SAMR), which would integrate the antitrust functions of the three agencies, as well as those of the AMC. In addition to antitrust enforcement, the SAMR would appropriate the other functions then assumed by the SAIC, the Administration of Quality Supervision, Inspection and Quarantine (SQSIQ) together with China Food and Drug Administration (FDA). The establishment of the SAMR put an end to the perennial turf war among the three administrative antitrust agencies. The change was ultimately heralded as a significant breakthrough in Chinese antitrust enforcement.

The SAIC emerged victorious in this specific round of government restructuring. The former head of the SAIC, Zhang Mao, was selected as Director General and Deputy Party Secretary of the SAMR. Bi Jinquan, the former bureau chief of the China FDA, was appointed Deputy Director General and Party Secretary. It is common for Chinese politicians to hold two titles simultaneously, one conferred by the administrative department and one bestowed by

---

[95] Yong Huang, *Pursuing the Second Best: The History, Momentum, and Remaining Issues of China's Anti-Monopoly Law*, 75 ANTITRUST L. J. 117, 125–26 (2008). *See also* NG, *supra* note 19, at 139.

the Party system. The leadership positions of Zhang Mao and Bi Jinquan paralleled each other as one held the utmost administrative post while the other held the highest Party post. In addition to Zhang and Bi, there were twelve other key Deputy Director Generals leading the SAMR. The sequence by which these twelve other leaders were introduced on the SAMR's website reflects their ranking within the organization. Along with Zhang, four other former SAIC officials were assigned seats on the SAMR's leadership board, where they were ranked at third, fourth, fifth, and twelfth. Moreover, three former officials from the SQSIQ were placed sixth, ninth, and tenth. The three officials accompanying Bi from the FDA were allocated to eighth, thirteenth, and fourteenth posts. The SIPO and the Central Party Discipline Committee each held one seat, ranking in eleventh and seventh respectively. In total, former SAIC members were handed five seats, FDA members were given four seats, and the SQSIQ three seats. Moreover, the seats occupied by the SAIC officials seem to be of paramount importance, signalling their prominent status in the new agency. In particular, Gan Lin, an ex-SAIC official responsible for directing antitrust and anti-unfair competition, online trade, and advertising departments was appointed as Deputy Director General, placing her at number four in the order. Gan is now leading the antitrust enforcement at the newly found agency. Notably, although the antitrust units of MOFCOM and the NDRC had been incorporated into the SAMR, neither MOFCOM nor the NDRC had a leadership seat in SAMR, making it difficult for the two agencies to continue exerting any influence over the SAMR.

Given the sway of the SAIC over the newly established agency, it is expected that the bureaucratic mission and the culture of the SAIC are most likely to be dominant in the new agency. As addressed earlier in this chapter, the SAIC was traditionally tasked with overseeing market activities and it had a solid understanding of law enforcement against violations in market regulations. Furthermore, its enforcement record in the past decade demonstrates its rather restrained approach. This suggests that Chinese antitrust enforcement will become more 'legalized' and professional. The SAIC's long history of law enforcement implies that the agency will be more cognizant of the requirements under Chinese administrative law and the requirement to observe the due process requirements. This bodes well for the future of Chinese antitrust enforcement.

This, however, does not suggest that the SAMR will keep to the same standard of due process as held in Western countries. The SAMR's enforcement strategies should still be understood in light of administrative law enforcement in China where the level of legal consciousness amongst government officials is low. As acutely observed by Randall Peerenboom, a Chinese law expert:

> Administrative officials [in China] today . . . tend to expect that people should defer to their better judgment and are disinclined to view themselves as servants of the people. They are more likely to pay attention to the shifting political winds and the dictates of their superiors than to the needs of the public or the individuals who come into contact with the system. And they still frequently disregard or circumvent the law when compliance would be inconvenient.[96]

Nor does the change suggest that the SAMR's decisions will be any less likely to be influenced by politics. The consolidation of the three former antitrust agencies occurred in the midst of a massive overhaul of the Chinese administrative system in 2018. Widely viewed as the most extensive round of government reorganization since 2008, the reform created a smaller number of 'super ministries', one of which is the SAMR. The NDRC lost its antitrust function and instead ceded some of its regulatory power to other ministries during the reorganization. According to Barry Naughton, the purpose of reducing the responsibilities of the NDRC was to induce the agency to channel its attention, energy, and resources towards macroeconomic issues rather than performing concrete interventions.[97] This looks like a market-friendly move. Even so, Naughton stressed that the main purpose was to make the bureaucratic machine more efficient and disciplined, making it easier for the top leadership to exercise command and control over an issue area.

3. Challenges Post Agency Consolidation

While many commentators have viewed the creation of SAMR as an encouraging and progressive step in the right direction, it has not changed the fact that the administrative enforcement of the AML will continue to be handled by a central ministry that belongs to the larger Chinese bureaucratic network. As such, the SAMR remains subject to the formal and tacit rules of the Chinese bureaucracy. These rules impose constraints upon Chinese agencies and set the boundaries for the work of the SAMR. They also form part of the continuing challenges that the new agency will face in the future.

---

[96] *See* PEERENBOOM, *supra* note 4, at 401–02.

[97] Barry Naughton, *Xi's System, Xi's Men: After the March 2018 National People's Congress*, 56 CHINA LEADERSHIP MONITOR 7 (17 May 2018).

3.1 Bureaucratic Hierarchy

Bureaucratic hierarchy will continue to be a significant constraint for the effective enforcement of the AML. As Chinese antitrust agencies are seldom challenged in court, the cost of their investigation and prosecution is lower in comparison to costs faced by government agencies in countries with established rule of law. However, defendants subject to antitrust investigations can lobby the relevant bureaucratic departments, transforming law enforcement into a bureaucratic process of bargaining and negotiation. As a consequence, the main battleground for administrative enforcement is not found in courts but within the government bureaucracy itself. This is particularly the case for SOE defendants who have relatively easier access to the government and can spend their resources more effectively on lobbying the relevant government departments. Chinese SOEs have traditionally enjoyed bureaucratic ranks determined by the levels of the government that supervise them. Even if the bureaucratic control of SOEs has gradually been abolished in the past few decades, the political pecking order of SOEs has persisted.[98] Today many top business leaders within SOEs remain appointed through the *nomenklatura* system and accordingly possess high bureaucratic rankings (which also implicitly determines the rankings of the SOEs) with accompanying benefits. This means that the leaders of SOEs have direct contact with the government. They do not need to work through business associations to relay their opinions or views and can instead engage in direct lobbying.[99] As such, the more politically powerful the SOE, the more resources it can utilize to lobby the government bureaucracy, translating into a higher cost for any Chinese administrative agency wishing to challenge its actions.

Accordingly, the political pecking order of the enforcement targets vis-à-vis the regulators is an important determinant of the cost that Chinese antitrust agencies face in enforcing the AML. Other things equal, the cost of bringing a case against a SOE would be higher than bringing one against a non-state firm; and the cost of challenging the action of a SOE owned by the central government would be higher than that of challenging a SOE owned by a local government. The cost further varies depending on the bureaucratic rank of the antitrust agency. The higher the agency's bureaucratic rank, the less opposition it will meet from SOEs. For example, the cost of prosecuting a local SOE would

---

[98] Barry Naughton, *Xi's System, Xi's Men: After the March 2018 National People's Congress*, 56 CHINA LEADERSHIP MONITOR (17 May 2018).

[99] Kjeld Eirk Brodsgaard, *Politics and Business Group Formation in China: The Party in Control*, 211 CHINA Q. 624, 627 (2012).

be lower for central enforcers than for local enforcers, as the former have a higher bureaucratic rank than the latter and for this reason are not subject to constraints imposed by local governments.

The NDRC's probe into the China Telecom/China Unicom case is a prime example. On 9 November 2011, the NDRC announced on the state-owned television network CCTV that it had been conducting an investigation into two large state-owned telecommunication firms for alleged price discrimination against rival companies upon receiving various complaints. Based on the complaints made by rival firms, China Telecom and China Unicom had sought out exorbitant fees from large Internet service providers (ISPs) for interconnection, which affected their ability to be competitive in the market. By contrast, it had fixed lower prices for non-competitors which are small ISPs. However, this differential pricing scheme developed into a situation of arbitrage in which small ISPs packaged their purchased bandwidth and resold it to large-scale ISPs. After detecting this, China Telecom disseminated a notice to its subsidiaries in 2010, barring resales of its services by small ISPs. Consequently, an Internet outage ensued for many large ISPs that had been dependent on the low-price bandwidth resold by small ISPs.

When the NDRC declared its investigation on national television, the public sentiment observed was overwhelmingly positive, as I will examine in Chapter 2. The case was widely applauded by Chinese intellectuals and considered a major breakthrough, but the situation quickly went downhill. A few days after the NDRC's announcement on CCTV, two editorials defending the two SOEs and harshly criticizing the NDRC's investigation were published in newspapers managed by the Ministry of Industry and Information Technology (MIIT), a telecom sector regulator. A few weeks later, both SOEs proposed a number of rectifications and requested a suspension of the state-led investigation. After the NDRC acknowledged the receipt of the settlement proposals from both two firms, no fines were ever levied upon them. Well-known antitrust scholars including Xiaoye Wang have expressed deep disappointment with the decision.[100]

Without recognizing the political dynamics at play between the relevant government actors, it would be difficult to understand the elusive outcome of this case. When the NDRC tried to regulate large SOEs such as China Telecom and China Unicom, it experienced potential backlash from many powerful

---

[100] See Xiaoye Wang, *The China Telecom and China Unicom Case and the Future of Chinese Antitrust*, in CHINA'S ANTI-MONOPOLY LAW: THE FIRST FIVE YEARS 478–86 (Adrian Emch & David Stallibrass eds., 2013).

actors. The first to resist NDRC's actions were the SOEs themselves. The leaders of China Telecom and China Unicom are appointed and supervised by the Organizational Department of the Central Committee of the Chinese Communist Party (the Party), enjoying ministerial ranks equal to that of the vice-minister at the NDRC. Thus, their bureaucratic ranks are higher than that of the head of the NDRC's antitrust bureau. This means that the Director General of the antitrust bureau was not in a position to give direct orders to the heads of these two telecom firms. The Director General would need to obtain support from a higher level of authority at the NDRC or from the upper echelons of the government—such as the State Council—in order to exert sufficient pressure to compel the SOEs to comply with their orders.

The second potential source of opposition against the NDRC was the State-owned Assets Supervision and Administration (SASAC), the Commission established directly under the State Council, responsible for overseeing the state's assets. The SASAC had emulated earlier campaigns in Japan and Korea, exerting great effort to develop national champions. Indeed, its main bureaucratic interest lies in fostering the growth of gargantuan and stronger SOEs. Accordingly, the SASAC has an incentive to 'protect' SOEs by granting them monopolistic resources. In recent years, the SASAC has become a powerful and vocal owner of the telecom sector, as was evident in its efforts to protect the financial interests of these two firms.[101] Hence, even if these two telecom firms had in fact abused monopoly power in order to maximize their profits, such behaviour was perfectly consistent with the SASAC's goal to maximize asset value. From the SASAC's perspective, harsh antitrust punishment of these SOEs would not only harm their reputation but also have significant impacts on their stock performance and asset value.

Another potential root of opposition could be attributed to the regulators overseeing the telecom sector. Sector regulation is often fragmented across a number of institutional bodies. When antitrust regulators are added to the mix, it further complicates the power dynamics between the government agencies with influence in the regulation of SOEs. As is the case with bureaucracies and firms alike, the more actors involved in a process, the pricier the output.[102] Indeed, the rectifications proposed by China Telecom and China Unicom, if accepted and enacted, would not just address the interconnection issues brought up in the NDRC's antitrust challenge but also 'greatly enhance the

---

[101] *See generally* Yukyung Yeo, *Between Owner and Regulator, Governing the Business of China's Telecommunication Service Industry*, 200 CHINA Q. 1013 (2009).

[102] POSNER, *supra* note 22, at 339.

penetration of fiber access and broadband access rates [and] reduce the unit bandwidth price for internet users by 35 per cent within five years'.[103] In March 2012, a deputy director from the NDRC's antitrust unit disclosed the developments of the case, revealing that China Telecom and China Unicom had at the time completed expanding their Internet broadband width by 100 gigabytes (G) and committed to reduce network tariffs for consumers.[104] The official also highlighted that China Unicom had further claimed that the penetration rate of 4 trillion-gigabyte bandwidth for public users would reach 50 per cent by the end of that year.[105]

Clearly, these ameliorative commitments exceeded the scope of the original antitrust complaint, raising the question of whether the NDRC was acting as an antitrust regulator or a telecom regulator. Regardless, the MIIT's uncompromising public campaign defending China Telecom and China Unicom and denouncing the NDRC's actions reveals much. Since the NDRC retains regulatory control over telecom fees, the MIIT saw the NDRC's antitrust intervention as an expansionist, strategic move in an attempt to encroach upon its regulatory turf.

This case offers a textbook example of how antitrust enforcement against Chinese SOEs takes place not in openly contested legal battles but through covert processes of negotiation and bargaining within a hierarchical bureaucracy. It also exposes how the utility function of an antitrust regulator such as the NDRC can effect its decision-making in tackling central SOE cases. As the regulation of telecom pricing is part of its designated responsibilities, antitrust intervention in this case could have helped the NDRC augment its policy control in the telecom sector. The final outcome of the settlement also appears to be a rational, utility-maximizing decision for the NDRC, as the compromise eventually reached significantly reduced its cost in handling the case. From the standpoint of the NDRC, the marginal benefits of imposing high fines on these two companies rather than settling with them would be low. By accepting their commitments to reduce telecom fees, the NDRC in large part achieved what

---

[103] For instance, China Telecom proposed that it would: (1) expand capacity with other backbone network operators such as China Unicom, China Railcom, etc., in a timely manner; (2) lower the price for direct connection with China Railcom, and further improve the interconnection quality to achieve sufficient interconnection; (3) further standardize the management of dedicated Internet access charges, deal fairly in accordance with market principles, and sort out the existing agreements to appropriately lower the current charge benchmark; and (4) greatly enhance the penetration of fibre access and broadband access rates, reduce the unit bandwidth price for Internet users by 35 per cent within five years, and commence implementation without delay. China Unicom has made similar commitments. *See* Wang, *supra* note 100, at 478–79.

[104] Id. at 479–80.

[105] Id. at 480.

it had wanted which was not only to retain existing powers but also expand its policy control in telecom regulation.

On the other hand, the SAIC never brought any high-profile cases against large central SOEs. As discussed above, the NDRC was often deemed more powerful than both the MOFCOM and the SAIC due to its pervasive policy control and its historical status as supra-ministerial. The SAIC was the weakest of the three as it had a relatively narrower mandate and the least policy control over SOEs amongst the three agencies. Although the SAIC was promoted to the status of a ministry-level agency in 2001, the formal upgrade did not translate into an actual enhancement of its political prowess. As such, the consolidation of the three agencies into the SAMR, which is mostly led by former SAIC leaders, potentially makes it even more difficult for Chinese antitrust agencies to tackle cases involving large and powerful SOEs. Bureaucratic hierarchy will therefore remain an impediment for the newly formed SAMR to prosecute politically mighty targets, particularly the large central SOEs.

3.2 Power Fragmentation

While many commentators have lauded the merging of the enforcement powers of the three former antitrust agencies into the SAMR, it is not a panacea for all inter-agency problems. The organizational structure of the AMC, a consulting and coordination organization established by the State Council in 2008, is quite telling in this regard. The agency was first headed by Qishan Wang, the then-vice premier in charge of the economic bureaucratic system.[106] The heads of the NDRC, the SAIC, and MOFCOM, as well as a deputy secretary-general of the State Council served as deputy directors. The AMC also consists of fourteen commissioners, including the incumbent deputy heads of various ministries and institutions under the State Council.[107] The AMC did not undertake any specific enforcement activity and operated only through meetings.[108] In

---

[106] Notice of the General Office of the State Council on the Main Functions and Members of the Anti-Monopoly Commission of the State Council (promulgated by the General Office of the State Council of the People's Republic of China, 28 July 2008) (LawinfoChina).

[107] In addition to the three former antitrust agencies, the AMC also include the SASAC, the MIIT, the Ministry of Transportation, the Ministry of Finance, the Ministry of Supervision, the State Intellectual Property Office, the China Banking Regulatory Commission, the China Security Regulatory Commission, the China Insurance Regulatory Commission, the State Electricity Regulatory Commission, and the Legislative Affairs Office of the State Council.

[108] *See* Regulations on Administration of the Establishment and Staffing of the Administrative Agencies of the State Council art. 6 (promulgated by Decree No. 227 of the State Council, 3 Aug. 1997, effective 3 Aug. 1997) 4 P.R.C. Laws & Regs III-01-01-201 (China).

practice, the commissioners rarely held formal meetings to discuss antitrust issues and the day-to-day work was simply assigned to MOFCOM. Regardless of the AMC's inactivity, it had officially bestowed authority upon various ministries and organizations to engage in antitrust affairs. The AMC's authority structures imply that no single ministry has the clout to make any important antitrust policy or decision unilaterally. It also sends a strong signal that the Chinese government does not view antitrust enforcement as an administrative task that should be handled independently by a specialized agency. Rather, inter-agency cooperation and coordination among different Chinese ministries is essential for antitrust enforcement.

This phenomenon of power fragmentation is not unique to antitrust. Political scientists have long observed that the Chinese government bureaucracy makes economic policy decisions according to the rule of 'management by exception'; at each bureaucratic level, agency representatives make decisions by the rule of consensus.[109] If the representatives at one level all agree, the decision is then automatically ratified at the higher level. Otherwise, the decision will be referred to authorities at a higher level who will either step in to make the decision or allow the matter to be dropped until a consensus can be reached. This method of decision-making has been used to alleviate information asymmetry for the Party leadership. Chinese ministries are organized either by function (e.g. education, culture, finance) or by economic sector (e.g. agriculture, telecommunication, transportation).[110] This complex structure gives virtual (i.e. non-electoral) representation to the economic groups and interests that the Party leadership depends on for political support.[111] This structure also creates some checks and balances among the agencies; each of the agencies has a particular mission and is expected to pursue it with fervour.[112] Therefore, when ministries and provincial leaders are called to convene to discuss a policy proposal, they are expected to represent and articulate the views of their units.[113] Accordingly, delegation by consensus is deemed more efficient because it relieves the trouble of constant interventions in the policy process for top Party leadership.[114] When a consensus cannot be reached, the issue is pushed to the top so that superiors can take advantage of and exploit the information obtained through different subordinate agencies.[115]

---

[109] LIEBERTHAL & OKSENBERG, *supra* note 20, at 23–24. *See also* SUSAN L. SHIRK, THE POLITICAL LOGIC OF ECONOMIC REFORM IN CHINA 116 (1993).
[110] SHIRK, *supra* note 109, at 93.
[111] Id. at 99.
[112] LIEBERTHAL & OKSENBERG, *supra* note 20, at 29.
[113] Id. *See also* SHIRK, *supra* note 109, at 98–99.
[114] SHIRK, *supra* note 109, at 117.
[115] Id. at 116–17.

One direct consequence of the 'management by exception' approach is that power often becomes fragmented during policy-making and implementation.[116] The existence of massive, parallel, and interdependent bureaucracies in addition to territorial administrations with overlapping jurisdictions further complicates this process. Kenneth Lieberthal and Michel Oksenberg, two leading experts on Chinese politics, proposed the 'fragmented authoritarianism' model to examine political processes in China.[117] By closely studying Chinese economic policy-making, they found that a centrally made policy was increasingly malleable to the political interests of various ministries and provinces responsible for enforcing that policy within their jurisdictions.[118] Within the energy sector, for example, they found that a single ministry or province lacked sufficient clout to launch or sustain a big project or new major policy.[119] This fragmentation of authority thus necessitates elaborate consensus-building efforts at every stage of the decision-making process.[120] China scholar David Lampton's studies on bargaining in Chinese politics offer similar insights in this regard.[121] He found that bargaining among bureaucracies with similar political resources and bureaucratic ranks is so frequent and ubiquitous that policy-making becomes protracted and inefficient.[122] As he noted: 'Americans sometimes see themselves as uniquely hamstrung by a "checks and balances system", the Chinese decision system often is hamstrung by a complex bargaining process and the need to build a consensus.'[123] Susan Shirk also observed that because each participant at the bargaining table has veto power, policies that emerge from this system tend to be incremental rather than radical.[124] Moreover, if there are more participants involved in the decision-making process, policy consensus becomes more elusive.[125]

The Chinese merger control process offers a good case for us to observe the power fragmentation in Chinese antitrust enforcement. Similar to most jurisdictions in the world, merger reviews are mandatory and suspensory (i.e.

[116] See LIEBERTHAL & OKSENBERG, *supra* note 20, at 22.

[117] Id. at 22–31. For more recent works on fragmented authoritarianism, *see* Andrew C. Mertha, 'Fragmented Authoritarianism 2.0': Political Pluralization in the Chinese Policy Process, 200 CHINA Q. 995, 995–96 (2009).

[118] Mertha, *supra* note 117, at 996.

[119] See LIEBERTHAL & OKSENBERG, *supra* note 20, at 23.

[120] Id. at 22–23.

[121] See David M. Lampton, A Plum for a Peach: Bargaining, Interest and Bureaucratic Politics in China, in BUREAUCRACY, POLITICS, AND DECISION MAKING IN POST-MAO CHINA 34–35 (Kenneth Lieberthal & David Lampton eds., 1992).

[122] Id. at 34–35, 57.

[123] Id. at 35.

[124] SHIRK, *supra* note 109, at 127.

[125] Id.

parties are not allowed to merge until they receive clearance) in China. As long as a transaction meets the notification thresholds in China, parties to the transaction have the obligation to notify the antitrust authority and the deal cannot be closed until the authority clears the transaction. The Chinese merger review system is modelled after that of the European Union, which has a body of competition law that is followed by many jurisdictions all over the world. But there are two features that have made China far more distinct in its approach.

First, the merger notification process in China is notoriously long. Large multinational companies increasingly find their merger transactions delayed by the antitrust authority's clearance decisions. For instance, in *Google/ Motorola*, China was the last jurisdiction to clear the transaction. In fact, the agency did not approve the transaction until the last day of the statutory review period. There were some cases in which the merging parties had not reached a desirable outcome with the antitrust authority, or the agency required or encouraged the parties to withdraw their previous filings and then re-file. Thus, in some cases, the administrative review time significantly exceeds the statutory review period. Moreover, it has been observed that, unlike other large merger jurisdictions—notably the United States and the European Union—where merger reviews are primarily economic based, China's antitrust authority often incorporates non-competition factors, particularly industrial policies into its analyses.[126] As such, the international business community has qualms about how the Chinese government applies the AML to protect domestic industries from foreign competition.[127]

To be fair, the Chinese antitrust authority is understaffed compared to other merger review antitrust agencies in large jurisdictions. The Anti-Monopoly Bureau of MOFCOM, previously in charge of reviewing hundreds of cases each year, only had a headcount of thirty-five. The number of employees responsible for merger enforcement at the current Anti-Monopoly Bureau of the SAMR is roughly the same. This fact alone, however, does not fully account for the hold-ups. The more decisive reason for the delay, one commonly known among experienced practitioners, is that the Chinese antitrust agency regularly confers with other government departments and organizations during merger reviews.[128] These government departments include bureaus at the NDRC and the MIIT that manage industrial policies, some sector regulators such as the

[126] Daniel Sokol, *Merger Control under China's Anti-Monopoly Law*, 10 N.Y.U. J.L. & Bus. 1, 14–16 (2013)

[127] Mario Mariniello, *The Dragon Awakes: Is Chinese Competition Policy a Cause for Concern?*, BRUEGEL POLICY CONTRIBUTION (Oct. 2013), at 2.

[128] Sokol, *supra* note 126, at 33.

Ministry of Agriculture as well as local governments in certain cases. As maintained by some observers, the industrial policy departments within the NDRC and the MIIT are the most frequently consulted government departments. The SAIC, local foreign investment approval authorities, and local government authorities are sometimes consulted. Because the NDRC and the MIIT are charged with broad mandates to oversee the growth and development of particular industries, commentators have noted that they have a tendency to provide input from the perspective of industrial policy.[129] The deliberation process is rather opaque and the antitrust agency does not discuss the information it has obtained from these government agencies with the disputing parties. In reality, the more government departments are involved in the negotiation process, the more unpredictable the situation becomes; sometimes, the delays are not within the antitrust agency's control. Moreover, because the final decision made by the antitrust authority is influenced by opinions and comments from other government agencies such as the NDRC and the MIIT, their decisions may sometimes appear inconsistent with economic-based principles and international standards.

Based on my interviews with government officials working at central ministries, I found that government officials did not view the antitrust agency's practice of consulting other agencies as 'unusual' at all; in fact, they thought it was the standard procedure for economic policy and decision-making in central ministries.[130] They pointed out that within the Chinese government bureaucracy, it was a customary practice for one agency in charge of economic policy or decision-making to solicit comments and opinions from other government agencies, this is typically known as the '*huiqian*' (meaning 'countersign') procedure in China. The *huiqian* procedure is a long-standing practice among ministerial agencies and has persisted in the absence of formal rules or procedures. The State Council Working Procedure Rules explicitly necessitate that the decision-making process used by each ministry and organization under the State Council be democratic and scientific. In addition, the State Council Working Procedure Rules specify that if the State Council needs to be notified of important matters, it will require extensive research and consulting by the ministry, including sufficient cooperation with other relevant government departments. In practice, government agencies that have been consulted will have a say in the policy-making process and therefore, the *huiqian* procedure is an important consensus-building mechanism among various government

[129] NG, *supra* note 19, at 249.
[130] Telephone interview with government officials at different central ministries, Jan. 2014.

actors. Consistent with prior studies conducted by political scientists on delegation by consensus, interviewees confirmed that policy proposals or administrative decisions that had been through the *huiqian* procedure are more likely to be ratified by the State Council. On the other hand, if the agencies were unable to reach a consensus on a matter, the decision would be relegated to the State Council.

Because large merger transactions often have an impact on the competitive structure of domestic industries, a merger review inevitably involves other government department functions, such as those responsible for industrial policy or those in charge of overseeing certain economic industry sectors. Consequently, even if the *huiqian* procedure constrains the antitrust agency's discretion to some extent, it also mitigates the risk of a decision negatively impacting the interests of the other government agencies at play. The *huiqian* procedure further helps the agency gain insight into the industry sectors in which the mergers take place. This was especially true during the early years of AML enforcement. With limited experience in merger review, the employees of MOFCOM had neither the capacity nor the sufficient expertise in various industry sectors to conduct the reviews. As MOFCOM could not solely rely on information provided by the merging parties, the *huiqian* procedure became part of an important investigation process into the market. In fact, if the antitrust authority made a critical merger decision without properly communicating with the relevant government departments, the legitimacy of its decision could be challenged internally within the government bureaucracy.

Although the Chinese antitrust authority has an interest in seeking out advice from other government departments, it does not necessarily embrace all of their opinions. As each government agency is presumed to maintain its own interests which compete with those of other agencies, conflicting views are inevitable. When this occurs, it is then left to a 'bargaining' process in which the antitrust agency and other government agencies must conceive a workable solution that is deemed satisfactory to all. Therefore, in many circumstances, a compromise is necessary because it is not usually possible to accommodate everyone. In fact, while some government agencies have complained that the antitrust authority had delegated far too much work to them through extensive consultation, they also grumbled that the opinions they had imparted during the discussions had not been fully adopted by the antitrust authority.

However, as the *huiqian* procedure is akin to a repeated game, an agency that refuses to cooperate with other agencies faces the possibility of future retaliation when it wishes to propose a decision or policy. Anticipating that they would need cooperation from the antitrust authority in the future, government agencies tend to seek a compromise. How often other agencies voice their opinions, how hard these agencies press their opinions, and how much the antitrust authority ultimately incorporates their opinions into a final decision depends on the relative power of the factional networks which those government agencies represent vis-à-vis the antitrust authority. In this regard, some commentators have observed that the antitrust authority on occasion was able successfully to fend off concerns of other government departments to focus on merger-specific competition issues.[131] However, when other departments express firm opinions against a transaction, the antitrust authority might from time to time find it necessary to take their concerns into account when making its decision.[132]

Indeed, power fragmentation and consensus building have been part of the bureaucratic routine in China. While the amalgamation of the three former antitrust agencies into the SAMR may have put an end to the power struggle between them, it cannot escape this trend. The regulatory authority of merger review remains fragmented among different central ministries. The SAMR will not be completely independent when conducting merger reviews and other ministries whose interests are at stake have a say in the process. Long delays and non-competition-related factors will continue to engender much uncertainty in China's merger enforcement, as I will further elaborate when examining the collapse of the *Qualcomm/NXP* deal in Chapter 5. In addition to merger reviews, it is similarly possible for other government departments to interfere in conduct investigations, as seen in the aforementioned China Telcom/China Unicom case.

3.3 Regional Inertia

Another bureaucratic constraint that antitrust agencies will continue to face is regional inertia, which stems from administrative decentralization. Most bureaucratic enforcement departments in China are simultaneously subject to supervision by two administrative organs: the local government at the same administrative level and the superior administrative agency. The local governments have control over personnel appointments and the budget allocation of the administrative agency. This ability allows them to issue binding orders, whereas the superior agency can only issue non-binding ones. For this reason,

---

[131] *See* NG, *supra* note 19, at 249.
[132] Id. at 250.

local governments are known to have 'leadership relations' with the agency and the superior administrative agencies instead have 'professional relations' with the agency.[133] However, the interests of the local governments are not necessarily aligned with those of the superior administrative agencies. In such circumstances, orders from the local governments are prioritized over those from the superior agencies, and local departments need to appease the local government.[134] This leads to the perennial problem of local protectionism.

One stark example that illustrates this is China's ineffectiveness in combating counterfeit products. While China has faced significant external pressure from foreign countries to improve its intellectual property protection, it has only succeeded in getting Beijing to promulgate satisfactory intellectual property laws and regulations.[135] Because most responsibilities for actual enforcement of intellectual property rights fall on the shoulders of local agencies, local officials often tolerate counterfeiting problems for the protection of the local government revenue and employment opportunities.[136] Moreover, local authorities lack incentives to crack down on local producers of counterfeit products when the products are sold to other regions such that the cost is borne by consumers in other provinces.[137] In some poorer areas, local enforcers rely on the collection of fines and license fees to cope with inadequate budget so regulatory activities become a revenue-generating activity. As a consequence, local officials prefer imposing financial penalties on infringing firms that operate the factories rather than shutting down the factories that produce the unsafe food themselves or initiating criminal prosecutions against them.[138] While the latter approach is deemed more effective in preventing illegal conduct, for the bureaucrats, it is analogous to 'killing the goose that lays the golden egg'.[139] Similar problems are prevalent in the areas of environmental protection[140] and food safety.[141]

The same challenge facing the SAIC in combating counterfeiting has likewise beleaguered antitrust enforcement agencies. For instance, based on decisions

[133] Andrew Mertha, *China's 'Soft' Centralization: The Parameters of Centralization: Shifting Tiao and Kuai Authority Relations*, 184 CHINA Q. 791, 797 (2005).
[134] DALI L. YANG, REMAKING THE CHINESE LEVIATHAN, MARKET TRANSITION AND THE POLITICS OF GOVERNANCE IN CHINA 97 (2006).
[135] MERTHA, *supra* note 5, at 15.
[136] Id.
[137] YANG, *supra* note 134, at 97.
[138] Wai Keung Tang & Dali Yang, *Food Safety and the Development of Regulatory Institutions in China*, 29 ASIAN PERSPECTIVE 5, 18 (2005).
[139] Id. at 19.
[140] Bejamin van Rooij, *Implementation of Chinese Environmental Law: Regular Enforcement and Political Campaign*, 37 DEVELOPMENT & CHANGE 27 (26 Apr. 2006).
[141] Tang & Yang, *supra* note 138.

disclosed by the SAIC, the vast majority of cases were initiated and enforced by local antitrust agencies. As of 2017, the SAIC concluded investigations of eighty-two antitrust violations. With the exception of the Tetra Pak case, all the other cases were brought by Regional Office of State Administration for Industry and Commerce (AICs). But considering the large nationwide network of AIC agencies, this is hardly an impressive feat. This local inertia in enforcing the AML can partially be explained by the local enforcers' lack of incentives. For local AICs, antitrust enforcement was viewed as an exciting new way to pursue greater policy control. This was particularly the case for AIC authorities because they shared overlapping responsibilities with other government agencies and thus had grown increasingly wary of other government departments encroaching upon their authority.[142] Notably, in some jurisdictions, local governments regard administrative fining as a revenue-generating business. To induce administrative agencies to generate more fining revenue, these local governments use the number of fines they receive as a benchmark for salaries and bonuses.

At the same time, local enforcers encounter severe constraints in enforcing antitrust laws against large local champions. Because the local governments control the local enforcers' budgets and personnel appointments, they are cautious enough to ensure that their antitrust enforcement efforts do not run against the interests of the local governments. Because regional monopolies are often deemed local champions that substantially contribute to the gross domestic product of local regions, they can often be shielded by local governments. This explains why cases initiated by local AICs tend to involve small as opposed to large local SOEs, with the exception of those cases in which the central agencies have actively chosen to intervene. By contrast, central enforcers have not experienced comparable constraints from local governments in prosecuting local SOEs. As they were higher in the political pecking order, their administrative control was not subject to that of the local governments. The extent of political opposition they faced was much lower than that those confronted by local offices.

The Shanghai gold retailer case illustrates the invigorated commitments from central officials. On 13 August 2013, the NDRC imposed a total fine of RMB 10 million on Shanghai Gold and Jewellery Association and five gold retailers for fixing the prices of gold and platinum. Despite widespread media coverage, few noticed that these five retailers were all SOEs controlled by the Shanghai government. At the time of the investigation, three remained owned

---

[142] Zhang, *supra* note 27, at 704.

by the city government even though the Shanghai government had sold off two of the retailers. What was also omitted from the NDRC's official decision was the fact that the Shanghai Price Bureau had been aware of such price-fixing arrangements among these retailers for more than a decade. In 2001, the Shanghai Price Bureau found that the price control measure among a group of eleven jewellery retailers (including those involved in this specific case) had been in fact a price alliance that violated the Price Law, a consumer protection law with a few antitrust provisions outlawing cartels. The Shanghai Price Bureau reportedly issued an administrative warning to these firms and ordered them to rescind their activities immediately, but no fines were imposed, even though the Bureau could have imposed a fine of up to five times the illegal gains made under the Price Law. Two months later, the Shanghai Gold and Jewellery Association made a petition on behalf of the jewellery retailers to the Shanghai government and applied for an administrative reconsideration of the penalty decision. The Shanghai government ruled in favour of the trade association and revoked the decision made by the Shanghai Price Bureau. No subsequent action was taken by the Shanghai Price Bureau until the NDRC in Beijing intervened in this case.

At the same time, the capacity of the central agency is very limited, and it is incapable of handling all of these regional cases on its own. Without the active intervention of central enforcers, antitrust enforcement against regional monopolies is unlikely to reap satisfactory results. As such, the consolidation of the three former separate agencies into a single unit has not resolved the inherent central versus local conflict. Unless the SAMR can exercise control over all local antitrust officials and become vertically integrated, the local inertia affecting antitrust cases will likely persist.

Summary

In this chapter, I have attempted to explicate a critical facet of Chinese antitrust exceptionalism, its bureaucratic underpinnings, by offering a bottom-up perspective to explain the rise of antitrust enforcement in China. As antitrust enforcement largely targets monopolies, central administrative enforcers are at the helm of agenda setting for antitrust enforcement. The stern sanctions under the AML have a strong deterrent effect over businesses, affording administrators great discretion to influence business activities. Such discretion is translated into power and prestige for the administrative agencies, which in turn, are more motivated to further advance antitrust enforcement. Business rivals and plaintiffs' lawyers also play important intermediary roles in facilitating the administrative agencies to propel enforcement forward.

In order to understand why Chinese government agencies behave as they do, it is crucial to understand the path-dependent nature of bureaucracies. None of the three former antitrust agencies were born in a vacuum; they were built on the foundations of previous agencies and therefore have ingrained institutional memories. The mission, culture, and structure of each of these administrative departments affected how each has carried out its enforcement duties. This is particularly apparent based on the observation of the NDRC's enforcement priorities and its controversial styles and tactics of enforcement. The absorption of the three agencies into a newly created agency, the SAMR, is a rare event that has disrupted this trend of bureaucratic inertia. The NDRC lost its clout over administering antitrust laws while the SAIC, one of the three former agencies, ascended to power by occupying the top leadership positions of the SAMR. As the SAIC has a long and distinct history of administrative law enforcement, it is expected that under its leadership, Chinese antitrust enforcement will become more professional and legalized.

Chinese antitrust enforcement is mostly administrative in nature. As decisions by administrative enforcement agencies have rarely been challenged in court, antitrust enforcement is largely dominated by a bureaucratic process, and day-to-day antitrust enforcement is subject to the formal and tacit rules that characterize all bureaucracies in China. As such, the constraints imposed by the Chinese bureaucracy—the bureaucratic hierarchy, power fragmentation, as well as local inertia—will continue to present obstacles to Chinese antitrust enforcement in the years to come.

2

Regulatory Hostage-taking and Shaming

In the sweltering summer of 2014, Chinese consumers were euphoric that foreign car makers such as Audi, BMW, Mercedes-Benz, Chrysler, and Jaguar
Land Rover were reducing prices of new cars and spare parts in China. These
manufacturers were not engaged in a price war. Instead, they were cutting prices to placate a regulator—the National Development and Reform
Commission (NDRC), one of the three former antitrust agencies. The NDRC
had been investigating the alleged resale price maintenance (RPM) practices of
luxury car manufacturers for weeks. RPM refers to a business practice whereby
a supplier restricts the freedom of the retailers to set prices for their products
below a certain level. As soon as the agency had announced its investigation,
the car makers immediately responded with admissions of guilt and promises
to rectify their behaviour. All of this occurred even before the agency had released any decision, but this response was hardly peculiar. All major RPM cases
previously investigated by the NDRC, encompassing local state-owned liquor
companies, optical lens makers, and infant formula manufacturers, ended in
a similar way. In one extreme example, a business executive from Wyeth appeared on the Chinese television together with NDRC officials and publicly
apologized for his company's behaviour.[1] This 'well-behaved' firm was ultimately rewarded with full immunity from punishment.

This pattern of acquiescing to an antitrust agency is highly unusual and
unique to China. In fact, antitrust regulators elsewhere can only dream of
enjoying such high levels of cooperation from firms under investigation. As
targeted firms rarely defended themselves, the NDRC saved a tremendous
amount of resources and time, thereby also significantly increasing its capacity
to take on more cases. More perplexingly, all those firms under investigation
took the extra step of reducing their prices despite having no legal obligation
to do so. Typically, for RPM violations, antitrust regulators only have the right
to ask infringing firms to rescind their practices, and under no circumstances

---

[1] CCTV, *Fan Longduan Nengfou Hanwei Women De Liyi* (反垄断能否捍卫我们的利益？）[*Can Antitrust Protect Our Interest*], DUIHUA（对话）[DIALOGUE] (25 Aug. 2013).

Chinese Antitrust Exceptionalism. Angela Huyue Zhang, Oxford University Press (2021). © Angela Huyue Zhang.
DOI: 10.1093/oso/9780198826569.003.0003

does the regulator have the right to request the company to reduce the prices of the wholesale products. One possible explanation for this peculiarity, as discussed in Chapter 1, is that the NDRC, which was also a price regulator that monitored prices and controlled inflation in China, coerced these merchants to lower prices.

At the same time, the NDRC's decisions were highly contentious from both substantive and procedural standpoints. In a *Johnson & Johnson* case dating back to 2013, the Shanghai High Court explicitly recognized the possible pro-competitive effects of RPM practices, and required the plaintiff to prove that the practices in question were anti-competitive.[2] The NDRC officials I spoke with claimed that the agency did conduct economic analyses during its investigations.[3] However, given the scant reasoning in the NDRC's decisions, it was unclear whether the agency had amassed enough economic evidence to prove the anticompetitive effects of RPM practices in the cases listed earlier and, if so, whether these effects outweighed the potential pro-competitive benefits. A general consensus among Chinese academics is that the standard of proof attained by the NDRC was usually much lower than what was required by the Chinese judiciary.[4]

Procedurally, the NDRC's practices have also been subject to fierce criticism, as discussed in Chapter 1. Amidst heightened antitrust scrutiny, foreign multinational companies continually raised complaints to their governments and chambers of commerce about the lack of transparency and due process violations in Chinese antitrust enforcement. In a survey of companies conducted by the US–China Business Council in 2014, 86 per cent of respondents indicated that they were 'somewhat' or 'very' concerned about the enforcement of China's Anti-Monopoly Law (AML), citing major concerns such as discrimination, lack of due process, little regulatory transparency, and the use of non-competition-related factors.[5] The reports released by the chambers

---

[2] Shanghai High People's Court, *Bangrui Yonghe Technology Trading Co., Ltd. v. Johnson & Johnson (Shanghai)Medical Equipment Co., Ltd. and Johnson & Johnson Medical (China) Ltd.*, [2012] Hu Gao Min San (Zhi) Zhong Zi No. 63, （北京锐邦涌和科贸有限公司诉强生（上海）医疗器材有限公司，强生（中国）医疗器材有限公司，（2012）沪高民三（知）终字第63号）1 August 2013 (hereinafter *Johnson & Johnson*). *See also* Chunfai (CF) Lui, *A Landmark Court Ruling in China: Resale Price Maintenance as Examined in the Johnson & Johnson Case*, 2 Competition Pol'y Int' Chron. 9 (2013).

[3] Interview with a NDRC official, Beijing, June 2016.

[4] Yong Huang & Yannan Liu （黄勇&刘燕南）, *Guangyu Woguo Fanlongduan Fa Zhuanshou Dingjia Weichi Xieyi De Falv Shiyong Wenti Yanjiu* （关于我国反垄断法转售价格维持协议的法律适用问题研究） [*Study Regarding the Resale Price Maintenance Law Under China's Anti-Monopoly Law*], 10 Shehui Kexue （社会科学） [Social Sci.] 82 (2013).

[5] US–China Business Council, *USCBC 2014 China Business Environment Survey Results: Growth Continues amidst Rising* (2014), at 20.

of commerce in both the United States and Europe also criticized China's hectic antitrust enforcement in recent years.[6] As the European Chamber of Commerce stated in August 2014:

> It [The Chamber of Commerce] had received numerous alarming anecdotal accounts from a number of sectors that administrative intimidation tactics are being used to impel companies to accept punishments and remedies without full hearings. Practices such as informing companies not to challenge the investigations, bring lawyers to the hearings or involve their respective governments or chambers of commerce are contrary to best practices.[7]

Given these legal ambiguities and procedural defects, it seems rather odd that none of those car manufacturers under investigation challenged the NDRC's decisions, and they were not alone. Since the enactment of the AML in 2008, no appeal has been lodged against any central enforcement agency in response to an antitrust decision, nor has there been any publicly disclosed administrative reconsideration directed at any government agency. So what is holding firms back?

Conventional wisdom suggests that these firms decided not to appeal because they had little trust in the Chinese judicial system and believed that they would be unlikely to succeed in an administrative suit. This is an appealing argument that seems to be evinced by unsuccessful appeals against the local antitrust agencies, as I will elaborate on later in this chapter. But there is an important factor that has not been accounted for by conventional perception. In a simple economic model, a party's decision to litigate or to settle depends on a number of factors, including the amount in dispute, each party's perceived chances of success, and each party's transaction cost of litigation.[8] If the plaintiff's expected gains at trial are higher than the defendant's expected loss at trial, then settlement will not occur, and vice versa. Thus, if a business is dissatisfied with an administrative decision and assumes that it can potentially gain more from suing the government than in settling the case it will appeal, even if the chance of success is low. As such, the unlikelihood of prevailing in an administrative suit is not necessarily the decisive factor holding firms back

---

[6] See US Chamber of Commerce, *Competing Interests in China's Competition Law Enforcement: China's Anti-Monopoly Law Application and the Role of Industrial Policy* (2014), at 77–78. See also European Chamber of Commerce, *European Chamber Releases Statement on China AML-Related Investigations* (13 Aug. 2014).

[7] European Chamber of Commerce, *supra* note 6.

[8] A. MITCHELL POLINSKY, AN INTRODUCTION TO LAW AND ECONOMICS 135–36 (4th eds. 2011)

from filing a suit. In fact, if the stakes for the business are extremely high, and the transaction cost of litigation remains relatively low, it is possible that the business would choose to battle the government, even though it faces a low probability of success. Conversely, a high probability of winning a case is not a sufficient condition for a company to appeal an antitrust decision either. This is because the direct payoffs from the lawsuit is not the only factor to consider. The cost of litigation can also bear on the parties' decisions. This cost of litigation not only includes the direct costs of handling the lawsuit but also indirect costs that may be incurred as a result of the lawsuit.[9]

In this chapter I argue that the transaction cost of launching an administrative appeal against a Chinese antitrust authority is so high that businesses refrain from appealing in the vast majority of cases, regardless of their likelihood of success in court. As explained in Chapter 1, each of China's three former central antitrust agencies, the NDRC, the State Administration and Industry and Commerce (SAIC), and the Ministry of Commerce (MOFCOM) were nestled within a large central ministry that operated like a conglomerate. Even after these agencies were consolidated in 2018, the new Anti-Monopoly Bureau is still housed within the State Administration and Market Regulation (SAMR), a big central ministry that oversees many aspects of market regulation. Thus, companies with business dealings in China, foreign or domestic, will presumably interact with the antitrust agency and its host ministry in the future. When a business decides to act, it must envisage how its current behaviour might influence the response of the regulator and in turn, affect its own future actions. In the early years of the enforcement of the AML, the NDRC was widely deemed the most powerful and aggressive of the three enforcers. It threatened companies with severe sanctions to dissuade firms from challenging the agency's decisions and generously granted cooperative businesses greater leniency, enticing them to settle. In addition to its antirust purview, the ministries that housed the former antitrust agencies also enjoyed broad discretion, retaining significant residual control in determining the interpretation of many other regulatory areas. Companies operating in China are therefore particularly susceptible to an array of regulatory attacks.

Legal sanction is not the only ammunition at the disposal of Chinese antitrust agencies. Although they are rarely subject to judicial challenge, they face acute bureaucratic constraints. As elaborated in Chapter 1, power is highly fragmented within Chinese bureaucracy, and antitrust regulators are often subject to lobbying and interference from other bureaucratic departments,

---

[9] Ronald H. Coase, *The Problem of Social Cost*, 3 J. L & ECON. 1 (1960).

especially when it comes to the regulation of rather large SOEs. In order to es-tablish a reputation as a tough antitrust regulator swiftly, the NDRC leveraged media to deter firms strategically from disobeying its orders and strong-armed them into obeying specific demands. The NDRC's successful media strategy was partly owed to the Chinese government's tight control of the media. In practice, once the agency had tactfully disclosed information concerning on-going investigations of particular firms, it could rile up populist sentiments against these firms and expose them to increased negative publicity. Such an outcome would deal a significant blow to companies, especially consumer product firms that hold dear to their brand image and reputation. Publicly listed firms could also face market sanctions and suffer the repercussions of slumping stock prices. As such, although antitrust fines can be astronomical and behavioural requirements can be severe, they are still tiny compared to the market damage that an antitrust agency can inflict on a company. Notably, the NDRC not only imposed 'shaming' sanctions on companies strategically but also shamed opposing antitrust experts to prevent them from challenging the agency's actions.

Game theorists have shown that a cooperative outcome can arise between antagonists if they anticipate repeated future interactions.[10] This theory aptly explains the cooperative outcome observed in Chinese antitrust enforcement. Needless to say, firms raided by Chinese antirust agencies are never happy. But since they foresee more penalties if they do not comply, they choose to capit-ulate instead of taking an aggressive and adversarial approach. Consequently, even if a business believes that the law is in its favour and that it maintains a good chance of winning in court, it will rationally decide that it is not cost ef-fective to sue the government. Sadly, the law does not really matter in these circumstances: the parties do not bargain in the shadow of the law—not even in the slightest. This explains why most businesses under Chinese antitrust in-vestigation prefer to accept their punishments, settle fines, and continue with their activities.

This chapter is organized as follows. I will begin by providing a general over-view of the administrative appeals system in China and recent administrative law reforms. I will then move on to explain the immense administrative discre-tion enjoyed by Chinese administrative agencies and how businesses are taken hostage by the government. By focusing particularly on the media strategy employed by the NDRC during antitrust enforcement, I will demonstrate

---

[10] *See generally* ROBERT AXELROD, THE EVOLUTION OF COOPERATION (1984).

how Chinese antitrust authorities can also regulate by shaming firms under investigation.

1. Suing the Chinese Leviathan

Like all other forms of government, an authoritarian regime faces the challenges of monitoring the performance of its departments and preventing abuse of administrative discretion.[11] Taking this into this consideration, the Administrative Litigation Law (ALL) of 1989 was created to complement the existing institutions with the aims of maintaining political control and tackling agency problems of lower-level officials.[12] A monitoring mechanism is also provided under the AML, giving dissatisfied parties the option to dispute a decision under Article 53. Specifically, if a firm is not satisfied with derived merger decision, it may first apply for an administrative reconsideration[13] before lodging an administrative suit in a Chinese court.[14] For non-merger antitrust decisions, firms have the choice to file for a reconsideration of the administrative decision or to bring lawsuits against the agencies directly. Despite this, few companies under investigation have chosen to challenge an antitrust decision, and the few appeals that were made have all fallen through.

1.1 Administrative Law Reform

There is no doubt that China has made remarkable progress with regards to the formal rules and procedures that have been incorporated into the administrative law regime. However, there remains a significant discrepancy between the law and enforcement.[15] In fact, some Chinese law specialists have observed

---

[11] Tom Ginsburg, *Administrative Law and the Judicial Control of Agents in Authoritarian Regimes*, in RULE BY LAW, THE POLITICS OF COURTS IN AUTHORITARIAN REGIME 58–72 (Tom Ginsburg & Tamir Moustafa eds., 2008).

[12] Randall Peerenboom, *Globalization, Path Dependence and the Limits of Law: Administrative Law Reform and Rule of Law in the People's Republic of China*, 19 BERKELEY J. INT'L L. 161 (2001).

[13] *See generally* Zhonghua Renmin Gongheguo Xingzheng Fuyi Fa（中华人民共和国行政复议法） [Administrative Reconsideration Law of the People's Republic of China] (1999) (promulgated by the Standing Comm. Nat'l People's Cong., 29 Apr. 1999, effective 1 Oct. 1999); *See also* Xin He, *Administrative Reconsideration's Erosion of Administration Litigation in China*, 2 CHINESE J. COMP. L. (2014).

[14] *See* Angela Huyue Zhang, *The Enforcement of the Anti-Monopoly Law: An Institutional Design Perspective*, 56 ANTITRUST BULL. 630, 637 (2011).

[15] Minxin Pei, *Citizens v. Mandarins: Administrative Litigation in China*, 152 CHINA Q. 832 (1992); Kevin O'Brien & Lianjiang Li, *Suing the Local State: Administrative Litigation in Rural China*, 51 CHINA J. 76, 75 (2005).

that suing the government agencies is as futile as 'attempt[ing] to crush stones with eggs'.[16] The statistics of Chinese administrative litigation seem to support this observation. Based on data provided by the Supreme People's Court, plaintiffs' success rate has never exceeded 15 per cent between the years 2006 and 2015, even dropping below 8 per cent during some years.[17] Simultaneously, there is an abnormally high withdrawal rate in administrative litigation cases.[18] Pursuant to the ALL, plaintiffs may apply for a withdrawal before the court makes a ruling in an administrative case, and the court has the authority to decide whether to allow the withdrawal.[19] In the year 2008, the Supreme People's Court laid out explicit criteria for considering withdrawal applications to ensure that plaintiffs' interests are protected.[20] Concerned with the possibility of coerced withdrawals, scholars have urged courts to serve as 'vigilant gate-keepers' while reviewing withdrawal applications.[21] In reality, however, withdrawal applications were rarely denied.[22] According to figures from the Supreme People's Court, the rate of withdrawal by plaintiffs never fell below 30 per cent from 1989 to 2014 and in some periods exceeded 50 per cent.[23]

However, these statistics only tell us the outcome of cases that were actually litigated. Klein and Priest have long pointed out a 'selection problem' in litigation: since litigated cases are not a random sample of disputes, using them to draw inferences about the status of Chinese administrative law can therefore be misleading.[24] While no conclusive inferences could be drawn from the available statistics, the overwhelming consensus amongst Chinese academics and

---

[16] See, e.g., Susan Finder, *Like Throwing An Egg against a Stone: Administrative Litigation in the People's Republic of China*, 3 J. CHINESE L. 1 (1989); Ji Li, *Suing The Leviathan—An Empirical Analysis of the Changing Rate of Administrative Litigation in China*, 10 J. EMPIRICAL LEGAL. STUD. 815 (2013); Xing Ying & Xu Yin, *Case Registration Politics and the Stagnation of Administrative Litigation: An Empirical Study of Two Northern China Basic Courts*, 6 L. & POLITICS FORUM 111 (2009).

[17] See Haibo He （何海波）, *Xin Xingzheng Susong Fa Shishi Yi Zhounian, Cong Quanguo Shuju Kan Chengxiao* （新行政诉讼法实施一周年，从全国数据看成效） [*One Year Anniversary of the New China's Administrative Litigation Law: Effects from Nationwide Statistics*], 3 Zhogguo Falv Pinglun （中国法律评论） [CHINA LAW REV.] (2016).

[18] He, *supra* note 17, at 261–63; *see also* Pei, *supra* note 15, at 842.

[19] Zhonghua Renmin Gongheguo Xingzheng Susong Fa （中华人民共和国行政诉讼法） [Administrative Litigation Law of the People's Republic of China] (promulgated by the Standing Comm. Nat'l People's Cong., 1 Nov. 2014, effective 1 May 2015) (hereinafter ALL), art. 51.

[20] See Supreme People's Court, *Zui Gao Renmin Fayuan Guanyu Xingzheng Susong Chesu Ruogan Wenti de Guiding* （最高人民法院关于行政诉讼撤诉若干问题的规定） [Rules of the Supreme People's Court in Regard to Certain Issues in Withdrawals in Administrative Litigation] (promulgated by Adjudication Comm. Sup. People's Ct., 14 Jan. 2008，effective 1 Feb. 2000), art. 2.

[21] He, *supra* note 17, at 264.

[22] Id.

[23] Id.

[24] George Priest & Benjamin Klein, *The Selection of Disputes for Litigation*, 13 J. LEGAL STUD. 1 (1984); *See also* Donald Whittman, *Dispute Resolution, Bargaining, and the Selection of Cases for Trial: A Study of the Generation of Biased and Unbiased Data*, 17 J. LEGAL STUD. 313 (1988).

policy-makers was that the ALL had not been effective in its original form.[25] This provided an impetus for amending the law.

In 2014, China revised the ALL and the newly amended law took effect on 1 May 2015.[26] The modified law seeks to alleviate the various difficulties experienced by plaintiffs during administrative suits. It extended the statute of limitations, allowing plaintiffs to file a complaint up to six months after they became aware of a disputed administrative act.[27] It also broadened the scope of administrative acts that can be challenged by private citizens.[28] Other improvements in this revision attempted to minimize the uncertainties for plaintiffs filing complaints. The new law requires the court to issue a receipt notice indicating the date of receipt of a complaint, and the court must decide whether or not to process the case within seven days.[29] If the court declines the complaint, it must issue a decision letter, which can be appealed by plaintiffs.[30] This registration procedure was introduced to guarantee a legal remedy for plaintiffs in case of an issued notices of refusal.

Moreover, to reduce the potential for local governments to exert influence over administrative suits, the new law also makes it possible for intermediate people's courts to try cases against administrative agencies above the county level.[31] In addition, high people's courts can designate certain courts to decide on cases from outside its jurisdiction, upon authorization from the Supreme People's Court.[32] The 2015 ALL revisions further attempted to address deficiencies in administrative reconsideration. Under the original 1989 ALL, if a higher administrative agency decided to sustain a lower-level administrative agency's decisions in a review case, then the lower-level agency would remain as the defendant.[33] However, if the higher-level agency decided to overturn the lower-level agency's decision, the higher-level agency would become the defendant. This gave an incentive for higher-level agencies to tolerate the actions of lower-level agencies to avoid becoming defendants in lawsuits. The 2015

---

[25] Xuan Hua（滑璇）, *Xingzheng Susongfa 25 Zhounian*（行政诉讼法25周年）[*The 25th Anniversary of the Administrative Litigations*] (29 Oct. 2015).

[26] Quanguo Renmin Daibiao Dahui Changwu Weiyuanhui Guanyu Xiugai Zhonghua Renmin Gongheguo Xingzheng Susongfa de Jueding（全国人民代表大会常务委员会关于修改中华人民共和国行政诉讼法的决定）[Decision of the Standing Committee of the National People's Congress on Revising the Administrative Litigation Law], Order No. 15 of the President (1 Nov. 2014).

[27] Art. 46, ALL.

[28] Art. 12, ALL.

[29] Art. 51, ALL.

[30] Id.

[31] Art. 15, ALL.

[32] Art. 18, ALL.

[33] Art. 25, ALL (promulgated by the Standing Comm. Nat'l People's Cong., 4 Apr. 1989, effective 1 Oct. 1990) (the 1989 version).

amendments resolved this problem by allowing plaintiffs to object to higher-level agencies sustaining the original administrative decisions of lower-level agencies.[34] The various measures introduced under the ALL revisions have generated a surge in administrative litigation nationwide. As soon as the new law was promulgated, the number of administrative cases accepted by People's Courts increased more than twofold in just one month.[35] The total number of administrative litigation cases in 2015 reached 220,398, representing a 55 per cent increase from 2014.[36]

Meanwhile, the number of actual withdrawal applications has plummeted after the ALL amendment. In 2015 the number of withdrawn cases remained at 22 per cent, the lowest recorded level since the ALL came into force in 1989.[37] Among these, the percentage of rescinded cases where the defendant altered their behaviour (such that the plaintiff could obtain some relief) increased from 5.5 per cent to 6.6 per cent.[38] The plaintiffs' prospects of success, though still low, have also risen to 13 per cent.[39] According to data published by the Supreme People's Court, from 2010 to 2014 Chinese courts at all levels handled 1.6 million administrative lawsuits in total, an increase of 16 per cent compared to the previous five years.[40]

1.2 The Anomaly of Antitrust Appeals

Despite the significant improvements brought about by the new ALL and the encouraging surge in acceptance rates for appeals, this trend does not extend to Chinese antitrust enforcement. In an empirical study about administrative litigation against Chinese tax authorities from Henan province, Ji Li found that firms with limited extractable resources, powerful allies in the government, and substantial stakes in the litigation were more inclined to sue the tax authorities, especially when the transaction cost of alternative dispute resolutions was high.[41] Li's findings are similar to what I have observed in the context of

---

[34] Art. 26, ALL.
[35] Hua, *supra* note 25.
[36] He, *supra* note 17.
[37] Id.
[38] Id.
[39] Id.
[40] Zhou Qiang（周强）, *Zuigao Renmin Fayuan Guanyu Xingzheng Shenpan Gongzuo Qingkuang De Baogao*（最高人民法院关于行政审判工作情况的报告）[*Report on Administrative Litigations of the Supreme People's Court*], NPC.GOV.CN (10 Nov. 2015).
[41] See Ji Li, *Dare You Sue the Tax Collector? An Empirical Study of Administrative Lawsuits against Tax Agencies in China*, 23 WASH. INT'L L. J. 57 (2014).

Chinese antitrust. Thus far, there have been only two cases where firms sought to launch a vigorous defence against a central antitrust authority. The first case is the NDRC's investigation of Qualcomm from 2014 to 2015. As discussed in Chapter 1, the stakes involved for Qualcomm were exceedingly high as the NDRC was demanding that the firm change its business model of its licencing fees charges, in effect drastically reducing its revenue. Finding itself in a precarious situation, Qualcomm was prepared to go to court to challenge the NDRC if the agency did not give concessions.

The second case is the NDRC's investigation of China Telecom/China Unicom, previously mentioned in Chapter 1 and further discussed in this chapter. Backed by other powerful central ministries including the Ministry of Industry and Information Technology (MIIT) and the State-owned Assets Supervision and Administration Commission (SASAC), the two state-owned telecom giants initiated a fierce attack to counter the NDRC's review. Notably, no litigation was launched against the NDRC in both cases. The Qualcomm case, though in the form of a penalty decision, resulted in a settlement, and the issued suspension in the China Telecom/China Unicom case was also considered a settlement reached among different bureaucratic interest groups. In all the other investigations made by the central authorities, none of the enforcement targets had powerful political allies in the Chinese bureaucracy the way that both China Telecom and China Unicom did. Nor were they in a paralysing position like Qualcomm. Thus, it is not surprising that they did not take legal action against antitrust authorities.

On the other hand, there have been a few unsuccessful attempts to appeal the decisions of local antitrust authorities. One such attempt was made when the Jiangsu Price Bureau investigated a cartel involving thirty-seven cement manufacturers and a cement association in Jiangsu province in August 2013. The agency imposed a total fine of RMB 37 million on the participating firms. Thereafter, three cement manufacturers filed an administrative lawsuit against the Jiangsu Price Bureau in April 2014. One company later withdrew its case and the case was ultimately dismissed by the court for exceeding the statutory limitation.[42]

Another case was brought by Yutai, a fish feed company, which was fined by the provincial authority of the NDRC in Hainan for RPM in 2017.[43] Yutai

---

[42] See NDRC, *Jiangsu Sheng Liangjia Lunningtu Qiye Bu Fu Fan Longduan Chufa Baisu* （江苏省两家轮凝土企业不服反垄断处罚败诉） [*Two Cement Manufacturers in Jiangsu Province Lost their Appeal against the Antitrust Penalty Decision*], NDRC.GOV.CN (8 Dec. 2014).

[43] See Lester Ross & Tingting Liu, *China's Supreme People's Court Rules RPM is Illegal Per Se*, WILMERHALE (3 July 2019).

appealed the decision of the local authority to the Haikou Intermediate People's Court. The latter validated the company's claims, making it the first administrative antitrust suit won by a private plaintiff in China. Troubled by the verdict and rather worried about the future loss of control of RPM cases, the NDRC officials travelled to Hainan to lobby the local government.[44] Its efforts proved successful, as the Hainan High People's Court subsequently overruled the decision of the Haikou court. In a departure from the judicial approach taken in previous RPM cases such as *Johnson & Johnson*, the Hainan High Court endorsed the NDRC's per se illegality approach and relieved the agency of the burden of establishing the anti-competitive effects in this case.[45] Yutai then appealed its case to the Supreme People's Court (SPC) in 2018 but the SPC upheld the decision of the High Court.[46] The SPC recognized the use of different standards when evaluating the illegality of RPM. Although it acknowledged that RPM could have pro-competitive effects, it nonetheless backed the NDRC's decision on the grounds that the Chinese market was not yet fully developed, and competition continues to be weak. The SPC expressed further concern that requiring the administrative agency to satisfy a high burden of proof could have a chilling effect on public enforcement.

This case was considered an important victory for the NDRC. There had been much scepticism surrounding the NDRC's aggressive prosecution of RPM cases and the Yutai case helped the agency gain legitimacy, emboldening its prosecution of additional RPM cases. The SAMR, the new antitrust authority created after merging three former antitrust agencies, has continued to apply the same approach in RPM investigations. Be that as it may, the Yutai decision also received scathing criticism from many within the SPC as the tenuous argument put forward about the different standards of proof required in civil and administrative cases found little support in Chinese law.[47] Moreover, even though a decision by the SPC has some precedential value, there is no stare decisis in China. Therefore, the SPC's decision on the Yutai case is not binding on the lower courts and there is no obligation for courts to use the decision as a guideline for similar cases. That said, even if the Yutai decision is overruled by a future court, it remains unlikely that businesses will choose to take issue with RPM decisions by a central antitrust authority in Beijing. Unlike local authorities with limited antitrust enforcement jurisdiction over a

---

[44] Interview with a judge who was privy to the case, Beijing, Nov. 2018.

[45] Peter Wang *et al.*, *China's Supreme Court Resets Resale Price Maintenance Analysis*, JONES DAY (Aug. 2019).

[46] Id.

[47] Interview with a judge who was privy to the case, Beijing, Nov. 2018.

business subject, the central authority maintains extensive administrative discretionary power and can strategically leverage state media to damage the reputation of firms under investigation, as elaborated below.

2. Regulatory Hostage-taking

Raymond Vernon, a renowned economist specializing in international investment, once proposed an obsolescing bargain model to describe the bargaining dynamics between foreign investors and a host country.[48] When a host country first tries to entice foreign investors, the initial bargain favours the investors. However, the relative bargaining power shifts over time to benefit the host government as the assets of the investors are taken hostage by the host government. The host country then begins to impose more conditions on the foreign investors in the form of higher tax rates along with greater stringent regulatory measures to expropriate the assets of the foreign investors. Consequently, the original bargain becomes obsolete.

This obsolescing bargaining model helps to explain the ever-changing relationship between foreign multinational companies and the Chinese government over the past few decades. When China first embarked on market reform and opened its doors to foreign investors in 1979, the central government ceded a significant degree of power to the local governments in an effort to attract foreign investment. Local governments throughout China rushed to give preferential treatment and economic concessions to foreign investors, ranging from reduced land use fees and labour to preferential tax breaks. Now, more than four decades later, China has become the world's largest recipient of foreign direct investment and the globe's second largest economy, with a market of 1.4 billion consumers that few multinational companies can afford to ignore. As the initial investment made by foreign investors has become a sunk cost, foreign investors are gradually ceding bargaining power to the Chinese government. Foreign multinationals operating in China have become increasingly alarmed by China's complex tightening of restrictions and new changes to the regulatory environment. A business climate survey by the American Chamber of Commerce and Deloitte in 2019 further confirmed these foreign sentiments, revealing that over half of the respondent companies agreed that

---

[48] RAYMOND VERNON, SOVEREIGNTY AT BAY: THE TRANSNATIONAL SPREAD OF U.S. ENTERPRISES (1971).

current Chinese regulatory enforcement has become a major source of unfair treatment and discrimination for foreign multinational companies.[49]

Indeed, law is never complete and inevitably, the executing agency retains a certain degree of discretion. This is particularly true of antitrust enforcement, which affords the Chinese antitrust agency enormous discretion in determining violations and imposing sanctions. Meanwhile, the weak institutional environment in China gives rise to a race-to-the-bottom scenario in terms of regulatory compliance. Foreign businesses operating in China are therefore susceptible to regulatory attacks on various fronts and often find themselves at the mercy of enforcement agencies. Furthermore, each of the three former antitrust authorities were, and the incumbent agency is, housed within larger ministries that possess broad overarching regulatory functions. Because companies under examination for antitrust violations are typically large and successful with significant market power, they envisage frequent dealings with the central ministries in the future. This explains the cooperative approach adopted by businesses when slapped with antitrust investigations in China as they fear that an adversarial approach will spur a greater backlash in the future.

2.1 Antitrust Discretion

A large grey area exists within the framework of administrative antitrust enforcement, enabling Chinese agencies to exert influence and exercise their discretion over outcomes.[50] Chinese antitrust authorities often offer scant reasoning for underlying theories of harm, and it is therefore difficult to bind agencies to the precedents made under their authority. Despite the promulgation of numerous rules and implementation guidelines there are still no clear procedural guidelines for the determination and application of penalties under the AML. Some commentators have expressed great concern about the absence of an effective mechanism for controlling the broad discretionary power bestowed to these agencies. They have also warned of the dangers of inconsistent decisions and unequal treatment.[51] On 17 June 2016, the NDRC released the Anti-Monopoly Commission's drafted guidelines on levying

---

[49] American Chambers of Commerce & Deloitte, 2019 China Business Climate Survey Report (2019).

[50] Xingxiang Zhang, *China's Anti-Monopoly Law Enforcement, A Quest for Transparency, Consistency, and Fairness*, RESEARCH CENTER FOR CHINESE POLITICS AND BUSINESS OF INDIANA UNIVERSITY (APRIL 2015).

[51] Dr Xu Liu is one of the most vocal critics of the AML enforcement. He maintained a blog on Sina Weibo.

fines in an effort to inject more transparency and predictability into the fining process.[52] Although this represented promising progress, ambiguities still abound as a large degree of authority is still retained by the current Chinese antitrust agency.[53] This problem is also common elsewhere. The European Commission (the Commission), even with its long-standing fining guidelines, has been criticized for imposing arbitrary and inconsistent fines.[54] Although the Commission's fining decisions are frequently disputed in EU courts, practitioners still lament the lack of a rigorous judicial review of the Commission's fines.[55]

As detailed in Chapter 1, the NDRC was adept at conducting administrative interviews, a pre-emptive method of intervention, during its inquiries. Such interviews simultaneously served as a promise and a threat to businesses. The NDRC enticed companies under investigation to comply by suggesting that they proactively reduce prices and credit these changes to the agency in public announcements. In return, the agency could vindicate them from wrongdoing or give them a reduced penalty. As Xu Kunlin, the former Director General of the antitrust subdivision at the NDRC, stated during a televised appearance: 'Regardless of whether your company is the subject of an investigation, if you give yourself up voluntarily and co-operate, you can receive a lesser punishment or avoid it altogether.' His remarks are consistent with the enforcement record of the NDRC, conveying that the agency has made good on this promise. For instance, referring back to the Infant Formula case, three key manufacturers including Wyeth, Beingmate, and Meiji received complete immunity after voluntarily relinquishing intelligence and pertinent evidence. But this practice of awarding immunity appears to run afoul of the NDRC's own guidelines which explicitly stipulate that only the first company to report willingly can receive immunity. The NDRC officials that I met with explained that they were entitled to grant immunity to multiple infant manufacturers because they viewed each firm's violation as a distinct and separate case.[56]

---

[52] NDRC, *Guanyu Rending Jingyingzhe Longduan Xingwei Weifa Suode He Queding Fakuan De Zhinan*, （关于认定经营者垄断行为违法所得和确定罚款的指南） [*Guidelines of the Anti-Monopoly Commission of the State Council on Determining the Illegal Gains Generated from Monopoly Conduct and on Setting Fines*], NDRC.GOV.CN (17 June 2016).

[53] *See* Comments of the American Bar Association Part of Antitrust Law and International Law on the Draft Guidelines of the Anti-Monopoly Commission of the State Council on Determining the Illegal Gains Generated from Monopoly Conduct and on Setting Fines (21 June 2016).

[54] Damien Geradin & David Henry, *The EC Fining Policy for Violations of Competition Law: An Empirical Review of the Commission Decisional Practice and the Community Courts' Judgments*, 1 EUROPEAN COMPETITION J. 401 (2005).

[55] Ian Forrester, *A Challenge for Europe's Judges: The Review of Fines in Competition Cases*, 36 EUROPEAN L. REV. 185 (2011).

[56] Interview with NDRC officials, Beijing, June 2016.

This explanation, however, is not tenable from an economic perspective. Economic theories dictate that there are two circumstances under which RPM can be considered anticompetitive. The first occurs when the RPM is imposed by a firm with substantial market power that wishes to leverage its market position to reinforce market power in another market. This cannot be applied to and is not what was observed in the Infant Formula case, as the manufacturers operated in a highly competitive market. The second is when the RPM can facilitate the formation of cartels amongst manufacturers. If the latter had been the NDRC's primary concern at the time of prosecution, then it would not have made sense for the agency to approach each violation individually. More fundamentally, these cases were related to RPM practices rather than secretive cartels, and thus it is equivocal as to why such exemptions were conferred in the first place.

On a similar note, after dawn raids, the NDRC routinely asked companies to submit reports of self-assessment admitting guilt without allowing them to see or respond to the implicating evidence.[57] Once companies agreed to sign the settlement offer, it became impossible for them to reverse their positions or file an appeal. These pre-emptive interventions and quick settlements helped the agency resolve cases quickly and efficiently, effectively shielding officials from legal challenges down the road. On the other hand, if the company endeavoured to defend itself and deny the allegations, it risked receiving a higher penalty for exercising its legitimate rights of self-defence.

Going back to the example in Chapter 1, during a private meeting with legal counsels from over thirty foreign multinational companies, one NDRC official explicitly warned companies not to employ lawyers to challenge their investigations, or they would risk doubled or tripled penalties.[58] Indeed, some NDRC officials viewed the right of legal defence as an 'obstruction' and imposed higher penalties on those who defended themselves, citing higher prosecution costs. According to my interview with an NDRC official involved in the Infant Formula case, Biostime received the harshest fine not because it had committed a more serious violation compared to the other infant formula manufacturers, but because the firm's legal counsel had wasted the agency's time and caused 'too much trouble' by defending the firm's business practices.[59] In fact, the NDRC's penalty for Biostime also explicitly indicated that non-cooperation was one of the main reasons why the firm had received a severe fine.

---

[57] Interview with two senior antitrust practitioners, Beijing, June 2016.

[58] Michael Martina, *Tough-talking China Pricing Regulator Sought Confessions from Foreign Firms*, REUTERS (22 Aug. 2013).

[59] Interview with a NDRC official, Beijing, June 2016.

Clearly, the NDRC's enforcement practices were in violation of Chinese administrative law. China's Administrative Penalty Law explicitly stipulates that administrative agencies are forbidden from imposing high penalties on parties simply because they tried to defend themselves.[60] The Law also invalidates an administrative penalty if the agency refuses to hear the claims of self-defence from the party in question.[61] Moreover, administrative agencies are required to hold a public hearing before imposing large fines.[62] In spite of this, no-one dared to challenge the NDRC's final decisions, and lawyers advised the firms subject to investigation to acquiesce and cooperate with the agency swiftly. As such, most companies subject to examination appeared readily willing to admit wrongdoing and promised to rectify their behaviour.

Notably, among the three former agencies, only the NDRC had perceptibly applied such high-pressure enforcement tactics. Since its absorption into the SAMR (along with the two other agencies) there have been fewer complaints about violations of due process. Thus, the aggressive enforcement style of the NDRC appears to have been highly correlated with the agency's culture and the leadership style of the agency head, as discussed in Chapter 1. Nonetheless, the NDRC's early practices have had a lasting impact on subsequent enforcement and compliance.

2.2 Hostage beyond Antitrust

Antitrust is not the sole legal challenge that businesses face when operating in China. In principle, a firm that has strong regulatory compliance should worry less about government retribution. However, all businesses operating in China, domestic or foreign, might be tempted to engage in extra-legal activities to grow their businesses and maintain their competitive advantage. As observed by a Chinese businessman: 'The law in China does not have only a few grey areas: it is one big grey area. The authorities can tolerate a practice for years then round people up on an arbitrary basis.'[63] Confronted with a choice between strong regulatory compliance with low profitability and weak regulatory

---

[60] Art. 32, Zhonghua Renmin Gongheguo Xingzheng Chufa Fa (中华人民共和国行政处罚法) [Administrative Penalty Law of the People's Republic of China] ((promulgated by the Standing Comm. Nat'l People's Cong., 13 Mar. 1996, effective 1 Oct. 1996) (hereinafter Administrative Penalty Law), art. 32.

[61] Administrative Penalty Law, art. 41.

[62] Administrative Penalty Law, art. 42.

[63] Jim Armitage, *China Charges GSK-linked Investigator and His Wife for 'Illegally Obtaining Private Information'*, THE INDEPENDENT (14 July 2014).

compliance with high profitability, firms may be more inclined to opt for the latter. This race to the bottom exposes firms to various regulatory risks. They become vulnerable to the administrative discretion of Chinese enforcement agencies. Companies operating in China, regardless of nationality, are generally averse to using a confrontational approach in dealing with the government. Instead, many of them try to wine and dine government officials in an effort to obtain better government services and protection.[64]

As a matter of fact, Chinese firms are not the only ones to have built their businesses on the fragile cornerstones of legal grey areas. As demonstrated by Jordan Barry and Elizabeth Pollman, many of the world's most high-profile and innovative companies such as Airbnb, Uber, and Tesla have devoted significant time and resources to operate businesses fraught with legal risks.[65] These companies are regulatory entrepreneurs: they first break the law, take advantage of legal loopholes, display the pretence of remorse, and then seek to expand their sphere of influence by mobilizing their users as a political force. For these companies, changing the law is an integral part of their business plan. A similar phenomenon also exists in China, where innovative technology companies like Didi and Alibaba tap into controversial business practices and consequently are on the verge of breaking Chinese laws.

Since the early 2000s, a large number of leading private businesses in China have encountered lurking regulatory risks as they try to use the variable interest entity (VIE) structure to raise funds from overseas stock markets. Typically, foreign investors acquire stakes in an offshore holding company, usually based in tax havens such as the Cayman Islands. The holding company then sets up a Chinese subsidiary, which signs contracts with a third-party company in charge of running the business and which then pledges to send profits to the Chinese subsidiary. This mechanism of complex contractual arrangements allows these foreign-owned companies technically to bypass the Chinese government's investment restrictions in the internet sector. However, it arguably contravenes the spirit of the law, and recent regulations drafted by MOFCOM have cast significant doubt on its legitimacy.[66] While the legality of the VIE structure has been ambiguous from the start, ambitious foreign and domestic entrepreneurs, along with investors, have chosen to take a gamble on the government's potential reaction. The survival of these companies therefore

---

[64] Hongbin Cai et al., *Eat, Drink, Firms, Government: An Investigation of Corruption from the Entertainment and Travel Costs of Chinese Firms*, 54 J. L. & ECON. 55 (2011).

[65] Jordan M. Barry & Elizabeth Pollman, *Regulatory Entrepreneurship*, 90 S. CAL. L. REV. 383 (2017).

[66] Gregory J. Millman, *Foreign Companies at Risk from Proposed Chinese Law*, WALL ST. J. (19 Apr. 2015).

depends not only on their performance in the market but also on the resolution of legal issues affecting core aspects of their business. Until the Chinese government intervenes decisively, these companies can continue to operate in and capitalize on the grey area and reap profits.

Other examples of legal grey areas abound in China. In 2014, GlaxoSmithKlein (GSK) paid an RMB 3 billion fine to the Chinese government in response to accusations of 'massive and systematic bribery' of government officials, hospitals, and doctors in order to boost its sales in China. GSK's senior executives were detained, and one was temporarily banned from leaving China. But industry experts noted that such bribery practices are quite common in the Chinese market, and in fact, the Chinese competitors of GSK are 'more brazen than their multinational counterparts'.[67] After the scandal was revealed, GSK revamped its sales incentive schemes.[68] Instead of a high-powered incentive model that pays sales representatives according to their sales performance, sales representatives are now rewarded with a higher base salary and a bonus scheme tied to their product knowledge, and other initiatives such as the number of meetings with doctors. This change made it less likely for doctors to receive benefits from prescribing GSK drugs, as their demands could no longer be entertained by GSK's sales representatives, nor were they paid to informally promote the company's drugs. The problem, however, is that this new practice also puts the GSK's business at a commercially disadvantaged position, since doctors are now less inclined to prescribe GSK drugs as other drug companies can offer them more incentives.

Notably, GSK is only one on a long list of foreign companies involved in corruption practices in China, as uncovered by the US government's recent aggressive enforcement campaign under the Foreign Corruption Practice Act (FCPA). In 2012, Pfizer reached a USD 45 million settlement with the Securities Exchange Commission (SEC) for FCPA charges. The SEC alleged that Pfizer had employed 'point programs' that incentivized doctors to prescribe its drugs in exchange for small gifts such as cell phones and tea sets. In 2015, Mead Johnson paid USD 12 million to settle an FCPA investigation. According to the SEC, Mead Johnson's employees at its Chinese subsidiary had paid doctors and nurses to recommend their infant formula to parents of newborn babies. In 2016, a Chinese subsidiary of Johnson & Johnson was revealed to have bribed employees of Chinese state-owned shipyards. Other

[67] Yanzhong Huang, *Three Take-Home Message from China's Glaxo Verdict*, FORBES (25 Sep. 2014).
[68] Andrew Ward & Patti Waldmeir, *GlaxoSmithKline Navigates Difficult Path in China after Scandal*, FIN. TIMES (27 Nov. 2015).

multinational companies found to have conducted bribery activities in China include Rio Tinto, Morgan Stanley, Daimler, UT Starcum, DPC, IBM, Siemens, Lucent Technologies, and Avon. This shows that a wide range of sectors have been implicated, including healthcare, equipment, finance, computer manufacture, and cosmetics.

Interestingly, most of these multinational companies were not investigated by Chinese regulators but by US regulators, exposing a regulatory lag in China. Out of all the aforementioned firms, only GSK and Rio Tinto were investigated by the Chinese authorities. China does not have an independent and forceful regulator that specializes in dealing with corruption practices. Rather, anti-corruption power is fragmented, and a number of regulatory authorities have jurisdiction over this area. As such, the market for corruption regulation is immense in China, and the Chinese regulators have only recently sought control over this market.

In addition to corruption, product quality and food safety have been major concerns for the Chinese government. Foreign companies have not been able to evade these either. In 2014, a number of global food chains such as McDonald's, KFC, and Subway were involved in a 'foul meat' scandal in China after Chinese regulators discovered that one of the chains' suppliers had been supplying expired meat. Walmart has also been fined multiple times and accused of selling poor-quality food to Chinese consumers.

For many multinational companies operating in China, the Chinese authorities' regulatory intervention is akin to a ticking time bomb that might explode at any point. According to a survey published by the AmericanChambers of Commerce, 'inconsistent regulatory interpretation and unclear laws' have been one of the top five challenges facing US businesses in the past five years.[69] In 2016, unclear laws was ranked as the most pressing business challenge for US companies operating in China.[70] But regardless of the opacity of the law, given the wide latitude the Chinese enforcement authorities have during enforcement, foreign firms are concerned that they might be arbitrarily targeted. A 2015 survey conducted by the American Chamber of Commerce on China's business climate indicated that over half of the respondents believed foreign firms had been singled out in the government's recent campaigns.[71] As one successful Chinese entrepreneur once said:

---

[69] The American Chamber of Commerce, *2016 China Business Climate Survey Report*, at 18.
[70] Id.
[71] American Chamber of Commerce in the People's Republic of China, *2015 China Business Climate Survey Report*, Feb. 2015, at 20.

The skills needed to run Chinese companies are different from those required to run European and U.S. companies. Europe and the U.S. have relatively complete legal systems, which result in relatively stable management styles. But it takes more ambition to run a Chinese company. Here's an analogy: If you manage a company in Europe or the U.S., the line between the red light area and the green light area is relatively clear, while there is only a narrow grey area in between. But in China, the grey area is too broad to ignore, and it takes ambition, wisdom and skills to deal with it.[72]

As there are so many grey areas in Chinese law and the government retains residual rights in interpreting the law, the government can easily go after a firm or an individual. As a consequence, foreign firms are careful to avoid directly confronting a government agency, as it is often deemed counterproductive and may jeopardize their relationship with the government. As one in-house counsel I interviewed put it: 'If you make their lives difficult, they will make your life even more difficult'.[73] The row between Alibaba and SAIC, a predecessor of SAMR, offers a textbook example of how a direct clash with an administrative agency could aggravate a regulatory conflict.

On 23 January 2015, the E-Commerce Supervision Department of the SAIC issued a report on its latest monitoring results of e-commerce platforms, show-casing how it had found thirty-two counterfeit products within a sample of fifty-one products purchased on Taobao.[74] Among these thirty-two products, twenty-two of them lacked certification, proper labelling, or were sold through unauthorized channels. This monitoring report disclosed more counterfeit products than an earlier report published by the SAIC in December 2014.[75] The SAIC's report prompted an open letter from an Alibaba employee four days later, claiming that the SAIC's research method was categorically flawed as

---

[72] Navigating the 'Grey Areas' of Business Management: An Interview with Mai Boliang, CEO of China International Marine Containers Co. (9 Aug. 2015), http://knowledge.wharton.upenn.edu/article/navigating-the-grey-areas-of-business-management-an-interview-with-mai-boliang-ceo-of-china-international-marine-containers-co/

[73] Interview with a senior in-house counsel, Beijing, 2016.

[74] E-Commerce Supervision Department of the SAIC, *Guojia Gongshang Zongju Fabu 2014 Nian Xiabannian Wangluo Jiaoyi Shangpin Dingxiang Jiance Jieguo* （国家工商总局发布2014年下半年网络交易商品定向检测结果） [*SAIC Releases E-Commerce Monitoring Results for Second Half of 2014*] (23 Jan. 2015).

[75] E-Commerce Supervision Department of the SAIC, *Guojia Gongshang Zongju Yanzheng Chengnuo Bufen Dianshang Pingtai Rengcun Shoujia* （国家工商总局验证承诺，部分电商平台仍存售假） [*SAIC Verification Promise, Some E-Commerce Platforms Still Sell Counterfeits*] (11 Dec. 2014). *See also* Wang Zhuoqiong & Meng Jing, *Online Firms Urged to Step Up Quality Checks*, CHINA DAILY (12 Dec. 2014).

it was based on a small sample size.[76] In an unusual move, the letter also plainly named the SAIC official in charge of the investigation, Director Liu Hongliang, and accused him of 'violating the regulations and blowing a black whistle'. The letter also stated that 'we are willing to accept your God-like existence, but we cannot agree with the double standard in various sampling procedures and your irrational logic'. In the employee's defence, the letter also argued that the SAIC's sampling method did not comply with the requirements laid out in the relevant regulations.

SAIC responded the next morning with a statement, asserting that the monitoring was completed 'according to the law'. Meanwhile, the SAIC released a White Paper on its website, condemning Alibaba for allowing merchants to operate without business licenses and enabling them to run unauthorized shops selling counterfeit products; the SAIC also denounced Alibaba employees for taking bribes and failing to mend errors related to the customer feedback and internal credit-scoring system.[77] The White Paper was in fact based on the SAIC's discussion with Alibaba earlier in July that year, but it took place behind closed doors as the agency did not want it to have a negative impact on Alibaba's initial public offering in the United States. Clearly, the prompt release of the White Paper was a retaliation directly targeted at Alibaba.

Shortly after the publication of the White Paper, Alibaba made an official statement criticizing Director Liu Hongliang's 'regulatory misconduct, behaviour of emotional enforcement, and using flawed methodologies to arrive at a biased conclusion'.[78] Joseph Tsai, a senior Alibaba executive later said, '[w]e believe the flawed approach taken in the report, and the tactic of releasing a so-called "White Paper" specifically targeting us, were so unfair that we felt compelled to take the extraordinary step of preparing a formal complaint to the SAIC'.[79] Alibaba, however, never filed a formal administrative complaint or administrative litigation. The White Paper was later removed from the SAIC's website and an SAIC spokesperson subsequently admitted that the White Paper had no legal force and was actually the meeting minutes.[80] But

---

[76] Taobao, Weibo post (27 Jan. 2015), reprinted in Sina (http://finance.sina.com.cn/chanjing/gsnews/20150127/144521408992.shtml).

[77] Zheping Huang, *The Chinese Government has Erased a Damning Report on Alibaba, but You Can Read it Here*, QUARTZ (29 Jan. 2015).

[78] Taobao, Weibo post (28 Jan. 2015, 14:58), reprinted in Sina, http://tech.sina.com.cn/i/2015-01-28/doc-iawzunex9478513.shtml.

[79] Alibaba Group, *Joe Tsai Addressed Recent Interaction with SAIC* (29 Jan. 2015), https://www.alibabagroup.com/cn/news/article?news=p150129a

[80] SAIC, *Guojia Gongshang Zongju Xinwen Fayanren Jiu Xingzheng Zhidao Da Jizhe Wen* (国家工商总局新闻发言人就行政指导答记者问) [*SAIC Spokesperson Responds to Reporters' Questions on Administrative Guidance*] (30 Jan. 2015). PEOPLE.CN.

the damage to Alibaba's reputation had been done. This incident dealt a significant blow to Alibaba's business, whose shares fell by 4.4 per cent in just one day, resulting in a market capitalization loss of USD 11 billion. Alibaba also faced a number of class action lawsuits for misleading investors with the non-disclosure of material information.[81] The Chinese media called this the 'most expensive quarrel' in history.

This case reveals the predicament of businesses in conflict with government agencies in China. SAIC's accusations may have suffered from procedural deficiencies, but Alibaba was not entirely in the clear. Counterfeiting is rampant in China and Alibaba's platforms have been plagued by this problem. There was plenty of scope for SAIC to go after Alibaba. The SAIC's issuance of the White Paper was a brinkmanship tactic that led both the agency and Alibaba closer to the edge of the cliff. Had Alibaba carefully assessed the risk of retribution and of the government's potential tit-for-tat strategy, it would probably not have resorted to this form of direct confrontation with the SAIC in the first place.

3. Regulation by Shaming

In addition to the vast administrative discretion afforded to these agencies, the Chinese central antitrust authorities have another potent weapon at their disposal: the Chinese media. While the Chinese antitrust authorities are subject to little judicial oversight, they are held back by two constraints. The first constraint is capacity. As newly established antitrust authorities, the three former Chinese agencies were severely understaffed and lacked experience and expertise to tackle large and complex cases effectively. The second, less conspicuous type of constraint was the bureaucratic constraint that beset these agencies. Although the former agencies were housed within large and powerful central ministries, each of them stood only at the bureau level. This rendered their policy-making susceptible to the influence of lobbying and interventions from both within and outside their own ministries. As such, the problem the former antitrust agencies was presented with was a thorny one: how can a newly established antitrust agency, faced with severe capacity and bureaucratic constraints, establish its legal authority to become an antitrust regulator commanding the attention of large and

---

[81] Qu Yunxu, *U.S. Law Firms Filed Class Action Lawsuit against Alibaba in New York*, Caixin (3 Feb. 2015).

powerful domestic and foreign businesses? Chinese administrative agencies, used to operating within weak legal institutions, found the answer in reputational sanctions.

Chinese antitrust enforcement offers an ideal setting to observe the transient stage of when a newly formed administrative agency tries to quickly establish its legal authority by strategically leveraging reputational sanctions. China only began to enforce the AML in 2008. As there were very few precedents available during the first few years of its enforcement, businesses were just starting to learn about the impact of legal sanctions under the AML. In the same vein, businesses had not fully understood the effect of a market sanction as an immediate consequence of a high-profile media announcement made by a regulator. As the agency's pattern of enforcement was not yet well established at that time, businesses were not very much deterred by the sanctions under the AML. Notably, out of the three former agencies, the NDRC appears to have been the most adept at imposing reputation sanctions on firms that were subjected to antitrust investigations. Thus, the first few cases in which the NDRC had applied reputational sanctions set important precedents for subsequent cases, and they became focal points of compliance for both businesses and practitioners.

Before we discuss the role of the media in Chinese antitrust enforcement, it is helpful to understand the relevant institutional environment in China. Once called the 'mouth and tongue' of the Party, the Chinese media is still tightly controlled by the government.[82] Although China has a highly dynamic media market, it remains one of the world's most restrictive.[83] Still, the Chinese media has undergone significant transformation in several rounds of government reform.[84] The first round of restructuring which was carried out in the 1990s led to the commercialization of many newspapers that centred on reporting financial and economic news. Unlike Party newspapers, which are to this day firmly controlled by the local communist Party organization and propaganda departments toeing the Party line, many commercial newspapers have become self-sufficient and no longer rely on public financial support. Other large-scale reforms involved fashioning conglomerates out of selected newspapers, thereby creating new media groups. While commercialized newspapers are

---

[82] Benjamin L. Liebman, *Watchdog or Demagogue? The Media in the Chinese System*, 105 COLUM. L. REV. 1, 17–18 (2005); SUSAN L. SHIRK, CHINA: FRAGILE SUPERPOWER 85 (2007).

[83] In 2020, Report Without Borders ranked China 177th out of 180 countries in its index of press freedom. *See* Report Without Borders, *2020 World Press Freedom Index*, RSF.ORG.

[84] DANIELA STOCKMANN, MEDIA COMMERCIALIZATION AND AUTHORITARIAN RULE IN CHINA 67–68 (2013).

still subject to political control by the Chinese government, they are financially driven and compete for readership by appealing to their tastes and demands.

There are several mechanisms through which the media can influence Chinese antitrust enforcement. First, economists have argued that profit-maximizing media can help overcome the rational ignorance problem of voters.[85] By collating, verifying, and summarizing relevant facts, the media mitigates the collective action problem associated with gathering information for a dispersed group.[86] Many Chinese state-owned enterprises (SOEs) hold entrenched and vested interests in concentrated industry sectors. These SOEs also enjoy a superior bureaucratic and political status, and they have more convenient channels through which to lobby, making it more difficult and costly for antitrust agencies to bring actions against them.[87] However, the media can help inform the public about antitrust policy, empowering policy entrepreneurs to mobilize public sentiments in order to challenge vested interests. As illustrated in the China Telecom/China Unicom case detailed below, news coverage of Chinese antitrust enforcement is not driven only by the intrinsic appeal of news but also by efforts exerted by the regulator.

Second, if Chinese state media strongly endorses an antitrust investigation, this sends a political signal that the investigation has gained endorsement from higher levels of the government. It also creates speculation that the Chinese government is tightening its regulation of a certain industry, with antitrust intervention being only one of its tools to achieve its policy objectives. As demonstrated in the Infant Formula case, an antitrust agency's strategic disclosure of cases can send discouraging signals to the market and cause significant damage to the stock prices of firms under investigation. To avoid further losses, businesses under these circumstances usually choose to settle with the agency quickly, accept the fines, and proceed with regular business activities. Indeed, if a firm vigorously defends itself, it might not only be viewed as resisting an antitrust agency's decision but also as trying to thwart the Chinese government's policy objectives. The fear of provoking the central government, coupled with the weakness of legal institutions and the lack of judicial checks, puts additional pressure on firms to conform to the antitrust agency's demands.

Third, Chinese media is not only the Party's mouthpiece but also serves as a news gatherer and watchdog for the Party.[88] Political scientists have long

[85] Alexander Dyck et al., *Media versus Special Interest*, 56 J. L. ECON. 521 (2013).

[86] Id.

[87] Angela Huyue Zhang, *Taming the Chinese Leviathan, Is Antitrust Regulation A False Hope*, 51 STAN. J. INT'L L. 195, 207–11 (2015).

[88] YUEZHI ZHAO, MEDIA, MARKET AND DEMOCRACY IN CHINA: BETWEEN THE PARTY LINE AND THE BOTTOM LINE (1998).

identified the function of the Chinese media as a bottom-up information transmission system, which helps Party leaders gather intelligence and monitor the performance of lower-level government officials.[89] Moreover, as the actions of Chinese antitrust agencies are seldom challenged in court, popular support is an important means through which Chinese enforcement agencies claim legitimacy for their actions. Public endorsement further helps the agency gain political credit from within the bureaucracy. It also enables an agency to overcome the political opposition it experiences when taking on powerful firms, as shown in the Qualcomm case thoroughly discussed below. In this case, an eminent Chinese antitrust expert, Zhang Xinzhu, who had provided expert consultancy to Qualcomm was dismissed from a prestigious government advisory body. Upon Zhang's dismissal, there was widespread media coverage condemning his action, discrediting the legitimacy of the defence he provided to Qualcomm.

Last but not least, consumer product firms operating in China are particularly sensitive to the negative publicity brought about by antitrust investigations. Economists have suggested that the effectiveness of the media strategy is predicated on two essential characteristics of the institutional environment. First, public shaming works when society as a whole repudiates the conduct exposed by the press.[90] Second, the magnitude of the penalty depends on the frequency and importance of the business' interactions with consumers, capital markets, and the government.[91] The Chinese market has long been inundated by concerns about poor quality and counterfeits. A solid and admirable reputation is therefore expensive to establish in China. An antitrust inquiry could smear a firm's hard-earned brand image, leaving consumers with the impression that they have been 'ripped off'. Thus, Chinese consumer product firms are most likely to suffer as a result of the negative publicity following an announcement that they are under examination for antitrust violations. Ironically, the less market power that a firm has, the more it fears the potential damage that could be done to its reputation because consumers can easily turn to other substitute brands. This is particularly the case for companies under scrutiny for RPM. Many cases that the NDRC investigated involved consumer product firms operating in highly competitive markets. These companies are therefore the most vulnerable to the negative publicity brought by an onslaught of media coverage of their cases.

---

[89] Id.

[90] Alexander Dyck et al., *The Corporate Governance Role of the Media: Evidence from Russia*, 63 J. FIN. 1093, 1101 (2008).

[91] Id. at 1102.

Notably, whether an administrative agency chooses to leverage the media has much to do with the leadership style of the agency head, as highlighted in Chapter 1. Of the three former antitrust agencies, the NDRC was the only agency that had actively and consciously employed a media strategy during its enforcement. Xu Kunlin, the former Director General of the antirust subdivision of the NDRC, was known as a savvy politician who actively harnessed the power of the media as a weapon to advance antitrust enforcement. During his tenure between 2009 and 2015, NDRC officials appeared twice on *Dialogue*, a popular talk show hosted by the state-controlled Central Television Network (CCTV), to broadcast their enforcement activities. Their first televised appearance took place on August 25, 2013, when the agency came to the fore with two high-profile investigations concerning the infant formula and white liquor industries. Surprisingly, an executive from Wyeth, an infant formula producer under investigation, also appeared on the talk show to announce publicly its determination to reduce prices in line with the NDRC's request. Wyeth's proactive cooperation set a prime example for other targeted companies to follow, and it ultimately won full immunity from punishment. On 15 February 2015, Xu and his team appeared on the *Dialogue* show again, expressing the challenges the NDRC were facing in proceeding with the Qualcomm investigation. In an attempt to rebut challenges from foreign media sources, Xu argued that the agency had not discriminated against foreign multinational companies during its enforcement of antitrust laws. He also firmly denied allegations of due process violations. Television appearances like these not only served to raise public awareness of the AML but also helped the NDRC establish its legal authority and legitimacy. In addition to on-air interviews, Xu also participated in interviews with various newspapers and magazines.[92]

At the same time, the NDRC adopted a passive approach in many cases and did not always disclose its investigations.[93] Xu Kunlin admitted that his agency had kept a low profile in order to avoid inflicting a 'double penalty' on firms. This is because many firms requested that the NDRC refrain from publicizing their cases for fear of reputational damage. The passive approach of disclosure took a variety of forms; sometimes the agency only revealed an investigation after the firm's self-disclosure, disclosed its investigation without specifying

---

[92] For instance, in June 2015, Xu Kunlin accepted an interview with a magazine in which he discussed the negotiation with Qualcomm at length. *Guojia Fagaiwei Jiagesi Sizhang Xu Kunlin: Qinli Zhongda Fan Londuan An* （国家发改委价格司司长许昆林：亲历重大反垄断案） [*Kunlin Xu from the Price Bureau of NDRC: The Experiences of High-Profile Antitrust Investigation*], Xinhua Net (20 June 2015).

[93] Angela Huyue Zhang, *Strategic Public Shaming: Evidence from Chinese Antitrust Investigations*, 237 CHINA Q. 174 (2019).

the names of the individual firms involved, announced its decisions without any prior disclosure of its investigations, or delayed announcement of its decision until months after the case was concluded. Some NDRC officials I spoke with indicated that the agency investigated many more cases than it had disclosed.[94] This is consistent with the data revealed in an obscure Chinese magazine entitled *Price Supervision and Check*. Mostly read by officials responsible for monitoring and control, this magazine exposed many cases that were investigated by the NDRC but never publicly named. In fact, many of these nonpublicized cases were 'harmonized' (i.e. resolved inside the bureaucracy) and no penalties were imposed.[95] This form of 'internal dispute resolution' appears to be quite common as these cases included a wide range of domestic targets, many of which were large central SOEs or local champions.

In contrast to the low-key approach taken on some occasions, the NDRC also served as a whistle-blower by leaking information to state media strategically. In the following discussion, I will focus on the NDRC's media strategy as seen in three high-profile investigations: the China Telecom/China Unicom case, the Infant Formula case, and the Qualcomm case. In order to conduct a systematic analysis, I used WiseNews to find relevant news coverage from the first public disclosure of each case to the day before the agency released its decision.[96] WiseNews, an online repository, collects news stories from a wide range of Chinese newspapers published on the mainland. I performed content analysis on the relevant news articles in the sample. I specifically included articles that expanded on the investigations and excluded those that made only a passing reference. Reading through each article, I reconstructed how the NDRC strategically exposed the nature of its investigations to state-controlled media, how the public reacted to the disclosures, and how media organizations covered the investigations. I also checked to see whether industry or legal experts had been interviewed, the types of comments these experts made, as well as subsequent responses from the convicted firms, the regulator itself, and other media outlets. Using a mixture of inductive and deductive reasoning, I started by anticipating the different themes based on my previous reading of similar news reports covering antitrust investigations, but I also added new coding as they emerged from the media analysis. I then documented the major themes of each article, how the issues had been framed, the institutional affiliations of the

---

[94] Interview with two NDRC officials, Beijing, June 2016.
[95] Interview with a NDRC official, Beijing, June 2016.
[96] For all these searches, I limited my search on news articles published by media outlets in mainland China.

cited sources in the articles, the underlying sources' comments, and the general tone of the article.

3.1 Strategic Public Shaming

It is not uncommon for Chinese government agencies to use shaming as a strategy during administrative enforcement. Indeed, scholars have seen this happening in regulatory areas such as securities law, environmental law, and intellectual property law.[97] But there is one crucial distinction between the shaming sanction applied by agencies in other areas and in the current antitrust setting. Previous literature has established that reputational sanctions imposed by administrative agencies are independent of a firm's corresponding response to the regulatory action. However, in the particular context of Chinese antitrust, shaming is employed strategically; that is, if a firm under investigation quickly acquiesces and accedes to the agency's demands, the agency will assist the firm in keeping a low profile. If not, then the NDRC played the role of informant and proactively leaked pertinent information to leading state media outlets, exposing the firm to a high level of negative publicity and adversely affecting its stock performance. This exerts pressure on firms to conform and deters them from defying orders. The China Telecom/China Unicom and Infant Formula cases illustrate this well.

On 9 November 2011, employees at China Telecom and China Unicom, two of China's largest state-owned telecommunication companies, were just heading out for their lunch break. They had no idea that their companies were going to be featured on the *30 Minutes News*, a popular news programme broadcast at noon, that day. The anchor began the segment by mentioning a recent expert report. The report in question noted that China's Internet speed ranked seventy-first in the world, which was less than one-tenth the average speed in OECD countries at the time. Chinese consumers were required, however, to pay double or even triple the global average price for this speed. Suddenly, Li Qing, a deputy director general at the antitrust unit of the NDRC, appeared on screen and proclaimed that her agency had launched an inquiry into China Telecom and China Unicom for antitrust violations. Director Li claimed that

---

[97] *See e.g.*, Benjamin L. Liebman & Curtis J. Milhaupt, *Reputational Sanctions in China's Securities Market*, 108 COLUMBIA L. REV. 929 (2008); Judith Shapiro, *The Evolving Tactics of China's Green Movement*, in ROUTLEDGE HANDBOOK OF ENVIRONMENTAL POLICY IN CHINA 48 (Eva Sternfeld ed., 2017); Peter K. Yu, *From Pirates to Partners (Episode II): Protecting Intellectual Property in Post-WTO China*, 55 AM. U. L. REV. 55, 952 (2006).

these two SOEs held dominant market positions and stated that together they controlled over two-thirds of the Internet access sector's market share. She further mentioned that these two SOEs had engaged in price discrimination against rival companies; if these allegations were ultimately proven to be true, the two SOEs would be subject to a fine of up to 10 per cent of their revenue in the previous year, or up to RMB 8 billion. In addition to antitrust accusations, Director Li asserted that the telecom networks of these SOEs had not been fully integrated, thus increasing the cost of Internet access for Internet service providers (ISPs). The CCTV programme also quoted estimates from the aforementioned expert report, adding that Internet access prices would fall by 27 per cent to 38 per cent in five years if this market was allowed to become truly competitive, saving Chinese consumers around RMB 10–15 billion. Director Li did not explain how the Internet speed was related to the issue of price discrimination but her message to Chinese consumers was clear: abusive behaviour by China Telecom and China Unicom had resulted in high Internet prices and low Internet speeds.

The NDRC's announcement on CCTV not only blindsided employees of the SOEs but also sent shock waves through the stock market. In an earlier study, I found that China Telecom experienced a statistically significant abnormal stock return of 2 per cent on the day of the announcement, while China Unicom suffered a negative abnormal return of 8 per cent.[98] As both companies were among the world's largest telecommunications companies, this meant a loss running into billions of dollars in market capitalization. Investors' prediction of this sort of significant value loss can be derived from several sources such as a high estimation of the fines that these companies would receive, the potential loss of profits after future price reductions, and other behavioural remedies these SOEs may ultimately need to offer the regulator.[99] But in the Chinese context, a high-profile regulatory announcement like this also sends another important signal. If the NDRC was so determined to charge these corporate giants, it meant that these companies were losing their political clout, which is a very important and valuable asset in China.[100] This is especially the case for SOEs, which have close ties with the Chinese government and access to convenient channels for lobbying.

---

[98] Zhang, *supra* note 93, at 186.

[99] Stijn Van den Broek et al., *Reputational Penalties to Firms in Antitrust Investigations*, 8 J. COMPETITION L. & ECON. 231 (2012).

[100] Yuen Yuen Ang & Nan Jia, *Perverse Complementarity: Political Connections and the Use of Courts Among Private Firms in China*, 76 J. POLITICS 318 (2014).

As revealed later in a report from state-controlled media *Xinhua News Agency*, the NDRC had begun its inquiry into the two companies seven months earlier.[101] By June 2011, the NDRC had already reached a preliminary conclusion, ascertaining that both SOEs had abused their monopoly power in the sector. Both SOEs then submitted feedback reports. But the investigation was kept classified during this period; even the employees involved were required to sign testimonies akin to confidentiality agreements after interviews with the NDRC. Four months later, the NDRC held a meeting with the Legal Department of the State Council, the Supreme People's Court, and the Ministry of Industry and Information Technology (MIIT). During this meeting, the NDRC's ongoing investigation met significant opposition, with these departments urging the NDRC not to reach a hasty conclusion before gathering substantial evidence against the firms. The NDRC promised that it would solicit further feedback from the SASAC and the MIIT before submitting its report to the State Council. The resistance that the NDRC encountered is not surprising. As discussed in Chapter 1, the power to regulate Chinese SOEs is deeply fragmented and the authority is divided among a number of bureaucratic departments with overlapping jurisdictions. When the NDRC tried to apply antitrust law to intervene in the pricing decisions of these two telecom giants, the SASAC interpreted this as an aggressive move that would undermine the value of the state sector it is responsible for overseeing, while the MIIT viewed it as a strategic attempt to encroach upon its turf and its oversight of the telecom sector.

The NDRC's formal announcement on CCTV therefore not only surprised the SOEs but also the SASAC, the MIIT, and various other government departments that had been consulted. According to *Xinhua News Agency*, the declaration on national television was a deliberate response to the arrogant attitude exhibited by China Unicom and China Telecom. My interviews with the participating NDRC officials corroborated the news report.[102] Insiders noted that the NDRC encountered considerable opposition from these SOEs and bureaucratic departments alike. By leaking the news to CCTV, the NDRC hoped to exert pressure on the two SOEs by turning public opinion against them, all the while making it even more difficult for other bureaucratic departments to intervene in the matter.

---

[101] Editorial, *Weiguan Fanlongduan Shou An* （围观反垄断首案） [*Examining the First Big Antitrust Case*], Xɪɴʜᴜᴀ Wᴀɴɢ （新华网） [Xɪɴʜᴜᴀ Nᴇᴛ] (11 Nov. 2011).

[102] Interview with two NDRC officials, Beijing, June 2016.

The NDRC's statement on CCTV generated quite a sensation in the Chinese media. Through WiseNews, I identified fifty-eight news articles from fifty-one media outlets covering the investigation the day after the news broke. As CCTV was the first to report this investigation, almost every news article (with the exception of one) relied heavily on the information disclosed by CCTV and cited the remarks made by Li Qing, the NDRC official who appeared on the TV programme, extensively. Additionally, 85 per cent of the remarks made by experts in these news reports expressed fervent support for the NDRC's actions. Wang Xiaoye, a prominent antitrust expert, stated that she was very pleased to see that the NDRC had initiated this investigation.[103] Professor Wang hailed the case as the first antitrust investigation of Chinese SOEs, adding that this was a milestone for Chinese antitrust enforcement.

With almost all news outlets relying heavily on the NDRC and CCTV as sources and the vast majority of experts' comments endorsing the investigation, the editorial slant was, unsurprisingly, skewed against the SOEs. Of the fifty-eight news reports released the day after the NDRC's announcement, 67 per cent adopted a hostile tone toward the telecom firms, either by reinforcing the one-sided allegations from the NDRC or by firmly endorsing the action as a major breakthrough in antitrust enforcement. Online public opinion was also overwhelmingly against the SOEs. A survey conducted by Sina Weibo, the Chinese Twitter, the day of the NDRC's announcement found that 96 per cent of online users believed that both SOEs held dominant positions in the broadband market, and 86 per cent of users were dissatisfied with their performance.[104] Indeed, the Chinese public had long loathed large Chinese SOEs, likening them to villains wreaking havoc on the Chinese economy.[105] At the same time, the overwhelming public support for the NDRC's action also revealed a confirmation bias amongst the Chinese public. Even without any substantial evidence, the Chinese public was eager to take a mere announcement by an antitrust agency of its investigation into SOEs as evidence of the firms' antitrust violations.

---

[103] Ma Xiaofang & Guo Liqing （马晓芳，郭丽琴）, *Dianxin Liantong Yiwai Zao Diaocha, Fanlongduanfa Shou Han Yangqi* （电信联通意外遭调查，《反垄断法》首撼央企） [*China Telecom and China Unicom were Subject to a Surprise Investigation, The First Attack on State-Owned Enterprises under the Antimonopoly Law*], Dıyı Caıjıng Rıbao （第一财经日报） [China Business News] (10 Nov. 2011).

[104] Yuanyue （袁悦）, *Fagaiwei Zhi Dianxin Liantong Shexian Longduan, Ying Weiguan, Gejie Fanying Buyi* （发改委指电信联通涉嫌垄断引"围观"各界反应不一） [*NDRC Alleged China Telecom and China Unicom were Monopolies, Mixed Feedback from Different Sides*], Renmıng Wang （人民网） (Renming Net), (9 Nov. 2011).

[105] Sheng Hong & Zhao Nıng, China's State-Owned Enterprises: Nature, Performance and Reform (2012).

Two days after the NDRC disclosed its investigation into China Telecom and China Unicom, *Xinhua News* published a lengthy report, calling the NDRC's investigation an attack on the deities that had no relevance to Chinese consumers.[106] A lawyer from a consumer association cited in the report condemned the NDRC's ambush on CCTV as an inappropriate move 'lack[ing] careful consideration'. The lawyer argued that the announcement was rather unfair to these firms and could result in adverse social consequences. As a leading Party news outlet, the criticism cited in the Xinhua report strongly conveyed the growing dissonance within the bureaucracy over the NDRC's action. The Xinhua report also quoted other misgivings expressed by many telecom industry experts over the antitrust investigation. For instance, Wu Songning, the editor-in-chief of People's Post and Telecommunication News (PPTN), clarified that the case actually involved the Internet service provider (ISP) access market as opposed to the broadband market as mentioned by the NDRC. He observed that the competition in the ISP market was fierce, with over 700 ISPs competing in the same market. Notably, PPTN is owned by MIIT, the telecom regulator that was distressed about NDRC's investigation and its extended authority. The Xinhua report subtly implied that many telecom experts had been reluctant to comment on the antitrust investigations, highlighting the sensitive nature of the matter.

On 11 November 2011, PPTN released an editorial on its front page entitled 'Confusing Facts Misleading the Public', in a direct rebuttal of CCTV's report.[107] It began by noting that the NDRC's announcement left the employees working at these two SOEs distraught and caused the stock prices of these two SOEs to tumble. It then went on to outline four ways in which the CCTV programme had been misleading. First, the case actually concerned the smaller ISP access market rather than the broadband market. Second, the CCTV programme duped the public into believing that the two SOEs held dominant positions in the ISP market; this was factually incorrect, as the market was highly competitive with the presence of many other players. Third, these two SOEs did not price discriminate; instead, they charged different firms varying prices on the basis of product differentiation. Finally, the mention of China's slow broadband speed compared with that of other OECD (Organisation for Economic

---

[106] Editorial, *supra* note 101.

[107] Xiaoya & Yangyang, *Hunxiao Shiting, Wudao Gongzhong: Bo Yangshi Dui Dianxin Liantong Shexian Jiage Longduan de Baodao* (混淆视听，误导公众：驳央视对电信联通涉嫌价格垄断的报道) [*Confusing and Misleading the Public: Rebutting CCTV's Coverage over the Alleged Price Monopoly of China Telecom and China Unicom*], REMIN YOUDIAN BAO (人民邮电报) (PEOPLE'S POST AND TELECOMMUNICATION NEWS) (11 Nov. 2011).

Co-operation and Development) countries was immaterial to the investigation. Additionally, the PPTN editorial argued that it was unfair to compare the Internet speed in China with those in advanced countries; a better comparison would be to measure China's progress against developing countries such as India and Russia. The editorial also criticized the lack of professional standards in the CCTV coverage, causing severe reputational and financial harm to these two SOEs. On the same day, *Telecommunication Industry News*, another newspaper owned by the MIIT, published its own editorial blasting the CCTV report.[108] It further argued that even if these two SOEs held dominant positions in the ISP access market, dominance in itself did not constitute a violation of the AML.

The scepticism exhibited by *Xinhua News* and the fierce rebuttal launched by the two MIIT newspapers ignited another round of debate over the legitimacy and relevancy of the investigation in state-controlled media. Three days after the publication of the *Xinhua News* editorial, *People's Daily*, another Party mouthpiece, circulated its editorial arguing that the case was not a quarrel between commercial deities, but rather an issue that affected the interests of millions of Chinese consumers.[109] It reiterated the message presented on CCTV that if market competition were allowed to flourish, the costs of Internet access would decrease 27–38 per cent for consumers, saving Chinese consumers RMB 10–15 billion. Moreover, it added that failing to integrate the networks of these two SOEs slowed Internet access speeds and raised the costs of Internet access. This editorial refuted the statements of the earlier *Xinhua News* editorial, which had casted doubt on the NDRC's actions.

The next day, CCTV aired another TV programme after retorts from the SOEs, in which a number of telecom and legal experts were invited to comment on the case.[110] Gao Hongbing, a telecom expert, argued that the two telecom firms had indeed violated antitrust law. He rebutted the claim that the investigation was irrelevant to consumer interests, noting that the failure of these two telecom firms to integrate fully harmed the interests of tens of millions of consumers. A few days later, *People's Daily* further endorsed the

---

[108] *Gongxin Bu Xiashu Liangjia Meiti Bo Dianxin Liantong Shexian Longduan Baodao* （工信部下属两家媒体驳电信联通涉嫌垄断报道）(*Two Newspapers Owned by MIIT Rebutted the Media Coverage over the Antitrust Violation of China Telecom and China Unicom*), ZHONGGUO XINWEN WANG (中国新闻网)[CHINA NEWS] (12 Nov. 2011).

[109] Chengchen （程晨）, *Fanlongduan Diaocha Bushi Shenxian Zhan* （反垄断调查不是"神仙战）[*Antitrust Investigation is not a Fight among Deities*], RENMIN RIBAO （人民日报）[PEOPLE'S DAILY] (14 Nov. 2011).

[110] Ma Xiaofang （马晓芳）, *Fanlongduan Yulun Zhan Di'er Chang: Yanshi Wang Quanmian Fanji* （反垄断舆论战第二场：央视网全面反击）[*The Second Antitrust Media Fight: The Combat of CCTV*], DIYI CAIJING RIBAO （第一财经日报）[CHINA BUSINESS NEWS] (16 Nov. 2011).

NDRC's intervention with a second editorial, entitled 'Applauding the NDRC's Actions'.[111] The editorial stated approvingly that the NDRC's actions appealed to the popular demand and sentiments of the Chinese people and set a milestone in Chinese antitrust enforcement.

The countervailing efforts made by the two SOEs appeared to do little to change public opinion. According to polling results compiled by state media outlet *Global Times*, as of 18 November 2011, over 80 per cent of the online users believed that the economic behaviour of China Telecom and China Unicom violated antitrust law; 70 per cent were not satisfied with their broadband services; and 30 per cent believed that the antitrust investigation would help resolve their broadband access problems.[112] On 2 December 2011, both China Telecom and China Unicom requested a suspension of the NDRC's investigation. Both SOEs issued statements with remedial proposals, promising to rectify their discriminatory conduct, accelerate their integration with other networks, and boost Internet speeds while lowering the costs of Internet access.[113] The NDRC acknowledged receipt of their request the very next day. There was no further assessment or information regarding the matter and neither company was fined. It thus seems likely that the dispute was subsequently settled internally within the bureaucracy.

The China Telecom/China Unicom case demonstrates the powerful feedback cycle connecting Chinese antitrust regulators, the Chinese media, and the Communist Party. As Susan Shirk points out, Party leaders, whose paramount priority is to maintain social stability, pay special attention to the media and public opinion as reflected in news coverage.[114] The NDRC's strategy of divulging its investigation on CCTV meant that the case became common knowledge nationwide. These reports successfully mobilized public sentiments. Such sentiments were then articulated through various online and print media, and this was then communicated back to Party leaders. Public endorsement

---

[111] Xiaoran （萧然）, *Renmin Ribao Wei Fagaiwei Fanlongduan Jiaohao, Kending Diaocha Dianxin Liantong* （人民日报为发改委反垄断叫好，肯定调查电信联通） [*Renmin Ribao Cheered for NDRC, Approving its Investigation of China Telecom and China Unicom*], RENMIN RIBAO （人民日报） [PEOPLE'S DAILY] 21 (Nov. 2011).

[112] Nie Lubing （聂鲁彬）, *Bacheng Shoufang Wangyou Renwei Dianxin Liantong Longduan, Huyu Diaocha Shiyou Hangye* （八成受访网友认为电信联通垄断，呼吁调查"石油"行业） [*Over 80% of Those Who Participated Online Believed China Telecom and China Unicom had Committed Antitrust Violation, Calling for Antitrust Investigation of the Oil Industry*], HUANQIU SHIBAO （环球时报） [GLOBAL TIMES] (11 Nov. 2011).

[113] Liu Yuying, *Zhongguo Dianxin He Zhongguo Liantong Tichu Zhongzhi Fanlongduan Diaocha shenqing* （中国电信和中国联通提出中止反垄断调查申请） [*China Telecom and China Unicom Applied for Suspension of Antitrust Investigation*], CHINA NEWS.COM (2 Dec. 2011).

[114] Susan Shirk, *Changing Media, Changing Foreign Policy*, in CHANGING MEDIA, CHANGING CHINA 239 (Susan Shirk ed., 2011).

thus helped the NDRC remove political obstacles, making it more difficult for the SOEs and their governmental allies to counter its investigation. However, despite public endorsement, it was never clear whether the NDRC had a valid basis to bring a case against the telecom giants and whether or not the outcome would benefit consumers. As the case was eventually suspended and no additional public information was revealed, there was very little the public could later learn about the case.

The media campaign utilized in the China Telecom/China Unicom case marks the first time that the NDRC leveraged state media to advance its position in a difficult antitrust investigation. Two years later, the agency further refined its media strategy by exposing firms in one particular case to different levels of publicity depending on the extent to which they cooperated. The curious pattern of disclosure in the Infant Formula case offers a prime example. On 1 July 2013, CCTV broadcasted that it had received confirmation from the NDRC that the agency was investigating Biostime and a few other manufacturers of infant formula at the time.[115] This was the earliest media confirmation of the NDRC's investigation, which indicates that NDRC had leaked the news to CCTV. CCTV seemed to target Biostime categorically: by referring to a report accessible on Biostime's website, CCTV identified Biostime as the largest player in the premium infant formula market in China, holding over 44 per cent of market share in 2011. Also, the report explicated that Biostime's infant formula business had grown by more than 61 per cent in the previous year, with its infant formula business accounting for 80 per cent of its overall revenue in 2012.

On the same day, *China Broadcast Net*, a newspaper owned by CCTV, published an article on its website attesting to the same facts.[116] The article similarly reported the phenomenon of an abnormal price hike in the infant formula market in recent years, with prices of foreign infant formula milk powder increased by 50 per cent from 2008 to 2013. It added that the prices of infant formula powder in China were by and large the highest in the world and that many Chinese consumers travelled abroad just to purchase milk powder. It further suggested that the NDRC's investigation was intended to quell this unusual trend. The day after CCTV's announcement, *People's Daily* disclosed the

---

[115] CCTV, *Fagaiwei Dui Heshengyuan Deng Rufen Qiye Jinxing Fanlongduan Diaocha* （发改委对合生元等乳粉企业进行反垄断调查） [*NDRC Launched Antitrust Investigation into Biostime and Other Milk Powder Companies*], PEOPLE.CN (1 July 2013).

[116] Feng Ya （冯雅）, *Fagawei Jiage Jiandu Jiancha Yu Fanlongduan Ju Dui Heshengyuan Jinxing Fanlongduan Diaocha* （发改委价格监督检查与反垄断局对合生元进行反垄断调查） [*NDRC Launched Antitrust Investigation into Biostime*], FINANCE.CNR.CN (1 July 2013).

names of five more companies also involved in the case, claiming that it too had obtained confirmation from the NDRC.[117] Mysteriously, there was no mention of Meiji, Fonterra, and Beingmate in the news, all of whom were associated with the case and under investigation. It therefore appears that the NDRC had exposed the firms under investigation to three different levels of negative publicity.

According to one NDRC official that I spoke to, these differential disclosures had to do with the firms' levels of cooperation rather than the severity of their conduct.[118] That is, if a firm vigorously defended itself and did not confess to its behaviour quickly, the NDRC would subject the firm to more negative media hype and inflict a higher penalty. He said that among the infant formula producers, Biostime was the most difficult to deal with during its investigation as the firm had aggressively defended its RPM practices. This was in contrast with other firms involved in the investigation; Meiji, for example, readily accommodated the agency's demands and even volunteered to submit all evidence of its resale price maintenance practices to the agency. Biostime's lack of cooperation meant that it became a scapegoat.

In earlier research, I investigated the economic consequences of the NDRC's shaming strategy and found that infant formula manufacturers subject to public disclosure experienced statistically significant adverse effects on their stock prices.[119] For instance, Biostime, the firm most heavily shamed by the NDRC, suffered the worst stock price damage from the NDRC's announcement. Despite the company's prior disclosure that it had been made the focus of an antitrust investigation, the NDRC's subsequent announcement still sent a very unfavourable signal to the market. Biostime's stock bore a cumulative negative abnormal return of 22 per cent soon after the NDRC's announcement in the three-day event window and 37 per cent in the seven-day event window. This illustrates that investors managed to gain new information from the NDRC's actions even though the government's announcement itself had contained no more information than Biostime's own disclosure. Since Biostime was the only firm that was named by CCTV, investors may have seen this as an indication that the NDRC had obtained substantial evidence of the firm's antitrust violations and severe infringement. Therefore, the loss of equity may reflect the investors' predictions of legal sanctions, including potentially high

---

[117] Zhu Jianhong（朱剑红）, *Fagaiwei Jinxing Diaocha, Duojia Naifen Qiye Shexian Jiage Longduan* （发改委进行调查，多家奶粉企业涉嫌价格垄断）[*NDRC is Launching an Antitrust Investigation into Milk Powder Companies Suspected of Price Monopolies*], PEOPLE.CN (2 July 2013).

[118] Interview with a NDRC official, Beijing, June 2016.

[119] Zhang, *supra* note 93, at 186–87.

fines that could be imposed under the AML, as well as behavioural remedies such as forced price reductions. After the NDRC condemned the excessively high prices of Biostime's products on a CCTV programme, Biostime found itself lambasted by a slew of Chinese media outlets in the following days. Many of these outlets employed an accusatorial tone, insinuating that the company had used aggressive distribution tactics to reap abnormal profits. Investors may have therefore projected a loss from potential shaming—that the widespread public criticism aimed at Biostime would result in a loss of trust from consumers and suppliers, thereby affecting the firm's sales and future performance.

On the other hand, Beingmate, the other Chinese infant formula manufacturer operating on a similar business model as Biostime, met a completely different fate.[120] Since it had not been mentioned in the news, investors were not able to learn about its involvement in the case. In fact, its stock prices even reacted positively to the NDRC's announcement referencing its competitors. Beingmate's stock prices only took a plunge on 4 July 2013 when the firm publicly admitted its participation in the case. The NDRC closed the case after deciding that Biostime would get the heaviest fines. The market, unexpectedly, reacted favourably to this news, and Biostime experienced a positive abnormal return of 7 per cent on the day of the decision. This suggests that the market had overreacted to the NDRC's announcement and probably overestimated the legal consequences that Biostime would have to face. As a matter of fact, the fine it eventually received was rather small in comparison to the enormous market losses it incurred as a result of the NDRC's shaming. As I demonstrated in a previous work, Biostime suffered an equity loss of almost RMB 4.39 billion from negative media coverage, which was twenty-six times larger than the fines it had to pay.[121]

It is important to note that none of the infant formula producers launched a countervailing media campaign to defend themselves. The lack of response might have been due to NDRC pressure and intimidation. Officials had reiterated that firms which chose to cooperate proactively with the agency would be rewarded with reduced fines, implying that any form of defence would lead to higher sanctions. It is also possible that infant formula manufacturers were concerned that launching a defence would further delay the agency's decision, prolonging stock price volatility. As one executive involved in the Infant Formula case told a newspaper soon after the announcement of the investigation: 'We

---

[120] Id. at 187–90.
[121] Id. at 191.

hope the NDRC will release its decision soon. The sooner it decides, the less impact it will have on our stock performance.'[122]

3.2 Shaming the Dissidents

In addition to shaming firms under investigation, the NDRC had also applied a similar strategy to suppress dissenting opinions. Antitrust is one of the fastest developing areas of legal practice in China. The austere sanctions that can be enforced under the AML incentivize businesses to expend resources defending their cases. However, the absence of procedural safeguards and judicial oversight of agency actions makes antitrust lawyers less effective in constraining the actions of administrative authorities. More often than not, firms acquiesce to rather than directly challenge the antitrust agency's actions and there is little market demand to challenge agency decisions in court. Private law firms, therefore, gain little by taking an adversarial approach in defending their clients. They risk burning their bridges, to say the least, if they antagonize the government.

For antitrust lawyers, it is also vital to develop a cordial relationship with Chinese regulators. Due to the opacity of the regulatory process and the great discretion afforded to antitrust agencies, lawyers who have well-established, genial, and personal relationships with antitrust officials reap additional benefits. They enjoy a competitive advantage by obtaining valuable insider information regarding the status of investigations as well as acquiring intelligence on the individual preferences of the officials managing the case. The more information procured by the lawyers from the regulators, the better informed their responses to their clients. Chinese antitrust lawyers thus play the critical role of what sociologist Ronald Burt called the information brokers.[123] Their position in the social network constitutes an important form of social capital.

Furthermore, Chinese antitrust lawyers and law firms are repeat players who have the opportunity to establish their reputations in antitrust practice.[124] Since interacting with the government is a routine part of their business, lawyers are obliged to build a reputation of cooperation. Compliant and accommodating

---

[122] Bihua Ye （叶碧华）, *Fagaiwei Shiyi Huishi Mianzao Zhongfa: Shouxian Jiangjia Shuaidui Rencuo* （发改委释疑惠氏免遭重罚：首先降价率队认错）[*NDRC Explained Why Wyeth got Exemptions from Penalties: Wyeth was the First One to Reduce Price*] (8 Aug. 2013).

[123] Ronald S. Burt, Brokerage & Closure: An Introduction to Social Capital 4 (2005).

[124] Ronald J. Gilson & Robert H. Mnookin, *Disputing through Agents: Cooperation and Conflict between Lawyers in Litigation*, 94 Colum. L. Rev. 509, 513 (1994).

lawyers can cultivate better relationships with the agencies, which in turn enhances their credibility before the regulators. For instance, in cartel investigations, the NDRC often requested suspected firms to self-investigate and self-report any cartel conduct. If a business asked a 'cooperative' law firm to follow through on the NDRC's request, it could increase the reliability of the self-report. This advantage, in turn, enables the lawyers to attract more clients. The more representations these lawyers accumulate, the more experienced and sought after they become.

As Gilson and Mnookin pointed out, law firms 'provide a larger repository of reputational capital.'[125] Therefore, defection by any one lawyer in a single case will jeopardize the entire firm's rapport with the government agency. As such, the larger and more established a firm's antitrust practice, the more reputational capital is at stake, and the more reluctant the firm will be to forfeit its reputation by representing a client that wishes to call into question an antitrust agency's decision.[126] In the worst-case scenario, a non-cooperative Chinese lawyer may even be boycotted by the regulator.[127] A boycott would be considered grievous to the lawyer, because being unable to represent the client in front of the regulator would render the lawyer useless. Moreover, as both the former and current Chinese antitrust authorities are housed within large central ministries that oversee various policies, law firms usually have repeated dealings with these ministries on various fronts. Therefore, law firms with established antitrust practices would not risk jeopardizing their relationship with central antitrust authorities by bringing suits against them.

Chinese antitrust academics encounter the same dilemma as lawyers. While Chinese enforcers have been subject to fierce criticism in the international media, these agencies meet surprisingly little opposition in China. Launching harsh criticism against the government is a hair-trigger issue, and academic freedom is limited in China.[128] Moreover, as businesses cannot take agencies to court, there is little market demand for academic criticism of agency decisions in China. Indeed, Chinese antitrust scholars are not just assessed by their scholarly works but more importantly, by their connections with and proximity to the antitrust regulators. Similar to Chinese lawyers, an important asset of a

---

[125] Gilson & Mnookin, *supra* note 124, at 530.

[126] Id. at 525. *See also* Benjamin Klein & Keith B. Leffler, *The Role of Market Forces in Assuring Contractual Performance*, 89 J. POL. ECON. 615 (1981).

[127] Michael Martina & Matthew Miller, *'Mr. Confession' and His Boss Drive China's Antitrust Crusade*, REUTERS (15 Sep. 2014).

[128] Gary King *et al.*, *How Censorship in China Allows Government Criticism but Silences Collective Expression*, 107 AM. POL. SCI. REV. 326 (2013). *See also* Perry Link, *Testimony of Perry Link at the Hearing on 'Is Academic Freedom Threatened by China's Influence on American Universities'*, US House Committee on Foreign Affairs (4 Dec. 2014).

Chinese legal academic is the collection of privileged sources of information to which they can access. Scholars favoured by the regulators are invited to advise on large and important antitrust cases, which provides them with valuable insights into regulatory legal practice. Leading scholars are invited to sit on the prestigious Expert Advisory Committee of the Anti-Monopoly Commission (AMC), giving them a window into the inner workings of antitrust enforcement. Thus, the last thing that antitrust experts want is to develop a reputation for criticizing the regulators at the expense of their connections with the latter.

Furthermore, through frequent interactions and repeated dealings with each other, Chinese antitrust regulators, academics, lawyers, and judges have formed a close-knit community. Robert Ellickson believes a group is close-knit when informal power is broadly distributed among group members and the information pertinent to informal control circulates easily among them.[129] As this cohesiveness is contingent on the existence of continuing relationships among the group, members of the group informally encourage each other to engage in cooperative behaviours. The prospect of a continuing relationship facilitates cooperation, since non-cooperation endangers the future welfare of all the parties. In the words of Oliver Williamson, for two people in a continuing complex relationship, the future welfare of one is held hostage by the other.[130]

But collective action is not easy, as Mancur Olson has long pointed out.[131] One important approach to ensure collective action, as is common with unions, is by bestowing selective incentives on its members. That is, the coalition imposes penalties on members taking actions that deviate from the goal of the coalition. Zhang Xinzhu, a pre-eminent Chinese antitrust scholar, represents one such outlier who has provoked and publicly criticized the antitrust agency. Zhang, a professor from the Academy of Social Sciences, received his doctoral degree from the Toulouse School of Economics under the supervision of Jean-Jacques Laffont. Unlike most antitrust scholars, Zhang is an expert in both telecommunication regulation and antitrust regulation. Long before he started advising on antitrust matters, he served as an advisor for Chinese telecom firms and the telecom regulator MIIT. Zhang also formerly sat on the Expert Advisory Committee to the AMC. The Expert Committee comprised twenty-one experts in law, economics, and other various industry sectors.

---

[129] ROBERT C. ELLICKSON, ORDER WITHOUT LAW: HOW NEIGHBOURS SETTLE DISPUTES 177–78 (1994).

[130] Oliver E. Williamson, *Credible Commitments: Using Hostage to Support Exchange*, 73 AM. ECON. REV. 519 (1983).

[131] MANCUR OLSON, THE LOGIC OF COLLECTIVE ACTION: PUBLIC GOODS AND THEORY OF GROUPS (1971).

During the NDRC's investigation of China Telecom and China Unicom, Zhang made scathing remarks about the agency's actions.[132] During an interview with a Chinese newspaper, he commented that there was insufficient evidence to conclude that the two SOEs had committed antitrust violations. Noting that the Internet retail access market had already been liberalized, he observed fierce competition in the market and argued that the differential pricing only reflected a plausible market outcome. He slammed the NDRC for inappropriately assuming the role of a telecom regulator. According to Zhang, the matter should have been jointly handled by both antitrust and telecom regulators. He suggested that a wiser solution for the NDRC would have been to promote institutional restructuring of these companies. He also expressed concern over the little-to-no participation from economists during the enforcement of the AML in the past three years, arguing that economists too should have taken a more prominent role in enforcing antitrust law. He further found fault with the NDRC's overzealous attempt to regulate while ignoring the proper rules or standards of antitrust enforcement. Finally, Zhang condemned the agency's tactic of using public opinion against these telecom SOEs and failing to make full disclosure of the case.

After the two SOEs requested the suspension of the investigation, Zhang further lambasted the NDRC's investigation by publishing another editorial in the Chinese press.[133] Zhang noted that the NDRC's proactive disclosure of the case on CCTV was a skilful move to leverage the public's resentment against state monopolies, and that the NDRC had successfully achieved its objective of mobilizing public sentiment. However, he pointed out that such a strategic move was problematic from the perspective of antitrust law enforcement. In his opinion, law enforcement should be grounded in facts and the law rather than being influenced by public opinion. He noted that no other antitrust enforcement agency in the world has used the media to influence antitrust enforcement outcome. He perceived that rival state-owned telecom firms also seemed to have played a contributing role in pushing the NDRC to investigate these two SOEs. He also urged antitrust regulators to be vigilant about the possibility of firms strategically using antitrust law to hurt rivals.

---

[132] Dong Dong et al., *Zhang Xinzhu: Cong Muqian De Xinxi Kan Lilun Shang Wufa Rending Longduan* (张昕竹：从目前的信息看理论上无法认定垄断) [*Not Sufficient to Conclude Antitrust Violation Based on Existing Evidence*], XINLANG CAIJING （新浪财经） [SINA FIN.] (11 Nov. 2011).
[133] Xinzhu Zhang （张昕竹）, *Dianxin Fanlongduan An Fansi: Chanquan Gaige Shi Nan Yi Yuyue Hong Gou* （电信反垄断案反思：产权改革是难以逾越鸿沟） [*Reflections on China Telecom Antitrust Case: The Reform of Property Rights is the Impossible Chasm*], XINLANG CAIJING （新浪财经） [SINA FIN.] (13 Dec. 2011).

In this editorial, Zhang provided much-needed legal analysis of the case, casting further doubt on the legitimacy of the NDRC's actions. He first clarified that the AML only prohibits abuse of the dominant position, and maintaining a monopoly position is not illegal per se. He then noted that it was uncertain whether China Unicom and China Telecom had held a dominant position in the relevant market in the first place. Even if they had, Zhang contended, the regulators would still need to satisfy a high burden of proof to demonstrate abusive conduct on the part of these two firms. Zhang later advocated for a rule-of-reason approach to analyse these two SOEs' alleged price discrimination. Moreover, he outlined a number of reasons for defending the pricing practices of the two telecom firms, arguing that the existing evidence gathered by the NDRC was insufficient to prove their alleged abusive conduct. Last but not least, he proposed that the fundamental solution for reforming the Chinese telecom industry lies in property reform. He reinstated that without such market reforms, there would not be effective competition in the telecom industry and warned against a scenario where an antitrust regulator becomes the de facto price regulator of the telecom industry. He also criticized the remedies sought by the NDRC to regulate the interconnection prices charged by these two SOEs, asserting that these were an undesirable form of price regulation that lacked any justification under the AML.

Out of all the Chinese antitrust experts serving on the Expert Advisory Committee for the AMC, Zhang was the only one who did not refrain from directing his criticism at an antitrust authority and its decision. But it is with this outcry that Zhang sealed his own fate. On 12 August 2014, news broke that Zhang Xinzhu had been sacked from the Expert Advisory Committee to the AMC after allegedly accepting a large sum for defending Qualcomm in a different antitrust case.[134] The news caused a stir in the Chinese media. It also shocked Zhang, who told a news reporter that he had not been aware of his sacking until he learned of it from the newspaper.[135] Zhang claimed that he had instead been dismissed from the Committee for 'speaking for foreign businesses'. He recalled that a few months earlier, the then-Chair of the Expert Advisory Committee, Zhang Qiong, had asked him to conduct a

---

[134] Neil Gough & Chris Buckley, *Adviser to Government in Chinese Investigation of Qualcomm is Ousted*, N.Y. TIMES (13 Aug. 2014).
[135] Shi   Dongdong   （是冬冬）,   *Zhang   Xinzhu   Huiying   Bei   Guowuyuan Fanlongduan   Weiyuanhui   Zhuanjia   Zu   Jiepin: Wo   Bang   Waiqi   Shuohua   Le* （张昕竹回应被国务院反垄断委员会专家组解聘：我帮外企说话了） [*Zhang Xinzhu Responded to the Dismissal by the Expert Advisory Committee to the Anti-Monopoly Commission of the State Council: I spoke for Foreign Firms*], PENGPAI (澎湃) [THE PAPER] (12 Aug. 2014).

self-assessment of his consulting practices for Qualcomm.[136] Zhang Qiong reprimanded Zhang Xinzhu for defending foreign firms and, in doing so, being fundamentally at odds with the government's objectives. Zhang made an analogy of his position to that of a criminal defence lawyer: 'It's like I am defending a criminal facing death sentence. Every case should have two sides, they can't deprive me of my right to speak.'[137] Zhang recounted that his involvement with the Qualcomm case was not the only trigger for his dismissal and the cynicism displayed towards his dogmatic behaviour.[138] As a vocal critic of the NDRC in *China Telecom/China Unicom*, Zhang elucidated that his comments had created many obstacles for the agency.

On 13 August 2014, the very next day, there was widespread media speculation in China that Zhang had accepted 6 million in compensation after speaking for Qualcomm, although it was not clear whether the figure was in US dollars or renminbi.[139] Zhang strongly denied this allegation, but the figure was widely reported by major newspapers. On the same day, *Xinhua News* published an editorial entitled 'Those Experts Who Have Fished in Troubled Waters, Living in Our Country While Leaking Secrets to Others Is Not to Be Tolerated'.[140] The opinion piece assumed a very harsh tone with reproachful remarks, condemning Zhang for using his title as a member of the Expert Advisory Committee to back foreign firms. The editorial also suggested that although Zhang was a knowledgeable expert, his behaviour should be denounced as unethical. It noted that some multinational companies had tried to use a variety of tactics to defend themselves and thwart investigations. It claimed that government experts working for foreign firms had violated disciplinary rules and that such conduct should be penalized. As *Xinhua News* is

---

[136] Li Wei （李伟）, *Fanlongduan Fanduizhe: Xiagang Zhuanjia Zhang Xinzhu* （反垄断反对者："下岗"专家张昕竹） [*Antitrust Opponent: The Jobless Expert Zhang Xinzhu*], CAIJING YAN （财经眼）[CAIJING EYE] (15 Aug. 2014).

[137] Han Zhe （韩哲）, *Fanlongduan Yaorang Zhengfan Fang Dou Shuohua* （反垄断要让正反方都说话）[*Both Voices Should be Heard in the Anti-Monopoly Investigations*], XINHUA WANG (新华网) [XINHUA NET] (14 Aug. 2014).

[138] Shi Dongdong （是冬冬）, *Zhang Xinzhu Huiying Bei Jiepin: Wobang Waiqi Shuohua Le Haiwei Shoudao Tongzhi* （我帮外企说话了，还未收到通知）[*Zhang Xinzhu Responded to Dismissal: I Spoke for Foreign Firms and Haven't Received Notice*], ZI MAO QU YOUBAO (自贸区邮报) [FTZ POST] (12 Aug. 2014).

[139] *Zhang Xinzhu Huiying Shouhui Gaotong 600 Wan: Chedan* （张昕竹回应受贿高通600万：扯淡）[*Zhang Xinzhu Responded to the Allegation of Accepting 600 Million Bribery from Qualcomm: Bullshit*], 21 SHIJI JINGJI BAODAO （21世纪经济报道）[21ST CENTURY BUSINESS HERALD] (13 Aug. 2014).

[140] Zhou Lin（周琳）, *Juebuneng Rang Mouxie Zhuanjia Hunshui Moyu, Chili Pawai* （决不能让某些专家浑水摸鱼，吃里扒外）[*Those Experts Who Fished in Troubled Water, Living on Our Country while Leaking Secrets to Others is Not Tolerated*], XINHUA WANG （新华网）[Xinhua Net] (13 Aug. 2014).

regarded as a Party mouthpiece, this editorial signalled that the Chinse leadership had set the tone for the incident and remaining events.

Around the same time, CCTV produced another programme discussing Zhang's case. The discussion revolved around his conflict of interest and the programme also interviewed Ren Yuling, a consultant for the State Council. Mr. Ren was concerned about the incident, saying that it was not a purely commercial matter and had ricocheting effects for the national interest. Ren hinted that Zhang was in a position to leak information to foreign firms and thus some degree of corruption may have been involved. Mr Ren then called for more laws to be promulgated to address similar problems. Meanwhile, several newspapers implied that Zhang could be subject to legal punishments. On 14 August 2014, *Global Times* circulated an editorial, noting that it was unclear whether Zhang Xinzhu had been privy to any state secrets while serving on the Expert Advisory Committee. If so, Zhang's consulting for Qualcomm could amount to treason—the selling of state secrets.[141] *Yangtze News* also presumed that Zhang may have had the capacity to obtain state secrets.[142] The article referred to Article 111 of the Criminal Law stipulating that a person involved in the sale of state secrets could be sentenced to life imprisonment.

In the database of WiseNews, I identified sixty news articles discussing the dismissal of Zhang Xinzhu from the date his dismissal was publicly announced to the day before the NDRC released its decision on Qualcomm. Among these articles, 93 per cent mentioned that Zhang Xinzhu accepted high compensation from Qualcomm for defending the firm and 46 per cent mentioned that he had accepted 6 million from Qualcomm; some articles denominated that figure in dollars, but others did not specify. Additionally, 47 per cent explicitly condemned and criticized Zhang's conduct. Public opinion was also relatively unreceptive towards him. A poll on Sina demonstrated that 80 per cent of those surveyed believed that Zhang Xinzhu had illicit dealings with Qualcomm.[143]

Regardless of whether or not the AMC was justified in ousting Zhang, his downfall created a chilling effect for Chinese antitrust academics. Ever since then, Zhang has remained silent and idle in the antitrust community. Academic supervision of administrative behaviour, an important form of external

---

[141] Shan Renping （单仁平）, *Guowuyuan Fanlongduan Zhuanjia Anzhu Waiqi Taibugai* （国务院反垄断专家暗助外企太不该） [*State Council Antitrust Expert Shouldn't have Secretly Assisted Foreign Firms*], HUANQIU SHIBAO （环球时报） [GLOBAL TIMES] (14 Aug. 2014).

[142] Yang Yuze （杨于泽）, *Zhang Xinzhu Shijian de Lunli Yu Falv* （张昕竹事件的伦理与法律） [*The Ethics and Law in the Zhang Xinzhu Incidents*] (15 Aug. 2014).

[143] Xinlang Caijing （新浪财经） [Sina Finance], *Ni Ruhe Kandai Fanlongduan Zhuanjia Bei Jieping* （你如何看待反垄断专家被解聘） [*How Do You View the Dismissal of Antitrust Experts?*], XINLANG DIAOCHA （新浪调查） [SINA INVESTIGATION] (15 Aug. 2014).

constraint on administrative departments, has been deemed largely absent in China. As Zhang told the *New York Times* in an interview: 'currently, China's administrative law enforcement is extremely dangerous, with investigative powers and law enforcement powers bound together'.[144] Zhang was pessimistic about the future of China's antitrust enforcement, as he lamented: 'from the viewpoint of administrative enforcement of the law, China's anti-monopoly law is at a dead end. The judiciary is the only hope'.[145]

3.3 The Backlash to Defence

With the exception of China Telecom and China Unicom, no other firms have launched their own media campaigns to defend their case so far. As revealed in the Infant Formula case, the potential retribution and the continuing negative impact on stock prices were important concerns holding firms back from challenging the agency, but there is an additional danger for companies initiating a defence: media backlash. This is particularly the case for consumer product companies whose reputational lifeline is conditional on consumer perception and loyalty. The Chinese public loathes high prices and applauds the antitrust regulator's vows to reduce consumer prices. As such, the media is more concerned about the effects of an antitrust investigation on consumer prices than the investigation's actual legitimacy. Unless a firm can offer compelling evidence to rebut the government's allegations, a defensive strategy could be depicted as arrogant behaviour, thus further inflaming public opinion and prolonging the firm's exposure to undesirable publicity. Foreign businesses face heightened risks, as a reluctance to admit guilt can easily stir up nationalist sentiments.[146]

This sort of backlash can be observed in other areas of market regulation, such as in the food and drug industry. Proctor and Gamble's (P&G) experience in handling the SK-II brand offers a memorable lesson. SK-II was P&G's only high-end skincare brand in China. In March 2005, a dissatisfied customer claimed that her skin suffered from negative side effects after using SK-II products.[147] She lodged a complaint with the Nanchang Business Bureau, accusing the firm of false advertising. She also brought a suit against P&G in the

---

[144] Gough & Buckley, *supra* note 134.
[145] Id.
[146] Shirk, *supra* note 114, at 45.
[147] Richard Farmer, *SK-II: Damage Control in China*, THE ASIA CASE RESEARCH CENTER, THE UNIVERSITY OF HONG KONG 3 (2008).

Nanchang District court for defrauding consumers. This case spiraled out of control and made national headlines overnight, as numerous newspapers, on-line discussion boards, and blogs speculated about the safety and effectiveness of SK-II products. In response to the crisis, P&G China denied the accusations of defective products and false advertising, claiming the products received approval from the Ministry of Health before being imported into the country, and that they had been fully compliant with the relevant regulations. However, the strong denial from P&G sparked a harsh online commentary for its arrogant approach in handling the consumer crisis.[148]

On 14 September 2006, the State General Administration of Quality Supervision, Inspection, and Quarantine (AQSIQ), the governing body for import and export quality control, announced through *Xinhua News* that nine SK-II skin cream products were found to contain traces of chromium and neodynmium, banned substances under Chinese law.[149] SK-II persistently denied these accusations and insisted that it had delivered safe products.[150] It also asked for a re-test by the AQSIQ to reassess its final decision.[151] Although it had offered to refund customers, its botched refund policy spurred further disapproval. *Southern Metropolis Daily*, a highly regarded newspaper based in Guangzhou, later printed a sensationalist editorial entitled 'The Arrogance of Procter and Gamble', lambasting the company for its arrogant and negligent misconduct and stoking nationalist sentiments. Just one week after the government's announcement, P&G suspended sales of its SK-II products and exited the Chinese market altogether.

What was omitted from the entire public debate was whether the SK-II products had actually complied with the relevant laws and regulations. Similar tests in Hong Kong found amounts of chromium and neodymium in SK-II products to be within the acceptable range, posing little to no health risks.[152] Moreover, other foreign cosmetic products, including those from Clinique, Estee Lauder, Christian Dior, Lancôme, and Shiseido, were all found to contain the same substances, some with even higher levels than those in SK-II's products.[153] However, none of these brands faced similar criticism in China. On 24 October 2006, the AQSIQ released a statement, admitting that SK-II's

---

[148] Cheng Guixiang（程桂香）, *SK-II De Aoman Shishui Guanchulai De?*（SK-II的"傲慢"是谁惯出来的？）[*What Contributed to SK-II's Arrogance?*], PEOPLE.COM.CN (26 Sep. 2006).

[149] Katherine Allred et al., *SK-II: Damage Control-China*, WORDPRESS.COM (May 2011).

[150] Mei Fong & Loretta Chao, *P&G Stumbles in China*, WALL ST. J. (25 Sep. 2006).

[151] *See* Jennie Tung, *SK-II China: Managing Public Relations*, STANFORD GRADUATE SCHOOL OF BUSINESS CASE IB-81, 7 (2007).

[152] *See* Tung, *supra* note 151, at 11.

[153] Id. at 12.

products had not violated Chinese law.[154] The statement clarified that although chromium and neodymium were banned in China, these substances were only illegal when used as added ingredients. As these substances had not been intentionally mixed into SK-II's products but were naturally occurring, their dosages were low enough to constitute no threat to humans, thereby establishing that the substances were safe for consumption in China.

But AQSIQ's clarification came too late. The reputational damage to P&G's business had been done. There is an overwhelming consensus that the public relations crisis faced by SK-II had stemmed from its unwillingness to apologize to consumers and its vehement denial of the results released by the government inspection authority.[155] In fact, P&G's defensive strategy provided the media with an opportunity to spin scandalous narratives of how premium foreign products are deceptive and deleterious. Their defensive strategy also helped the media fuel a nationalist debate. In 2006, Sino-Japanese relations had reached a freezing point, further contributing to the media's interest in stoking public anger against Japanese-manufactured products.[156] In this case, the focal point was not the law. AQSIQ ultimately admitted that its earlier accusation had been a misunderstanding and that SK-II had committed no wrongdoing. However, SK-II's denial of the government's charges did not restore the company's reputation. To the contrary, it caused a backlash and aggravated the reputational damage. The Chinese media was extremely critical of the firm's misconduct and did not allow for alternative views. In the end, SK-II won its legal battle but lost the Chinese market.

Businesses under antitrust investigations face similar difficulties if they choose to adopt a defensive strategy when handling disputes with the government. Just like product safety issues, excessive pricing is a highly sensitive topic amongst Chinese consumers. Whenever a foreign firm is involved, state media see it as a golden opportunity to frame the situation as a nationalist story and accuse foreign firms of exploiting Chinese consumers. Unless these companies offer immediate and compelling evidence to dispute the allegations, a defensive strategy will be most likely to antagonize Chinese consumers. Indeed, although there is wide consensus among economists that resale price maintenance (RPM) practices are generally benign, it is exceedingly arduous for firms to proffer economic evidence to justify RPM conduct. Appeals can also take years. By the time a case is tried in court, the damaging publicity would have

---

[154] *See* Farmer, *supra* note 147, at 7.

[155] William R. Crandall *et al.*, *When Crisis Management Goes Abroad: The Demise of SK-II in China*, http://www.aib-midwest.org/uploads/4/2/3/2/42320691/p21_crandall.pdf

[156] *See* Tung, *supra* note 151, at 13.

already dealt a severe blow to a firm's sales. Business executives who are shrewd in their risk assessment would hesitate to file an appeal against a Chinese antitrust agency; the costs of doing so are immediate and substantial, while the future benefits pale in comparison to the present costs. Even when a firm's reputation can be restored after a victorious lawsuit in court, this can barely reclaim the losses that the firm would have likely already suffered in the interim. This explains why consumer product firms would rather accede to an antitrust agency's demands by lowering their prices and paying the fines, as this minimizes both the stock price volatility and the risks associated with the firm's exposure to prolonged negative publicity.

Summary

In this chapter, I have explained another facet of Chinese antitrust exceptionalism pertaining to how China regulates by demystifying the rareness of appeals against antitrust agencies in China. As documented in Chapter 1, Chinese antitrust agencies' idiosyncratic approach to enforce the AML have deeply troubled foreign firms operating in China. Yet appeals against their decisions are few, and foreign firms have displayed an unusual readiness to cooperate with the government. I identified two important factors holding firms back from challenging the government. First, China's former and current antitrust authorities, as well as the central ministries that host these agencies, hold vast administrative discretion over companies operating in the country. As many grey areas for doing business exist in China, companies can be held hostage by these regulatory authorities. As a consequence, businesses are averse to taking a confrontational approach in dealing with the antitrust authorities for fear of future retribution. In addition to formal regulatory tools, the Chinese central antitrust agency can leverage the state media strategically to inflict shaming sanctions on firms that are subject to an investigation. The additional sanctions help the agencies overcome their capacity and bureaucratic constraints in tackling China's powerful state-owned behemoths, and further deters private businesses from countering agency actions and facilitates their cooperation with the agency. Sadly, in those circumstances, the law does not matter. Even if the prospects of winning an administrative appeal in a Chinese court improve, the prohibitive transaction costs associated with initiating a lawsuit would still discourage companies from challenging an antitrust agency.

The various antagonistic enforcement tactics employed by the NDRC provide a good illustration of the formal and informal regulatory tools at the disposal of Chinese administrative authorities. It remains to be seen whether the new antitrust agency, the SAMR, will adopt such an aggressive approach to push ahead with its enforcement. Just like the NDRC, the SAMR would face few institutional checks if it chooses to follow the NDRC's path. It all comes down to the decision of the agency head, who will decide when and how to employ such regulatory tools.

While this chapter focuses on antitrust, many of its findings can be extended to a more general setting that explains the imbalance of power between the government and businesses in China. Although China's recent administrative law reforms have made significant progress in encouraging and facilitating suits against the government, they do not appear to have enhanced the bargaining power of large businesses dealing with China's powerful and resourceful government agencies.

PART II

HOW CHINA IS REGULATED

This Part explores the other dimension of Chinese antitrust exceptionalism by focusing on the antitrust challenges that Chinese firms experience overseas. I will detail the exceptional way that Chinese firms have been treated by Western regulators and how such regulatory outcomes are also deeply rooted in China's distinct political economy, particularly its decentralized economic structure and state-led model of governance. In the wake of the large influx of Chinese capital into Europe over the past decade, Chapter 3 elaborates on the EU's dilemma when applying the existing merger review framework to scrutinize acquisitions by Chinese companies. It assesses the feasibility of using foreign investment review as a complement to antitrust review, particularly the EU's recent regulatory proposal to tighten scrutiny over state-backed acquisitions. Chapter 4 delves into the US judicial inquiry into Chinese export cartels amid America's growing anxiety over China's dominance in essential medical supplies. In particular, it spotlights the 2018 decision handed down by the US Supreme Court relating to a group of Chinese vitamin C producers and discusses the dilemma facing US judges in handling Chinese export cartel cases.

3

The EU Merger Probe into China, Inc.

In March 2016, the European Commission (Commission) issued a decision that that could fundamentally change the way in which China and its state-owned enterprises (SOEs) conduct business in Europe. The Commission had been scrutinizing a proposed joint venture between two state-owned nuclear energy companies—France's Électricité de France (EDF) and China's China General Nuclear Power Corporation (CGN). The two companies were planning jointly to construct and operate three nuclear power plants in the United Kingdom. Under the proposed terms of the agreement, China's CGN agreed to take a 33.5 per cent stake in the ongoing Hinkley Point C project, the construction of a new nuclear power plant in Somerset, and the two companies would partner to build and manage two additional power plants in Suffolk and Essex. Under the Commission's rules at the time, it did not have authority to review this proposed deal. Because China's CGN had little turnover (i.e. revenue) in Europe, any deals that it engaged with in Europe would be considered too small to trigger the Commission's merger review.

The Commission had been under growing pressure to change the way it scrutinized mergers associated with Chinese state-owned enterprises (SOEs). Ever since the Great Recession, European regulators had been alarmed by the enormous influx of Chinese capital being channelled into Europe. From 2011 to 2015, annual Chinese foreign direct investment (FDI) in Europe amounted to more than EUR 10 billion, compared to an average of EUR 1 billion yearly in the previous five years.[1] In 2015 alone, Chinese companies invested EUR 20 billion in the European Union (EU), a 44 per cent increase from the previous year.[2] This number further grew to EUR 35 billion in 2016, rising by 77 per cent from 2015.[3] Many regulators were also concerned about possible strategically

---

[1] Thilo Hanemann & Mikko Huotari, *A New Record Year for Chinese Outbound Investment in Europe*, MERCATOR INST. FOR CHINA STUD. 3 (Feb. 2016). Many of the footnote references in this book are online materials and they can be easily accessible online.

[2] Id.

[3] Thilo Hanemann & Mikko Huotari, *Record Flows and Growing Imbalances: Chinese Investment in Europe in 2016*, MERICS PAPERS ON CHINA 3 (Jan. 2017).

Chinese Antitrust Exceptionalism. Angela Huyue Zhang, Oxford University Press (2021). © Angela Huyue Zhang. DOI: 10.1093/oso/9780198826569.003.0004

and politically motivated takeovers by Chinese enterprises, particularly those in which the Chinese government held a controlling interest.

Under growing external pressure and internal anxiety over the continued encroachment of Chinese influence in European markets, the Commission decided that it needed to review the EDF/CGN case. In its judgement, the Commission ruled that all Chinese SOEs operating in the energy sectors including CGN would be treated as a single entity.[4] In this manner, the Commission was able to treat all Chinese SOEs operating in the energy sector as part of a single, unified, Chinese conglomerate—China, Inc. Even if CGN's turnover by itself did not meet the threshold for review by the Commission, the turnover generated by all Chinese energy firms operating in Europe was certainly large enough to allow the Commission to gain jurisdiction over the deal and conduct its assessment.

In some ways, the Commission had been heading in this direction for several years. Ever since 2011, the Commission has applied a 'worst-case scenario' approach when reviewing merger transactions involving SOEs.[5] Under this cautious approach, the Commission considers whether the proposed transaction could produce anticompetitive harm if all Chinese SOEs in the same sector were assumed to be part of a single entity. This approach in part foreshadowed the *EDF/CGN* decision as it had contemplated the consequences of considering a large part of the Chinese economy as one firm: China, Inc. This view had previously never caused any issues; until the end of 2015, the Commission unconditionally cleared all such transactions because even under the 'worst-case scenario', there was no anticompetitive risk, and the Commission did not have to take a definite stance on its position. By the time the *EDF/CGN* deal came about, however, the Commission's hand was forced, and it was required to make a decision.

Even though the Commission ultimately cleared the *EDF/CGN* deal in 2016 and there were signs that this shift in approach was on its way, the Commission's decision still shocked the European antitrust community. Law firm partners rushed to notify their clients advising them on the potential implications. Several European scholars and commentators lauded the Commission's decision and encouraged the Commission to take a bolder and more uncompromising approach in scrutinizing future Chinese investment. Alan Riley, a senior fellow for the Institute for Statecraft, urged the Commission to view all

---

[4] Commission Decision No. M.7850 (EDF/CGN/NNB), slip op. ¶ 49 (10 Mar. 2016).

[5] *See* Angela Huyue Zhang, *Foreign Direct Investment from China: Sense and Sensibility*, 34 Nw. J. INT'L L. & BUS. 395, 435 (2014).

SOE collectively, not just within each sector, as one entity in their merger re-views, essentially forming a grand China, Inc.[6] Nicolas Petit, professor at the University of Liège, went further, arguing that all Chinese firms with a Party link should be treated as a single entity, regardless of their ownership status. He was of the opinion that all Chinese firms are part and parcel of a Party-led syn-dicate, reminiscent of super-trusts that stimulated social demand for antitrust regulation in the twentieth century.[7]

The repercussions of the *EDF/CGN* decision are significant. From a proce-dural standpoint, the Commission's power and reach has greatly expanded. The decision endowed it with the power to investigate many more deals, which will be likely to face more delays in Brussels; instead of focusing on a few targets, it now has the authority to zero in on a specific firm along with *all* Chinese SOEs in the same sector, perhaps even the entire Chinese public economy. These ex-pansive assessments will significantly increase potential horizontal and ver-tical overlaps between the parties, possibly affecting transactions adversely. It may also impact the remedies available; if all Chinese SOEs in a sector are con-sidered as a single entity, no SOEs can purchase a divested business that others may jettison to clear merger review.[8]

Practitioners have warned that the problems could transcend antitrust law. If other European regulators such as those in charge of securities regulation take a similar stance, a Chinese SOE may be required to provide the financial dis-closures for all other Chinese SOEs operating in the same sector, as they would be considered concert parties. Some Commission officials have also suggested that treating multiple Chinese SOEs as China, Inc. may complicate state-aid law enforcement. For example, they noted that two Chinese SOEs thought to be part of a single entity in a competition case would have trouble complying with the unbundling rules of the Third Energy Package, a regulation used to open up the energy and gas markets, in the European Union.

At the same time, this new, seemingly vigilant approach is also fraught with legal risks. The act of treating multiple Chinese SOEs as part of China, Inc. may jeopardize the Commission's future jurisdiction over cases pertaining to SOEs.[9] If Chinese SOEs in the same sector are regarded as part of a single entity, then

---

[6] Alan Riley, *Nuking Misconceptions: Hinkley Point, Chinese SOEs and EU Merger Law*, EUR. COMPETITION L. REV. (2016), https://ssrn.com/abstract=2778229; *see also* Sebastian Heilmann, *Europe Needs Tougher Response to China's State-Led Investments*, FIN. TIMES (9 June 2016).

[7] Nicolas Petit, *Chinese State Capitalism and Western Antitrust Policy* 15–16 (22 June 2016), https://ssrn.com/abstract=2798162; *see also* Heilmann, supra note 6.

[8] Geneviève Lallemand-Kirche et al., *The Treatment of State-Owned Enterprises in EU Competition Law: New Developments and Future Challenges*, 8 J. EUR. COMPETITION L. & PRAC. 295, 305 (2017).

[9] *See* Angela Huyue Zhang, *The Single Entity Theory: An Antitrust Time Bomb for Chinese State-Owned Enterprises?* 8 J. COMPETITION L. & ECON. 805, 825–26 (2012).

agreements, as well as mergers between them, could arguably be exempted from EU competition law. The EU's ability to act in such cases may be crucial if they pose a threat to European consumers. Therefore, the Commission's decision not only creates uncertainties for the business community but also carries grave legal risks for the Commission itself.

How should we respond to this paradoxical facet of the Chinese antitrust exceptionalism? The solution, I argue, actually lies beyond the existing EU Merger Regulation (EUMR) framework. The fundamental question facing the Commission is not how to define and incorporate China, Inc. into the existing merger framework but rather, how can the Commission properly identify the anticompetitive effects of state ownership. But this is easier said than done. When dealing with SOE cases, recognizing the clear inadequacy of its current framework in this context, the Commission narrows its assessment of control from de jure to de facto control. This approach fundamentally switches merger review from a form of ex ante enforcement, turning purely on structural incentives, to an ex post form emphasizing proof of communication and government directives. In practice, however, it is extremely difficult to compile evidence of actual coordination by the Chinese state. This coordination does not require verbal communication between that state investor and management, nor is communication required for the anticompetitive effect to occur if a Chinese SOE indirectly obtains a minority stake in a competing business. Chinese SOEs may also wield power and control exceeding their formal minority shareholder rights owing to their superior political and economic status.

Given this regulatory dilemma, it is not surprising that the Commission has been tightening its foreign investment control since 2017. In June 2020, the Commission published a White Paper aiming at tackling state-backed acquisitions.[10] Although China is not explicitly referenced in the policy, Chinese SOEs will unequivocally become the main targets of this new rule. This ambitious and interventionist move by the Commission shows that the line between competition review and security review is increasingly blurred in the European Union.

This chapter proceeds as follows. I will first analyse the rationale behind the EUMR provisions concerning the assessment of mergers between SOEs. After comparing the Commission's precedents pertaining to European and Chinese SOEs, I will show that the Commission has applied a double standard in its current approach to Chinese SOEs. I will then move on to examine how the

---

[10] European Commission Press Release, *Commission Adopts White Paper on Foreign Subsidies in the Single Market* (17 June 2020).

EUMR has failed to address the fundamental problem of anticompetitive effects of state ownership, resulting in both overinclusive and underinclusive outcomes. Finally, I caution against adopting a formalistic approach to address state ownership and put forward the solution of using foreign investment review as a complement to antitrust review of acquisitions by Chinese SOEs.

1. The Dilemma of the EUMR

Delineating the boundary of an 'undertaking' is the central inquiry in establishing whether and what type of EU competition law applies.[11] Article 101 of the Treaty on the Functioning of the European Union (TFEU) applies to agreements and concerted conduct *between separate undertakings*,[12] whereas the EUMR only covers corporate reorganization *between undertakings*.[13] The boundary of an undertaking is also germane for the assessment of liabilities and fines. At the same time, finding a consistent and coherent method to determine the boundary of any given undertaking has become an intractable problem for regulators. While it has perennially fascinated European policymakers and academics, scholars have tried in vain to identify a logically sound solution.

Nevertheless, the EUMR is built on this very concept. In particular, Article 3(2) of the EUMR defines control as the 'possibility of exercising decisive influence over an undertaking.'[14] Since 'concentrations' within the meaning of the EUMR hinges on changes in control,[15] a merger between SOEs belonging to the same state would not trigger a change in control. Therefore, any consolidations between SOEs of the same state would be exempt from EU regulation. To avoid this apparent prejudice between the public and private sector, EUMR includes an exception, Recital 22. It stipulates that in merger cases between SOEs belonging to the same state, the Commission must consider whether the merger results in the undertakings becoming an economic unit with independent power of decision, 'irrespective of the way in which their capital is held or of

---

[11] *See generally* Alison Jones, *The Boundaries of an Undertaking in EU Competition Law*, 8 EUR. COMPETITION J. 301 (2012).

[12] Consolidated Version of the Treaty on the Functioning of the European Union art. 101, 9 May 2008, 2008 O.J. (C 115) 47 [hereinafter TFEU].

[13] Council Regulation 139/2004, 2004 O.J. (L24) art. 3 [hereinafter EUMR].

[14] *See* id. art. 3(2).

[15] Commission Consolidated Jurisdictional Notice under Council Regulation (EC) No 139/2004 on the Control of Concentrations Between Undertakings 2008 O.J. (C 95), ¶ 51 [hereinafter *Jurisdictional Notice*].

the rules of administrative supervision applicable to them'.[16] The Commission's Jurisdictional Notice further states:

> [W]here a State-owned company is not subject to any coordination with other State-controlled holdings, it should be treated as independent for the purposes of Article 5, and the turnover of other companies owned by that State should not be taken into account. Where, however, several State-owned companies are under the same independent center of commercial decision-making, then the turnover of those businesses should be considered part of the group of the undertaking concerned for the purposes of Article 5.[17]

But is it ever possible for an SOE to have independent decision-making power when the state, as the main controlling shareholder, can influence the firm's corporate governance? If not, then in what manner can Recital 22 be applied, if at all? To answer these questions, I will first analyse the logic of Recital 22, then compare the governance structure of Chinese and French SOEs, followed by discussion about the challenges the Commission has faced when applying this provision to Chinese SOE cases.

1.1 The Logic of Recital 22

As demonstrated by Oliver Hart's Nobel-winning scholarship, the defining feature of ownership is the owner's retention of residual control.[18] As it is rarely the case that there are zero transaction costs, contracting parties can never draw out a contract envisioning all the contingencies. Consequently, not all rights conferred by ownership will be contracted away and an owner will always retain some residual control over their property. As Wouter Wils succinctly points out:

> [I]f the parent company has the possibility to exercise decisive influence over the strategic commercial behaviour of the subsidiary, the subsidiary cannot have real freedom to determine its course of action on the market. Even if the parent company happened not actually to exercise its influence,

---

[16] *See* EUMR, *supra* note 13, ¶ 22.

[17] *See* Jurisdictional Notice, *supra* note 15, ¶ 194.

[18] OLIVER HART, FIRMS, CONTRACTS, AND FINANCIAL STRUCTURE 29–55 (1995).

the subsidiary's apparent freedom would only exist by the parent company's grace, which could change at any time.[19]

The application of this logic to SOEs entails that a state owner will always retain some degree of residual control over its SOEs. It is through these residual rights of control, that the state has the power to influence such firms, regardless of whether this influence has been exerted or explicitly stated. Therefore, no SOE can enjoy decision-making powers that remain completely independent of the state.

Furthermore, any requirement mandating SOEs to run their businesses independently of their owning states would run counter to sound corporate governance. Fundamentally, corporate governance exists to address the agency problem, an intrinsic concern of any modern corporation where ownership and control are separate.[20] In light of this, it is essential for the state investor, to safeguard its interests, actively exercise its voting rights as a shareholder of the SOE, and engage in the company's corporate governance. If a large investor completely cedes control of the firm to the management, the management will be subject to scant monitoring from shareholders. For this reason, Ronald Gilson and Jeffrey Gordon have advocated using the law to encourage the practice of activist investing in the United States, as activist investors—shareholders who effect organizational change by putting pressure on the board of directors beyond the normal process—are more motivated than large institutional shareholders to achieve vigorous corporate governance.[21] In a similar vein, it would be efficient for a state shareholder to participate actively in the governance of the firms it owns.

Therefore, the state, by simply voting its stock, can always sway the SOEs' decisions. If it is presumed that the state is solely profit driven like a conventional firm, then it will have the incentive to coordinate its SOEs to maximize joint profit. In this case, it would not be necessary to engage with the de facto question of whether such coordination has actually occurred.

So, for Recital 22 to even make sense, it must assume two things. First, that a state has a utility function different from an ordinary commercial entity. Second, the key issue lies in examining de facto, rather than de jure, control;

---

[19] *See* Wouter P.J. Wils, *The Undertaking as Subject of E.C. Competition Law and the Imputation of Infringements to Natural or Legal Persons*, 25 EUR. L. REV. 99, 107–08 (2000).

[20] Eugene F. Fama & Michael C. Jensen, *Separation of Ownership and Control*, 26 J. L. & ECON. 301, 304 (1983).

[21] Ronald J. Gilson & Jeffrey N. Gordon, *The Agency Costs of Agency Capitalism: Activist Investors and the Revaluation of Governance Rights*, 113 COLUM. L. REV. 863, 896–97 (2013).

that is, while the state *in theory* can influence its SOEs, if the SOEs *in fact* operate independently from each other, then a merger between them will deprive the market of two real competitors. This would provide a basis for the Commission to intervene. This interpretation is consistent with the Commission's own Jurisdictional Notice, which focuses on whether the state in fact attempts to coordinate competition among its SOEs.[22]

This legal framework, however, changes the intrinsic nature of merger review. The merger review, as a form of ex ante enforcement, focuses on whether the integration of two separate competitors *could* result in a substantial lessening of competition. The loss of competition depends on how each firm's incentives to compete have been decreased due to the changes in market structure. Furthermore, in line with this logic, Article 3(2) of the EUMR defines control as 'the *possibility* of exercising decisive influence on an undertaking', and 'it is therefore not necessary to show that the decisive influence is or will be actually exercised'.[23] And this makes sense, from a practical standpoint. As Wouter Wils points out, de facto control is exceptionally difficult and costly to identify.[24] Indeed, explicit communication is not necessary for a state to exert control over its SOEs. In the absence of direct state participation in the SOE activities, the state can appoint executives to the board to partake in important decision-making including budgeting, business planning, and commercial strategies. The firm's management may be spurred to pursue state objectives to display its loyalty to the state. Therefore, despite being outwardly passive, the state investor still has the opportunity to influence the actions of SOEs indirectly by simply exercising its basic voting rights. This applies to all SOEs, irrespective of whether it is Chinese or non-Chinese.

Furthermore, a state can design incentive packages for SOE executives that discourage competition with state-owned rivals. This is especially true in cases where the structure of executive compensation ties the firm's profitability to the industry or competitor standards.[25] Recently published empirical research on common shareholding by institutional shareholders demonstrates that commonly owned firms are more likely to compensate chief executive officers (CEOs) based on industry performance rather than on performance relative to competitors.[26] CEOs are therefore incentivized to soften competition with rivals to maximize their own compensation.

---

[22] Jurisdictional Notice, *supra* note 15, ¶ 194.

[23] Id. ¶ 16 (emphasis added).

[24] Wils, *supra* note 19, at 107.

[25] David Gilo, *The Anticompetitive Effect of Passive Investment*, 99 MICH. L. REV. 1, 26 (2000).

[26] Miguel Antón et al., *Common Ownership, Competition, and Top Management Incentives* 3–5 (ROSS SCH. OF BUS., WORKING PAPER NO. 1328, 2017).

Even if the state holds absolutely no voting power, it still has other means of exerting control that are not available to ordinary commercial investors. For instance, managers could be motivated to adhere to the state if the government can somehow influence their future employment prospects, particularly if the managers ultimately want to pursue political careers in the long run. Similarly, the state can impact a firm's commercial decisions if it can entice the firm with cheap financing or promises of a bail out if the firm runs into trouble. The corporate governance of Chinese and French SOEs illustrates the challenges that the Commission faces in applying Recital 22.

1.2 Comparing Chinese and French SOEs

China has an unusually large state-owned sector. At the end of 2017, there were 58,000 central SOEs, and 116,000 local SOEs in China.[27] According to the Rhodium Group, SOEs still account for 28 per cent of China's industrial assets as of June 2018.[28] Meanwhile, China applies a centralized model to oversee its extensive state assets, with major industrial SOEs falling under the supervision and purview of the State-owned Asset Supervision and Administration Commission (SASAC), a special commission directly subordinate to the State Council. In the pre-reform era, all industrial Chinese SOEs were owned and managed by various central ministries. After several rounds of market reform, the control rights were transferred from the ministries to SASAC, an independent agency created in 2003. Therefore, the establishment of SASAC, a move intended to separate the government's public sector role from its capacity as an investor, was an important step in China's market reform. Local governments—including provincial and municipal governments—were also instructed to set up their own local SASACs, representing the local government's ownership of assets and not subordinate to the central SASAC.

Notably, SASAC's role in the management of state assets was only formally recognized in 2008, upon the promulgation of the Enterprise State-Owned Assets Law (the 'State Assets Law').[29] The State Assets Law explicitly designates SASAC as a fiduciary for the state's ownership interest. It also gives SASAC

---

[27] Daniel H. Rosen et al., *Missing Link: Corporate Governance in China's State Sector, An Asia Society Special Report with Rhodium Group* (Nov. 2018), https://asiasociety.org/missing-link-corporate-governance-chinas-state-sector, at 12.

[28] Id. at 9.

[29] Zhonghua Renmin Gongheguo Qiye Guoyou Zichan Fa （中华人民共和国企业国有资产法） (Law of the People's Republic of China on the State-Owned Assets of Enterprises) (promulgated by the Standing Comm. Nat'l People's Cong., 28 Oct. 2008, effective 1 May 2009).

the rights accorded to a shareholder, including returns on its investments and approval of any major ownership decisions of the firm, such as mergers, bankruptcy, and the issuance of new securities. The SASAC also has the authority to appoint directors, managers, and supervisors of wholly state-owned enterprises and nominate directors and supervisors in partially state-owned enterprises. However, apart from that, SASAC is prohibited from direct management of the firm or day-to-day operations. The central SASAC further propagated rules for local SASACs to ensure compliance with government mandates.[30]

While the establishment of SASAC has ostensibly weakened the administrative ties between the Party and SOEs, the inextricable link has been far from severed. Richard McGregor, the former bureau chief of the Financial Times, detailed this relationship in his influential book, *The Party*, by providing a glimpse into the Party's shadowy affiliations and murky control over various aspects of the Chinese political economy.[31] In the book, McGregor coined and popularized the collective term 'China, Inc', depicting vivid narratives of how the Party has maintained a tight grip on the Chinese state-owned behemoths in the oil, mineral, and the banking sectors. The book's success has generated greater misgivings about the independence of the Chinese SOEs under SASAC's supervision than had existed prior to its publication. One of the Party's most effective methods of exerting control over SOEs is through personnel appointment.[32] Although SASAC, in theory, is entrusted with the task of appointing and selecting managers, in practice, these decisions are made under the shadow of party control. The top leaders of the fifty-three central companies whom are considered the bureaucratic equivalent of vice-ministers, are directly appointed by the Department of Organization, the human resources department of the Party.[33] Moreover, executives in Chinese SOEs are not solely rewarded based on financial performance but also with career advancement opportunities. Indeed, for the top executives at leading central SOEs, their career paths after leaving the firms are determined by the Party.[34]

China is not distinct in its application of a centralized model to manage state assets.[35] Similar models have been adopted in several European countries,

---

[30] ORG. FOR ECON. CO-OPERATION AND DEV. [OECD], OECD REVIEWS OF REGULATORY REFORM: CHINA—DEFINING THE BOUNDARY BETWEEN THE MARKET AND THE STATE 59 (2009).

[31] RICHARD MCGREGOR, THE PARTY: THE SECRET WORLD OF CHINA'S COMMUNIST RULERS (2010).

[32] *See* Jiangyu Wang, *The Political Logic of Corporate Governance in China's State-Owned Enterprises*, 47 CORNELL INT'L L. J. 631 (2014).

[33] *Wang, supra* note 32, at 659.

[34] *See* Nan Lin, *Capitalism in China: A Centrally Managed Capitalism (CMC) and Its Future*, 7 MGMT. & ORG. REV. 63, 74 (2010).

[35] *See generally* Maria Vagliasindi, *Governance Arrangements for State Owned Enterprises* (WORLD BANK SUSTAINABLE DEV. NETWORK, WORKING PAPER NO. 4542, 2008).

including Denmark, the Netherlands, Spain, Norway, Sweden, Belgium, France, and Poland, often as a result of privatization reforms.[36] Among them, France's model bears the most resemblance to China's because it too established a specialized independent agency in 2004, the Government Shareholding Agency (APE), to manage state assets.[37] Operating under the joint authority of the Minister of Finance, the Public Budget, along with the Minister for the Economy, Industry and Digital Affairs, the APE's statutory mission is to preserve the French government's patrimonial interests and pursue state-shareholder goals in French SOEs.[38] By mid-2017, the APE had managed eighty-one SOEs on behalf of the French government and oversaw assets exceeding EUR 100 billion.[39] French state ownership was most concentrated in the energy sector (49 per cent), followed by the defence (24 per cent), transport (7 per cent), and telecom sectors (7 per cent).[40] The APE has the power to appoint representatives to a firm's board of directors, supervisory board, or other deliberative bodies, if the agency directly or indirectly owns more than 50 per cent of the capital in that firm.[41] The APE may also assign other representatives to the firm's deliberative bodies if it owns more than 10 per cent of the capital in the firm.[42] According to APE's 2016 annual report, the French government appointed 824 directors to the boards of directors or the supervisory boards of French SOEs that specific year.[43] The legislation in place makes it permissible for French state representatives to exercise the same rights and powers as those afforded to other members of the board of directors, supervisory boards, or governing bodies.[44]

On paper at least, the French model of state-holding closely parallels the Chinese model. Consider EDF, one of the largest French SOEs and one of the parties in the EDF/GCN case. The French government owns 83 per cent of

---

[36] Id. at 11–14.

[37] AGENCE DES PARTICIPATIONS DE L'ÉTAT, THE GOVERNMENT AS SHAREHOLDER: 2016-2017 ANNUAL REPORT, https://www.economie.gouv.fr/files/files/directions_services/agence-participations-etat/Annual_Report_APE_2016-2017.pdf [2016 Annual Report].

[38] Décret 2004-963 du 9 septembre 2004 portant création du service à compétence nationale Agence des participations de l'Etat [Decree 2004-963 of 9 September 2004 establishing the national service State Shareholding Agency], JOURNAL OFFICIEL DE LA RÉPUBLIQUE FRANÇAISE [J.O.] [OFFICIAL GAZETTE OF FRANCE], 10 Sept. 2004, at 341.

[39] 2016 Annual Report, *supra* note 37, at 13.

[40] Id. at 27.

[41] Ordonnance 2014-948 du 20 août 2014 relative à la gouvernance et aux opérations sur le capital des sociétés à participation publique [Ordinance 2014-948 of 20 Aug. 2014 on the governance and capital transactions of publicly controlled companies], JOURNAL OFFICIEL DE LA RÉPUBLIQUE FRANÇAISE [J.O.] [OFFICIAL GAZETTE OF FRANCE], 23 Aug. 2014, 14011.

[42] Id.

[43] 2016 Annual Report, *supra* note 37, at 14.

[44] Ordonnance 2014-948, *supra* note 41, at 14011.

EDF, according to the APE's 2016 annual report.[45] In fact, EDF's statute restricts non-state ownership to 30 per cent.[46] Of the eleven EDF directors appointed at the general meeting of shareholders, five were recommended by the French state, one of whom was an APE representative, and six directors were elected by employees.[47] The chairman and CEO of EDF are both appointed by French presidential decree upon recommendation of the board of directors. Any major commercial decisions, such as mergers and acquisitions, investments, and executive compensation also require approval from the French state. Therefore, even with the adoption of a passive investment strategy, the French government can subtly influence the EDF's commercial strategy through the appointment of high-level executives. For instance, Gérard Magnin, who resigned from the EDF board because he opposed the EDF/GCN project in 2016, was appointed by the French government in 2014.[48] Given Magnin's professional background in alternative energy, his appointment was widely speculated to be a strategic move by the French government to induce increased investment in renewable energy sectors. The French parliament introduced a new decree back in 2014, granting long-term shareholders automatic double voting powers, provided that the firm's articles of association did not forbid it.[49] Some commentators suggested that the aim of the new law was to permit the state greater flexibility with regards to divesting its holding in SOEs while retaining or even strengthening its control over SOEs in strategic industries.[50] The new law also enables the French government to fend off undesirable takeovers of French companies. For instance, the French government now has double voting rights in EDF, thus empowering the government with the ability to exert considerable influence on the firm's commercial activities beyond its existing shareholding rights.

---

[45] 2016 Annual Report, *supra* note 37, at 25.

[46] Loi 2004-803 du 9 août 2004 relative au service public de l'électricité et du gaz et aux entreprises électriques et gazières [Law 2004-803 of August 9, 2004 relating to the public service of electricity and gas and to electric and gas companies], Journal Officiel de la République Française [J.O.] [Official Gazette of France], 11 Aug. 2004, 14256 (noting in Article 24 that the state retains 70 per cent of the capital of the company).

[47] EDF, *2019 Facts and Figures*, https://www.edf.fr/sites/default/files/contrib/groupe-edf/espaces-dedies/espace-finance-en/financial-information/publications/facts-figures/facts-and-figures-2019.pdf, at 49.

[48] Graham Ruddick, *Resignation of EDF Director Paves Way for Hinkley Point Go-Ahead*, Guardian (28 July 2016).

[49] Tony Barber, *Illusionary French Sell-Off Plan Lacks Authenticity of Old*, Fin. Times (26 Nov. 2014); *see* Loi 2014-384 du 29 mars 2014 visant à reconquérir l'économie réelle [Law 2014-384 of 29 Mar. 2014 to reclaim the real economy ('Loi Florange')], Journal Officiel de la République Française [J.O.] [Official Gazette of France], 1 Apr. 2014, 6232

[50] Curtis Milhaupt & Mariana Pargendler, *Governance Challenges of Listed State-Owned Enterprises Around the World: National Experiences and a Framework for Reform*, 50 Cornell Int'l L. J. 473 (2017).

In addition, as is in the case in many Chinese SOEs, political appointments of representatives at large French SOEs are not uncommon. As an Organisation for Economic Co-operation and Development (OECD) report points out, '[i]n a number of cases there is a direct political dimension to the nomination with the direct involvement of the Council of Ministries or even the President, such as in France for Chairmen and CEOs of some large SOEs'.[51] A recent example is the French socialist government's move to oust Henri Proglio in 2014 as chief executive of EDF France due to his close association with the former centre-right president Nicolas Sarkozy.[52] Anecdotal evidence suggests that the French government had interfered in the daily operation of SOEs as well. The French government reportedly put pressure on its SOEs to buy Alstom products to prop it up.[53] On another occasion, the French government's concern about unemployment caused it to spend EUR 600 million on a high-speed train to rescue and revive a failing Alstom engineering plant.[54]

A comparison of the corporate governance structures of Chinese and French SOEs thus illustrates telling commonalities. First, as fiduciaries of the state, both SASAC and APE assume the management role of safeguarding state as-sets. As such, they must be involved in the SOEs' commercial decision-making, either directly or indirectly. It is an unrealistic expectation for the state to tie its hands completely in order to give SOEs sole autonomy of operations. Such a de-mand is not efficient from a corporate governance perspective either. Second, both SASAC and APE can influence the commercial strategies of the SOEs in-directly through the appointment of executives, even if these agencies are not directly involved in day-to-day decision-making and have delegated a great deal of operational discretion to management teams. Neither agency needs to rely on any explicit mechanism to control the SOEs' management; nor is di-rect communication necessary. As long as the government retains the power to govern decisions over personnel appointments within the SOEs, the intricate yet close-knit relationship between government and SOEs cannot be severed entirely. Finally, even though French SOEs have instituted a more reputable corporate governance structure, incorporated more transparency in its opera-tions, and provided better public disclosure about its management procedures

---

[51] OECD, Corporate Governance of State-Owned Enterprises: A Survey of OECD Countries 91 (2005).

[52] Michael Stothard & Hugh Carney, French Government Ousts Proglio at EDF, Fin. Times (15 Oct. 2014).

[53] Simon C.Y. Wong, Improving Corporate Governance in SOEs: An Integrated Approach, 7 Corp. Governance Int'l 9, 13 (2004).

[54] Ann-Sylvaine Chassany, France to Buy Unneeded Train to Save Belfort Factory, Fin. Times (4 Oct. 2016).

in comparison to their Chinese counterparts, they are not completely immune from political interference. Thus, the question confronting the Commission is not about whether SOEs have independent decision-making power. None of them do. The real question is the degree to which an SOE's decision-making power allows it to compete in the market independently of other SOEs.

1.3   Applying a Double Standard

Ostensibly, Recital 22 is applied evenly and uniformly to all SOEs, irrespective of nationality. And Commission officials stressed that the same criteria were applied consistently to every case.[55] In reality, however, the Commission's approach has been anything but consistent. While the Commission focuses on issues of actual change in control when scrutinizing European SOE cases, it applies a more onerous test when reviewing cases involving Chinese SOEs.

In *Neste/IVO*, a merger transaction between two Finnish SOEs in 1998, the Commission discovered that the Finnish government was able to exercise its shareholding rights and vote on important commercial issues such as mergers and acquisitions as well as listings.[56] The Commission, though, found no indication that Neste's and IVO's commercial conduct had ever been coordinated; rather, the Commission determined that the two SOEs' operative matters were administered independently by their respective operating managements. The Commission, therefore, concluded that these two Finnish SOEs acted separately from one another in the market.

In another merger transaction, *EDF/Segebel*, EDF sought to acquire Segebel, a Belgian electricity company, in 2009. The Commission then proceeded to deliberate whether GDF Suez, the largest electricity company at the time and also a portfolio company of APE, should be deemed independent from EDF.[57] The Commission acknowledged that APE was responsible for managing the French state's shareholding in both SOEs, but the Commission identified that the role of the APE was 'clearly limited' and did not appear to affect 'the commercial and business autonomy of these companies'. The Commission also ruled that these two SOEs were independent, based on three findings: first,

[55] Joaquin Almunia, Speech at the Eighteenth St. Gallen International Competition Law Forum ICF: *Recent Developments and Future Priorities in E.U. Competition Policy* (8 Apr. 2011); Cecilio Madero Villarejo, Deputy Director General for Antitrust Directorate General for Competition European Commission, Speech at the Seventh International Conference on Competition Law and Policy in Beijing: *Recent Trends in EU Merger Control* (1 June 2011).

[56] Commission Decision No. IV/M.931 (Neste/IVO) (17 Sept. 2002).

[57] Commission Decision No. COMP/M.5549 (EDF/Segebel) (12 Nov. 2009).

EDF could impartially set its business plan in relation to GDF Suez in accord-ance with its own commercial interest; second, there was no interlocking di-rectorship between the two SOEs; and third, there were adequate safeguards to ensure that commercially sensitive information would not be shared between these two entities. The Commission, based on the totality of the circumstances, concluded that EDF and GDF Suez were separate undertakings.

In both *Neste/IVO* and *EDF/Segebel*, the Commission explicitly recognized that the states involved had voting power in the SOEs, presumably giving the states power to intervene in important commercial decisions, including the appointment of board executives. However, the Commission seemed unper-turbed by the de jure control, noting that the state's power and role in these situations were constrained. The Commission, instead, focused on de facto control; that is, whether the underlying SOEs did in fact coordinate competi-tion between themselves.

This emphasis on de facto control is in stark contrast with the Commission's approach to reviewing non-EU SOEs. For instance, during its review of a trans-action involving Rosneft, a Russian SOE, the Commission pinpointed circum-stantial factors such as Russia's authority to assign and remove board members, and depicted these as important evidence to show the Russian government's discretion over commercial and strategic decisions.[58] But this influence is a norm of all SOEs. If this feature was not source for concern in *Neste/IVO* and *EDF/Segabel*, why did it suddenly become a problem with Rosneft, a Russian national champion? It is probable that the Commission was sceptical of the Russian government's influence over the commercial decisions of Rosneft and other SOEs. However, because of the difficulty in finding direct evidence of such coordination, the Commission fell back on evidence of de jure control. This is exactly what occurred in cases involving Chinese SOEs.

The first case where the Commission questioned the independence of Chinese SOEs was *Bluestar/Elkem*, a proposed acquisition of the Norwegian silicon producer Elkem by China National Bluestar in 2011.[59] China National Bluestar was a subsidiary of ChemChina, reporting directly to the central SASAC. The parties argued that ChemChina's decision-making power was in-dependent of the central SASAC, the latter only enjoys 'basic ownership func-tions on behalf of the Chinese State as a non-managing trustee'. The parties also argued that the local SASAC themselves were autonomous from the central SASAC, pointing out that the central SASAC had no authority to appoint the

[58] Commission Decision No. COMP/M.6801 (Rosneft/TNK-BP), slip op. ¶ 7(8 Mar. 2013).
[59] Commission Decision No. COMP/M.6082 (China National Bluestar/Elkem) (31 Mar. 2011).

management staff of SOEs operating under regional SASACs, with this jurisdiction residing exclusively with local governments and political organs. The
parties in *Bluestar/Elkem* also reiterated that the SASAC's key functions were
limited to actions such as nominating members to top management, reviewing
the annual results of the SOEs and ensuring that the SOEs operate within their
permitted license. The parties further argued that the level of state intervention
in the industry sectors relevant to the specific transaction was very minor, with
the SASAC remaining aloof when it came to critical decision-making such as
the approval of business plans or budgets.

The parties provided three pieces of evidence to demonstrate this negligible
level of state intervention: first, there was no sharing of proprietary information, the SASAC had never asked for commercial information from the SOEs
or impacted their commercial operations through other means; second, the
dividend policy of the SOEs had not been dictated by the SASAC on an individual company basis but was rather kept consistent across all central SOEs;
and third, management was compensated based on a point system, taking
into account various factors apart from financial performance. The parties in
Bluestar/Elkem also noted that the SASAC possessed limited capacity to su-
perintend the SOEs. At that time, the central SASAC oversaw 125 large central
SOEs and employed 800 individuals.

The Commission's findings from its own market investigation seemed to val-
idate the parties' position. First of all, the underlying market for silicon metal
was highly fragmented with more than 200 firms, many of which were privately owned. Second, nearly all Chinese state-owned firms in the market belonged to local governments, with ChemChina being the sole SOE reporting to
the central SASAC. Finally, European customers did not believe that there was
any coordination among the producers. These findings suggested that local
SOEs, together with private domestic firms, had introduced effective competitive constraints targeting ChemChina. Thus, had the Commission applied the
same de facto standard as it had in *Neste/IVO* and *EDF/Segebel*, it should have
endorsed the parties' position.

The Commission, however, was reluctant to do so. After summarizing previous precedents dealing with European SOEs, the Commission noted that the
overall assessment was 'guided by the *possible* power of the State to influence
the companies' commercial strategy and the *likelihood* for the State to actually
coordinate their commercial conduct, either by imposing or facilitating such
coordination'. The weight given to the 'probabilistic' nature of the state's power
to influence SOEs deviated from the Commission's jurisprudence in previous
European cases. Unconvinced by the parties' arguments, the Commission then

carried out a detailed assessment examining the product overlaps between Elkem's activities and the activities of ChemChina along with other SOEs under the administration of both central SASAC and the local SASACs. After extensive inquiries, it cleared the merger, having found no competition concerns.

Similar issues arose during the Commission's assessment of a joint venture between Koninklijke DSM N.V. (DSM), a Dutch company, and Sinochem, another SOE supervised by central SASAC. The Commission still remained incredulous, questioning the degree of Sinochem's independence from SASAC.[60] The Commission pointed to the State Assets Law and the associated information on SASAC's website as evidence suggesting that SOEs did not have independent decision-making power. The specific language quoted by the Commission was as follows:

> SASAC guides and pushes forward the reform and restructuring of state-owned enterprises, advances the establishment of modern enterprise system in SOEs, improves corporate governance, and propels the strategic adjustment of the layout and structure of the state economy [and]

> SASAC is responsible for the fundamental management of the state-owned assets of enterprises, works out draft laws and regulations on the management of the state-owned assets, establishes related rules and regulations and directs and supervises the management work of local state-owned assets according to law.

It is unclear why such language raised doubts because it appears simply to outline the normal functions of a state asset management firm. The Commission also cited an OECD report and a book by Barry Naughton, a China expert, suggesting that the Chinese state could influence Chinese SOE decision-making via both formal channels, such as the SASAC, and less formal channels. The Commission remarked that SASAC's own official statements supported this assertion, quoting a sentence from Sinochem's Annual Report: 'As [a] key state-owned enterprise, Sinochem Group is dedicated to serving the greater good of the national political stability, economic development, and social progress.'

True, the Commission's evidence brought forth during the assessment of the Sinochem deal does suggest that SASAC can sway the decision-making of its supervised SOEs in its favour. It does not, however, provide any indication that SASAC *had actually exerted influence* to limit the competition between Sinochem and its industry sector counterparts. The results from the market

---

[60] Commission Decision No. COMP/M.6113 (DSM/Sinochem) (19 May 2011).

investigation, though, are mixed. On the one hand, the Commission found that these SOEs may not be able to act as independently as private enterprises. In the undertaken study, some expressed concern that the proposed joint venture and other Chinese SOEs might be incentivized to coordinate in certain markets and that this was a likely outcome. There were others noting that the transaction was part of a scheme by Chinese SOEs to gain more leverage in the markets concerned. Europe-based customers and one customer in China stated that Chinese suppliers do indeed compete with one another to a certain degree.

The Commission revisited the same issue in subsequent cases but ultimately left open the question of how to determine the degree of SOE independence in its official decisions. But it could not dodge the issue during *EDF/CGN*.[61] As CGN had minimal turnover in Europe, the Commission could only exert jurisdiction over the transaction by enlarging the latitude of SOEs involved in the case. However, the Commission justified its jurisdiction by identifying a few factors.

First, the Commission pointed to the State Assets Law and its interim measures allowing SASAC to vote on important business decisions ranging from strategies and business plans to budgets. The Commission portrayed these provisions as evidence that SASAC could influence the commercial decisions of the SOEs it manages. This is puzzling, as SASAC—like all state investors, irrespective of EU and non-EU—would need to exercise its basic voting rights in order to govern the SOEs under its supervision. What the Commission perhaps saw as most troubling in the *EDF/CGN* case was its effect on the nuclear industry, a highly sensitive and vital industry sector. Once again, the Commission relied on specific diction as set out in the State Assets Law, noting that the Chinese government sought to facilitate and advance the centralization of state-owned capital in important industries appertaining to economic lifeline and national security. Given the critical importance of the nuclear power industry, the Commission believed that the Chinese government had a strategic as well as a calculated interest in coordinating competition in this industry. While the Commission could not identify any explicit evidence of coordination, it nonetheless found evidence of a strategic alliance formed among Chinese nuclear companies. As quoted by the Commission, the creation of the China Nuclear Industry Alliance was 'directed by the [Chinese] government to achieve some synergy' and was 'designed to eliminate detrimental or unseemly

---

[61] Commission Decision No. M.7850 (EDF/CGN/NNB Group of Companies), slip op. §§37–42 (10 Mar. 2016).

competition in export market'. While this may indicate that Chinese nuclear power companies may engage in export cartel conduct, it can be rendered insufficient evidence to conclude that they were acting as a single firm. Moreover, it would set a dangerous precedent if the Commission chose to do so. If these Chinese nuclear companies do in fact participate in export cartel behaviour, such conduct is clearly prohibited under Article 101 of the TFEU.[62] But if the Commission decided to treat all Chinese SOEs operating in the energy sector as a single firm, Chinese nuclear companies may then defend themselves as if it were a single firm.

Finally, the Commission brought up CGN's joint venture agreement with CNNC, another SOE in the nuclear sector, for the development and global marketing of a nuclear technology. While strategic links may be subject to additional antitrust scrutiny[63] it is far from clear evidence of single firm conduct. Based on these facts, the Commission decided that the Central SASAC could interfere in Chinese SOEs' strategic investment decisions and facilitate coordination between firms, at least in the energy sector. The Commission as such established that CGN and other Chinese SOEs in the energy sector should be taken as a single entity, and that their turnover should be aggregated for the purpose of merger notification. Ultimately, the transaction was cleared because even if all Chinese SOEs in the energy sector were viewed as a single entity, the deal would not pose any competitive concern. The Commission did not resolve the issue of how to treat other Chinese SOEs, including those that are not operating in the energy sector and those that are owned by local governments. This left much to ambiguity.

Recital 22 thus places the Commission in a difficult conundrum. While the regulator is right to assume that the SASAC—and the Party, by extension—may be working behind the scenes to effect the competitive strategies of SOEs under their control, evidence of coordination is extremely hard to ascertain. Consequently, the Commission, in its decisions, falls back on evidence of de jure control to infer de facto control. This is clearly inconsistent with the standard applied to European SOEs, jeopardizing the Commission's hard-earned reputation as an impartial and non-discriminatory regulator.

---

[62] A complicated issue, however, is whether such a cartel would be treated as compelled by the state and thus may be exempt from antitrust law. This decision would turn on the specific facts of the case. *See* more details in Chapter 4 of this book.

[63] Economic links like this may form the basis for a finding of collective dominance as the General Court decided in *Italian Flat Glass*. Joined Cases T-68/89, T-77/89, and T-78/89, Società Italiana Vetro SpA v. Comm'n, 1992 E.C.R. II-01403. However, collective dominance is no longer the enforcement priority for the Commission in recent years. *See* Thomas K. Cheng & Kelvin H. Kwok, *A Neglected Theory of Harm: Joint Ventures as Facilitators of Collusion Across Markets*, 5 J. ANTITRUST ENFORCEMENT 434, 437–58 (2016).

In short, the challenges that the Commission faces in applying Recital 22 to SOEs are deeply rooted in the legal framework upon which the EUMR has been built. As will be further elaborated below, a formalistic application of the EUMR will lead to both overinclusive and underinclusive problems when it comes to Chinese SOEs.

2 The Failed Application of the EUMR to Chinese SOEs

The EUMR is applied to 'concentrations' that have met EU notification thresholds.[64] As such, the delineation of an undertaking's boundary becomes a question of threshold, the answer to which will determine whether the Commission can exert jurisdiction and conduct a competitive assessment. This legal design, however, is premised on two assumptions: first, the ultimate controlling entity of the undertaking is incentivized to coordinate competition among the firms it controls; and second, it has the ability to do so. While this normally makes sense for commercial entities, these assumptions are not self-evident when it comes to SOEs, especially Chinese SOEs.

2.1 The Problem of Overinclusion

As economists Holmstrom and Tirole have demonstrated, competition acts as an effective safeguard to ensure satisfactory firm performance.[65] The Chinese leadership has embraced this logic, permitting the entry of private capital into most economic sectors. As non-state firms compete intensively with SOEs in liberalized sectors, the government has little incentive to coordinate competition among SOEs in those sectors. Even if the Party maintains political control over these SOEs, this does not necessarily translate into control over their competitive strategies.

Moreover, the Chinese state, despite its power and influence, is not omnipotent. While political power is highly centralized in the hands of the Party, the economic governance is in fact highly decentralized. Consequently, there is a lack unity and interest among SOEs owned by local governments—which account for the majority of the SOEs in China—to even coordinate competition.

---

[64] EUMR, *supra* note 13, art. 9.
[65] Bengt R. Homstrom & Jean Tirole, *The Theory of the Firm*, in HANDBOOK OF INDUSTRIAL ORGANIZATION 94, 96–97 (Richard Schmalensee & Robert Willig eds., 1989).

In any case, even if there was sufficient interest to coordinate competition, the existence of rampant agency problems in SOEs across all levels makes coordination a significant challenge.

2.1.1 The Utility Function of the Chinese State

Barry Naughton has tried to resolve the paradox of how China has sustained high economic growth without the adequate protection of individual property rights.[66] The answer, he argues, is the establishment of a mechanism that allows for thriving competition which in effect disciplines SOEs.[67] According to Naughton, competition from private domestic firms and foreign-invested firms exerts pressures on state-owned incumbents and forces them to up their game.[68] The history of Chinese economic reform is a testament to Naughton's theory.

When China embarked on market reform in 1978, the Chinese economy was predominantly controlled by the state. All prices and quantities were determined under a centrally planned system modelled on that of the former Soviet Union. There is little doubt that, at the time, the Chinese economy was run like a giant China, Inc. But such a model is plagued with serious agency problems. As the input and output prices were fixed by the Chinese government while other figures were inflated, it proved impossible for the government to evaluate the management performance of the SOEs' by simply observing the firm's profitability.[69]

To tackle this problem, the government introduced a series of SOE reforms in the 1980s, with the main goal of granting autonomy to SOEs and motivating them to pursue both profit and growth.[70] The decisions permitting SOEs to buy some of their inputs from the market and to sell some of their outputs to the market had partially contributed to the growth of non-state firms, especially township and village enterprises (TVEs).[71] The success of these TVEs, in turn, put significant pressure on the SOEs to be competitive, prompting the Chinese government to deepen and accelerate economic reform.[72] Empirical evidence shows that managerial incentives and total factor productivity of SOEs significantly improved due to increased autonomy of the management

---

[66] *See generally* BARRY NAUGHTON, GROWING OUT OF THE PLAN: CHINESE ECONOMIC REFORM, 1978–1993 (1995).

[67] Id. at 8–11.

[68] Id. at 200–43.

[69] *See* Justin Yifu Lin et al., *Competition, Policy Burdens, and State-Owned Enterprise Reform*, 88 AM. ECON. REV. 422, 423 (1998).

[70] BARRY NAUGHTON, THE CHINESE ECONOMY: TRANSITIONS AND GROWTH 92 (2007).

[71] *See* Lin et al., *supra* note 69, at 424.

[72] Id. at 425.

and competitive pressures from TVEs.[73] The profits of Chinese SOEs, however, declined sharply, as they could no longer derive monopoly rents in many markets.[74] This provided the impetus for China to conduct a round of privatization reforms in the late 1990s, causing a massive reduction in the number of SOEs between 1994 and 2000.[75] Large SOEs also underwent partial privatization by listing some of their best high-performing assets on domestic and foreign stock exchanges.

However, market reform is not yet complete in China, and SOEs still maintain a powerful presence in the Chinese economy. China is also a vast country with an enormous, fragmented bureaucracy.[76] As each component of the bureaucracy may have its own interests, the goal of the Chinese state is not necessarily coherent when it comes to the economic policy of SOEs. The SASAC, coincidentally a product of China's market reform, has emerged as a powerful and vocal bureaucratic department attempting to advance its own agenda regarding SOE policy. The Central SASAC's apparent objective is to encourage the consolidation of SOEs, turning them into 'national champions', thereby directly growing its own bureaucratic clout. The growth of SOEs signals the strength of Chinese state capitalism, and the entrenched interest of these giant SOEs helps further enhance the interests of the SASAC as a state asset management bureaucracy.

At the same time, other bureaucratic departments have different policy goals. As noted in Chapter 1, the Price Supervision and the Anti-Monopoly Bureau within the National Development and Reform Commission (NDRC) was tasked with controlling price inflation and tackling anticompetitive conduct. If prices are too high, the whole economic system can suffer from instability which may even lead to political turmoil jeopardizing the legitimacy of the governing party. But, because prices were liberalized, the agency had few traditional tools it could use to control prices. Accordingly, the NDRC employed antitrust as an effective tool to discipline firms, including SOEs, for inflating prices. The past record of Chinese antitrust enforcement demonstrates this, as revealed by the China Telecom/China Unicom case discussed in Chapters 1 and 2. The other frequent antitrust targets were local SOEs such as

[73] See generally Wei Li, The Impact of Economic Reform on the Performance of Chinese State Enterprises, 1980-1989, 105 J. POL. ECON. 1080 (1997); Lixin Colin Xu, Control, Incentives and Competition: The Impact of Reform on Chinese State-Owned Enterprises, 8 ECON. TRANSITION 151, 165–66 (2000).

[74] See Lin et al., supra note 69, at 425; see also Li, supra note 73, at 1084.

[75] NICOLAS R. LARDY, MARKETS OVER MAO 45 (2014).

[76] Angela Huyue Zhang, Bureaucratic Politics and China's Anti-Monopoly Law, 47 CORNELL INT'L L. J. 671, 684 (2014); Yasheng Huang, Managing Chinese Bureaucrats: An Institutional Economic Perspective, 50 POL. STUD. 61, 66–67 (2002).

premium white liquor manufacturers, gold retailers in Shanghai, large cement manufacturers, insurance companies, and auto manufacturers.

The utility function of the Chinese state is, therefore, highly complex. On the one hand, the government endorsed competition and liberalized most of its economic sectors over the past couple of decades. The Chinese government also allows non-state firms to compete freely with SOEs in those liberalized sectors.[77] But on the other hand, as elaborated in Chapter 1, power is fragmented within the Chinese bureaucracy and each governmental department has its own self-serving interest in promoting or limiting competition for SOEs. The SASAC, for instance, advocates for the expansion of the state sector and approves of the monopoly positions held by the largest Chinese SOEs. This is often incompatible with market reform and discourages competitive behaviour from private companies. It is also in conflict with the objectives of other departments, such as the price supervision department of the NDRC, which campaigns for consumer welfare.

2.1.2 The Limits of the Chinese State

Antitrust takes for granted that a controlling owner can coordinate firms under its control; it assumes that the owner can dictate the firm's actions. When that owner is a state, however, the question becomes a more nuanced one. There are two inherent problems of the Chinese economy that have made it extremely difficult for the state to exercise effective control to coordinate its SOEs. One is the highly decentralized Chinese economy and the other is the severe agency problems that exist in SOEs.

Economist Chenggang Xu characterized the Chinese economy as a 'regionally decentralized authoritarian regime' where a centralized, one-party, authoritarian state presides over a dynamic, decentralized economy.[78] Indeed, if we measure degree of decentralization statistically, China is the most decentralized country in the world.[79] In 2008, local governments' share of fiscal revenue and expenditure was 40 per cent and 73 per cent respectively, significantly exceeding the OECD averages of 19 per cent and 32 per cent.[80] A recent empirical study found that local information is key to understanding the governance of SOEs in China.[81] Professor Zhangkai Huang and his co-authors found that

---

[77] Fan Gang & Nicholas C. Hope, *The Role of State-Owned Enterprises in the Chinese Economy, in* US-CHINA ECONOMIC RELATIONS IN THE NEXT TEN YEARS pt. II, 7–10 (2013).

[78] Chenggang Xu, *The Fundamental Institutions of China's Reforms and Development*, 49 J. ECON LITERATURE 1076, 1078 (2011).

[79] ARTHUR R. KROEBER, CHINA'S ECONOMY: WHAT EVERYONE NEEDS TO KNOW 111 (2016).

[80] Id. at 111–12.

[81] *See generally* Zhangkai Huang et al., *Hayek, Local Information, and Commanding Heights: Decentralizing State-Owned Enterprises in China*, 107 AM. ECON. REV 2455 (2017).

the farther a SOE was from the government (the government had less direct observation over the firm), the more likely it was considered decentralized (i.e. managed by a lower level of government).[82] This correlation, however, is muted when it comes to central SOEs in strategic industries.[83] Notably, large, centrally owned SOEs only account for one-third of the total number of SOEs in China and control slightly less than half of all the state assets.[84] In other words, most SOEs and state assets belong to the local governments.

This decentralization, despite the lack of stable institutional support, has been viewed as the driving force behind China's phenomenal economic growth for several reasons.[85] First, local governments have greater incentive to foster their local businesses since their owners are cronies of the local leadership.[86] Formally, the success of the local businesses increases the tax revenues received by local governments, expands the employment base and helps the local government officials obtain political credit for economic achievements in their designated areas.[87] Informally, local business owners can reward officials with bribes and even grant them a high stake in the business.[88] Local officials thus morph into high-power incentive agents with vested interests in local businesses. As China is a vast country, thousands of local governments are effectively competing with each other.[89] While each local government is incentivized to erect barriers of entry to protect its own cronies, the existence of competition from other cronies fostered by other local governments counteracts the negative effects arising from local protectionism.[90]

The automobile industry provides one example. The automobile industry is a strictly regulated sector where foreign car makers must partner with Chinese domestic SOEs to access the Chinese market.[91] The central government initially aimed to nurture three large state-owned automobile manufacturers and refused to grant licences to other companies.[92] As a result, in the early 2000s, the Chinese automobile market was dominated by a few large state-owned players that had partnered with foreign firms, one of the most well-known

---

[82] Id.

[83] Id.

[84] KROEBER, *supra* note 79, at 99.

[85] Chong-En Bai et al., *Crony Capitalism with Chinese Characteristics* 3 (May 2014) (unpublished manuscript), http://cowles.yale.edu/sites/default/files/files/conf/2014/ma_song.pdf.

[86] Id. at 2–3.

[87] Id.

[88] Id. at 2.

[89] Id. at 3.

[90] Id.

[91] MICHAEL J. DUNNE, AMERICAN HEELS, CHINESE ROAD: THE STORY OF GENERAL MOTORS IN CHINA 8 (2011).

[92] Bai et al., *supra* note 85, at 5–7.

partnership being between Shanghai Automotive Industry Company and General Motors (SAIC-GM).[93] However, during this period, a number of small start-up car manufacturers, sponsored by the local governments, began to appear and soon developed into serious rivals of these large SOEs.[94] One example is Chery, initiated in 1997 and backed by the Wuhan city government.[95] Michael Dunne, a veteran of the Chinese auto industry, recounted the tale of how Chery was able to trump SAIC-GM after launching of a new car model similar to the one that SAIC-GM had wanted to release.[96] Although both SAIC-GM and Chery are both ultimately controlled by the Chinese state, in reality they belong to different owners (i.e. different levels of the Chinese state) and are fierce competitors.

While decentralization has stimulated China's astounding economic growth in the past few decades, it has also led to undesirable consequences. The Chinese government has had to confront severe overcapacity in many industry sectors, a point I will return to in Chapter 4.[97] Local governments are generally reluctant to close down businesses as this results in loss of gross domestic product (GDP) growth and employment, which also threatens the social stability in the region.[98] For this reason, local governments have the incentive to prop up SOEs even if they are in terminal decline.[99] The central government has repeatedly tried to orchestrate competition among SOEs in these sectors but it has often failed to do so. The steel industry is one example where, despite the numerous attempts to reduce competition among Chinese steel manufacturers, the severe problem of overcapacity persists. In response, the central government recently encouraged the tie-up between Baosteel and Wuhan Iron and Steel, two large state-owned steel makers. Clearly these two SOEs were not completely independent from the Chinese state since the state influenced their merger decision. However, if the government had been able to coordinate competition perfectly between these two SOEs, a merger between the two would not have been required in the first place.

The cases investigated by the Commission so far are also good illustrations of China's economic fragmentation. In *Bluestar/Elkem*, the Commission found that the silicon market was highly fragmented where SOEs were engaged in

[93] Id.
[94] DUNNE, *supra* note 91, at 125–36.
[95] Id. at 125.
[96] Id. at 125–36.
[97] Shuaihua Wallace Cheng, *Overcapacity a Time Bomb for China's Economy*, SOUTH CHINA MORNING POST (28 Sept. 2015).
[98] KROEBER, *supra* note 79, at 114.
[99] Id.

head-to-head competition with private firms.[100] In fact, ChemChina is the only centrally owned SOE in the silicon metal market; the rest all fall under the authority of local governments. The evidence from the Commission's market investigation also confirmed that these local SOEs and private firms constituted effective competitive constraints on ChemChina. This seems to suggest that the fragmented nature of the market makes it costly for the government to coordinate these firms even if it wants to do so. The Commission identified a similar phenomenon in *DSM/Sinochem/JV*, though the evidence gathered during that particular market investigation was mixed.[101] Given the extent to which these two SOEs compete, it would be problematic to treat them as a single entity for the purpose of antitrust assessment. It is true that the competition between these SOEs may have been stronger had the government not intervened, but it is indisputable that a merger between these SOEs would also reduce competition.

Similarly, the Commission's decision in *EDF/GCN*—treating all SOEs in the energy sector as a single entity—is unnecessarily broad and falls short of understanding the competitive landscape of the energy sector. The energy sector has been regarded as highly important for the Chinese economy and belongs to the 'key' and 'pillar' industries as identified by SASAC. Energy, though, is a gigantic industry that includes oil, gas, electricity, nuclear power, coal, and renewable energy, many of which remain very fragmented. For instance, Nicolas Lardy, an expert on the Chinese economy, denotes that in the coal mining sector alone, there were 880 SOEs as of 2011.[102] Even after assuming the Chinese government wants to coordinate competition between these SOEs, the cost of coordination would be prohibitively high. Moreover, private firms exert competitive pressures on these SOEs. As highlighted by Lardy, trade liberation and foreign direct investment are also important constraints on the SOEs.[103]

Agency problems further prevent the state from exercising effective control over SOEs. As Milhaupt and Pargendler have succinctly outlined, there are many unique challenges to SOE governance, including the weak exit options enjoyed by citizens as opposed to shareholders, the collective action problem faced by citizens in monitoring SOEs, and the ambiguity of government's objectives, as well as the means through which the government seeks to achieve these objectives.[104] Agency problems are not unique to Chinese SOEs but they

---

[100] Commission Decision No. COMP/M.6082 (China National Bluestar/Elkem) (31 Mar. 2011).

[101] Commission Decision No. COMP/M.6113 (DSM/Sinochem), slip op. ¶¶ 15, 24 (19 May 2011).

[102] LARDY, *supra* note 75, at 24.

[103] Id. at 36–37 (noting that the ratio of imports to GDP has increased since China joined the World Trade Organization and that subsidiaries of foreign firms also sell to the domestic market).

[104] Milhaupt & Pargendler, *supra* note 50.

present serious problems due to their size and unique bureaucratic status. Many Chinese SOEs in the strategic sectors are among the largest companies in the world. These companies were spun off from large central ministries, the latter then in turn dissolved and transferred most of the administrative, institutional, and personnel capacity to the SOEs. Even though these SOEs continue to be subject to regulation, this regulatory power tends to be dispersed, and agencies often lack sufficient political clout and resources to effectively monitor them, as was evident in the China Telecom/China Unicom case. In fact, some Chinese SOEs have overstepped the authority of industry regulators and have come to dominate the government.[105] In these situations, regulatory agencies rely heavily on SOEs and defer to them for important policy questions.[106] As was also discussed in Chapter 1, Chinese SOE executives still hold bureaucratic positions. Currently, the chairmen of the top fifty-three central SOEs have a bureaucratic status equals to either the head of the central SASAC or a vice-minister. Similar to the antitrust regulators, the SASAC often finds itself lacking the political clout to effectively check large SOEs.

Indeed, empire building is one important factor behind Chinese SOEs' overseas forays.[107] In China, the size of an SOE matters. The larger an SOE, the more powerful it becomes; the more powerful it is, the easier it becomes for the firm to obtain resources to expand further and become even bigger. China's oil and gas sector is one example of this phenomenon. China's national oil companies (NOCs) are the most active players in overseas acquisitions. Outwardly, the Chinese government appears to play a key role in coordinating these NOCs in their quest for oil and natural gas assets; the reality, however, is that these NOCs themselves were driving their ventures overseas. As Erica Downs observes, the political clout of a NOC is determined by the volume of high-quality assets it possesses.[108] The more valuable the assets that a NOC acquires, the more likely it is to obtain diplomatic and financial assistance from the Chinese government for future investments. This explains the lack of coordination among Chinese NOCs in their race for overseas expansion.

In fact, the lack of coordination has motivated the SASAC to promote consolidation among large central SOEs in recent years. One example of this is

---

[105] Bo Kong, China's International Petroleum Policy 93–94 (David L. Goldwyn & Jan H. Kalicki eds., 2010); Erica Downs, *Business Interest Groups in Chinese Politics: The Case of the Oil Companies*, in China's Changing Political Landscape: Prospects for Democracy 121, 122 (Cheng Li ed., 2008); Edward A. Cunningham, *China's Energy Governance: Perception and Reality*, MIT Center for Int'l Stud. Audits of Conventional Wisdom (Mar. 2007).

[106] Kong, *supra* note 105, at 16.

[107] Zhang, *supra* note 5, at 441–48.

[108] Erica S. Downs, *The Fact and Fiction of Sino-African Energy Relations*, 3 China Sec. 42, 50 (2007).

the tie-up between two state-owned rolling stock companies, China CNR Corporation and CSR Corporation, which merged to become the China Railway Rolling Stock Corporation. According to the Chinese media, the two firms had been ruthlessly competing with one another to win bids on overseas projects, and the merger was expected to bolster their combined competitive strength internationally. Since 2015, China has witnessed a new wave of mergers among its SOEs. In addition to the *CNR/CSR* merger, another ten megamergers between large Chinese SOEs have occurred in industries stretching from steel, shipping, energy, and construction to commerce.[109] These consolidations may even exacerbate the agency problem by reducing the Chinese government's bargaining power against these corporate behemoths, making them even more difficult to rein in. In any event, the European Union would benefit from intervening in those transactions if they pose a threat to European consumers. However, the Commission would have no basis to do so if it adopts the view that Chinese SOEs are to be treated as one single entity.

To constrain these rampant agency problems, President Xi has, since 2016, openly called for the Party to exercise stronger and improved leadership over SOEs.[110] A series of subsequent policy documents enhanced Party building within the SOEs and granted the Party members within the SOEs more power to exercise oversight.[111] While this is clearly a deliberate government attempt aiming at tightening political control over SOEs, this increased control and influence does not necessarily translate into anticompetitive effects. In some cases, it may in fact curb anticompetitive activities. The enduring challenge faced by Chinese leadership is how to strike the balance between granting autonomy to the management in order to pursue growth and profits while retaining sufficient control to ensure good corporate governance so that state assets are not looted by the management.

For instance, it is well-known that top Chinese SOEs have routinely rotated senior corporate and party leaders between them.[112] Some academics have portrayed this as evidence of the Chinese government's attempt to coordinate competition among them.[113] Western scholars, however, have overlooked the

---

[109] Wendy Leutert & Francois Godement, *Big is Beautiful? State-Owned Enterprise Mergers Under Xi Jinping*, EUR. COUNCIL ON FOREIGN REL. (30 Nov. 2016).

[110] Keith Zhai & Yinan Zhao, *Xi Boosts Party in China's $18 Trillion State Company Sector*, BLOOMBERG NEWS (7 July 2016).

[111] Lucy Hornby, *China Rows Back on State-Sector Reform*, FIN. TIMES (June 14, 2016); Zhuang Liu & Angela Huyue Zhang, *Ownership and Political Control: Evidence from Charter Amendments*, 60 INT'L REV. L. & ECON. (2019).

[112] *See* Li-Wen Lin & Curtis J. Milhaupt, *We Are the (National) Champions: Understanding the Mechanisms of State Capitalism in China*, 65 STAN. L. REV. 697, 740 (2013).

[113] Riley, *supra* note 6, at 21 & 30.

fact that the move was primarily motivated by a desire to curb nepotism and corruption.[114] The top executives at large SOEs have enormous influence, and their most important source of power lies in their control over personnel. As such, long tenure at a large SOE enables top executives to create large personnel networks within the firm. Those within the network collude with each other to share risks and illegal profits.[115] In his book on corruption in China, political scientist Minxin Pei investigated fifty cases of illicit dealings and found that the practice of buying and selling appointments along with promotions was widespread in Chinese SOEs.[116] A scandal at China National Petroleum Corporation, one of the largest state-owned oil firms, exemplifies this practice. Jieming Jiang, the former chairman of the firm who later briefly became the head of the SASAC, stole a vast fortune from the state.[117]

2.2 The Problem of Underinclusion

Many economic studies have shown that minority shareholding in rival businesses can cause anticompetitive harm.[118] However, there is currently is a gap in EU regulation as it does not completely address acquisitions of non-controlling interests.[119] The EUMR defines control as the power to exercise decisive influence over a firm. Generally speaking, a firm will be deemed to have control over another firm if it owns more than half the voting interest in that entity.[120] Meanwhile, the Commission's Jurisdictional Notice also recognizes de facto control through minority interest.[121] For instance, if a minority shareholder

---

[114] Shu Wang (王姝）, *Yangqi Yibashou Da Nuoyi, Weisha?* (央企一把手'大挪移'，为啥？）[*Why Rotate the Heads of Central SOEs?*], XIN JING WANG（新京网）[NEW BEIJING NET] (18 Sept. 2015).

[115] MINXIN PEI, CHINA'S CRONY CAPITALISM: THE DYNAMICS OF REGIME DECAY 172–73 (2016).

[116] Id.

[117] Id. at 170–73.

[118] Gilo, *supra* note 25; PATRICIA YPMA ET AL., EUR. COMMISSION, SUPPORT STUDY FOR IMPACT ASSESSMENT CONCERNING THE REVIEW OF MERGER REGULATION REGARDING MINORITY SHAREHOLDINGS (2016); OECD, *Antitrust Issues Involving Minority Shareholding and Interlocking Directorates*, at 9, OECD Doc. DAF/COMP(2008)30 (23 June 2009); *see* Steven C. Salop & Daniel P. O'Brien, *Competitive Effects of Partial Ownership: Financial Interest and Corporate Control*, 67 ANTITRUST L.J. 559 (2000); *see generally* David Gilo et al., *Partial Cross Ownership and Tacit Collusion*, 37 RAND J. ECON. 81 (2006).

[119] In 2014, the Commission published a White Paper proposing a 'targeted transparency system' specially designed to handle notifications of acquisitions of minority interests. However, the Commission's proposal received fierce criticisms during public consultations and the new EU Competition Commissioner Margrethe Vesteger stated in 2016 that she was not convinced that the EUMR needs changing. As a consequence, the plan to tackle minority shareholding issue was put on hold indefinitely. *Commission White Paper Towards More Effective E.U. Merger Control*, at 12, COM (2014) 449 final (9 July 2014).

[120] Jurisdictional Notice, *supra* note 21, ¶ 56.

[121] Id. 59–60.

has the right to manage company activities, or if the other shareholders are dispersed and small, then even a minority stake is deemed to confer control.[122] For joint ventures, control can also be established in deadlock situations where a minority shareholder can block a strategic commercial decision.[123] However, beyond the circumstances described above, a minority investment would fall outside the jurisdiction of the EUMR.

This has two implications when the EUMR is applied to minority-stake acquisitions by state investors. First, if a state investor acquires a significant but non-controlling interest in a European firm then it would not be considered to have acquired control in that firm. The transaction would not be seen as a concentration and not be subject to the EUMR. Second, if an SOE holds a significant but non-controlling right in a firm where private investors have majority control, that firm would be treated as a privately owned firm (POE), rather than as an SOE. If the POE then acquires control over a European firm, the SOE would not be judged as the ultimate controlling entity and would not be regarded as part of the same undertaking as the European firm. In these two scenarios, the SOE directly or indirectly acquires a minority interest in a European firm, but its action is completely outside the scope and scrutiny of the EUMR.

The concern relating to the legal vacuum in dealing with minority shareholding is not new, but acquisitions by Chinese SOEs have raised particular competition issues. Take the following hypothetical example. Suppose an acquiring Chinese SOE has a subsidiary that competes with the target European firm in the same product market. The acquisition by the Chinese SOE could create incentives for the target to compete less aggressively in the relevant market. If the Chinese SOE manages to raise prices and reduce the output of the target firm, some of the target's customers will move to its competitors, including the Chinese SOE's subsidiary, and the Chinese SOE is entitled to its profits. Anticompetitive effects, therefore, could occur when the SOE has the incentive and ability to invest in a concentrated sector heavily. Conversely, if a Chinese SOE has a minority interest in a POE, the SOE may find it profitable to raise prices and reduce output of its subsidiary. Since some of its sales will presumably shift to the European target, it is entitled to a share of that POE's profits. The coordinated effects also become more likely because of the common ownership of the Chinese SOE in both its subsidiary and the European target firm. One may even envisage the case that if Western regulators, such as the

Commission, increased scrutiny over Chinese SOEs, then Chinese SOEs may try to use POEs as vehicles for overseas acquisitions to avert the Commission's inquiry.

This may be puzzling: if the Chinese state lacks the incentive and ability to coordinate the SOEs in which it holds a majority control, would it not be even less likely for SOEs to coordinate firms in which they only have minority interests? This is not necessarily the case. There is a fundamental difference between coordination among Chinese SOEs and coordination between firms in which a single SOE owns multiple minority interests. The former is premised on the state (via central or local SASACs) coordinating competition among supposedly independent SOEs, whereas the latter assumes that a single SOE would coordinate firms that it partially owns. Although the incentive and the ability of SASAC to coordinate a large number of SOEs belonging to multiple levels of government in different regions is somewhat ambiguous, the incentive and ability of an SOE to do so is firmly grounded in economic circumstances, as will be discussed shortly.

2.2.1 Direct Acquisition of Minority Interest

Minority shareholding is an increasingly popular means of investment for Chinese SOEs when they expand overseas. In fact, some of the largest deals made by Chinese firms in Europe in recent years have been minority acquisitions, including but not limited to ChemChina and SAFE's USD 7.86 billion investment in Pirelli.[124] Despite not conferring majority control, such investments may nonetheless pose competition concerns.

The acquisitions of State Grid, a Chinese SOE supervised by central SASAC, offers a case in point. State Grid now ranks as the world's largest public utility company by revenue and was the fifth-largest company on the Fortune 500 List in 2019, having generated over USD 387 billion in revenue that year.[125] Since 2011, it has made several high-profile acquisitions in Western Europe, all of which have been of minority interests. Its first acquisition was in 2012, when it purchased a 25 per cent stake in Redes Energeticas Nacionais (REN), the largest energy network in Portugal.[126] State Grid became an active investor in REN and sent its senior executives to Portugal to participate in the firm's management.[127] State Grid is now the single largest shareholder in REN, which

---

[124] Id.

[125] *State Grid*, FORTUNE, https://fortune.com/global500/2019/state-grid/.

[126] Peter Wise & Leslie Hook, *China's State Grid to Take 25% Stake in Ren*, FIN. TIMES (3 Feb. 2013).

[127] Id.; Geert De Clercq et al., *China State Grid Quietly Builds Mediterranean Power Network*, REUTERS (10 Aug. 2014).

has a fragmented share structure with 35 per cent in public shares and the rest being held by seven investors.[128] Two years later, State Grid spent USD 2.8 billion to acquire a 35 per cent interest in Casesa Depositi e Prestiti, an Italian energy grid unit.[129] State Grid also actively participates in the management of Casesa Depositi e Prestiti and controls two of the five seats on the board of directors of the Italian grid.[130]

Over the last few years, State Grid attempted further forays into Western Europe. In June 2016, it won a bid to acquire a 14 per cent stake in Eandis Assets, a Belgian gas and power distribution firm.[131] The deal was later blocked by the Belgian authority, citing concerns of a possible takeover of distribution networks by the Chinese investors.[132] The deal would have given State Grid three seats on the forty-member board of directors.[133] In late 2016, State Grid purchased a 24 per cent stake of ADMIE, a Greek power transmission company.[134] State Grid's overall expansion into Europe was highly strategic. According to China Daily, State Grid was 'considering building an ultra-high-voltage global power network to transmit electricity from country to country and continent to continent, a goal that may cost US$50 trillion to develop by 2050'.[135] So far, State Grid has pushed its overseas investment over USD 10 billion in Europe, South American, and Asia, and it is only expected to increase its investments to USD 50 billion by 2020.[136] State Grid's minority acquisitions in Europe seem to be the key starting place to help it realize its ultimate vision of building a global power super grid. Thus far, it is not entirely clear if European firms that State Grid invested in compete with each other, as energy distribution networks tend to be natural monopolies. However, when such networks become more integrated within the European Union,[137] there is a foreseeable risk of anticompetitive behaviour.

Additionally, even if the SOE never casts a vote to sway management in its favour, its minority investment could nevertheless hinder competition under

---

[128] *Shareholder Structure*, REN, https://www.ren.pt/en-GB/investidores/estrutura_acionista.

[129] Chu Daye, *State Grid Buys Stake in Italian Firm for $2.8 Billion*, GLOBAL TIMES (1 Aug. 2014).

[130] Id.

[131] *China State Grid in Talks to Buy 14 Percent of Belgium's Eandis*, REUTERS (3 June 2016).

[132] NERA Econ. Consulting, *Global Energy Regulation: China's State Grid Fails to Acquire Shares in Flemish Distribution Network 4*, NERA.COM (Oct. 2016).

[133] Id.

[134] Ilias Bellos, *China Extends Penetration of Greek Market*, EKATHIMERINI (8 Jan. 2017).

[135] Zheng Xin, *State Grid Takes Stake in Greek Power Network*, CHINA DAILY (20 Dec. 2016).

[136] Shunsuke Tabeta, *China Power Giant Gobbling Up Foreign Players*, NIKKEI ASIAN REV. (25 Jan. 2017).

[137] *Second Report on the State of the Energy Union: Communication from the Commission to the European Parliament, the Council, the European Economic and Social Committee, the Committee of the regions and the European Investment Bank*, at 13, COM(2017) 53 final (1 Feb. 2017).

certain circumstances, especially if the SOE invests in concentrated sectors. As much of antitrust literature has demonstrated, passive investment without voting power may still cause anticompetitive harm.[138] Sovereign Wealth Funds (SWFs) remain a specific concern, as they regularly invest in minority interests.[139] Empirical studies have also found that SWFs are not purely passive investors and, in many instances, they actively monitor their investments or seek to influence firms' commercial activities.[140] Moreover, as SWFs possess proprietary information owing to their proximity to governments, and they can influence government policy to their benefit, investors of a target firm generally react positively to a SWF's investment and negatively to a SWF's divestment.[141] So, even if a SWF possesses no formal voting interest in a firm, the management may be motivated to cater to a SWF's preferences as the loss of a SWF's long-term investment would be reason for alarm, adversely affecting the firm's stock performance and causing them to tumble.[142]

Take China Investment Corporation (CIC) as an example. As China's official SWF, the fund was ranked the country's fourth largest in 2016.[143] CIC's operation is opaque, with little to no public disclosure about its investment activities. The information gathered by intelligence agencies, however, revealed some insight into its footprints in recent years. Since its establishment in 2007, CIC has been aggressively investing overseas.[144] The data collected by the American Enterprise Institute and the Heritage Foundation shows that CIC has invested widely in the financial, energy, real estate, and agriculture sectors.[145] In Europe, CIC had invested in real estate, energy, utilities, technology, and transport industries.[146] It often acquires a significant interest in target firms[147] but does not simply embrace a passive investment strategy. Since 2010, CIC has gained influence on the board of four companies in which it acquired a stake of 10 per cent or more.[148]

---

[138] Salop & O'Brien, *supra* note 118, at 568–84; *see also* Gilo, *supra* note 25, at 8–28.

[139] *See generally* Ronald J. Gilson & Curtis J. Milhaupt, *Sovereign Wealth Funds and Corporate Governance: A Minimalist Response to the New Mercantilism*, 60 STAN. L. REV. 1345, 1350–54 (2008).

[140] Kathryn L. Dewenter et al., *Firm Values and Sovereign Wealth Fund Investments*, 98 J. FIN. ECON. 256, 274 (2010).

[141] Id. at 258.

[142] Li Jing, *State as an Entrepreneur: A Study of the Investment Contractual Terms and Level of Control of China's Sovereign Wealth Fund in Its Portfolio Firms*, 3 PEKING U. TRANSNAT'L L. REV. 1, 21 (2015).

[143] *Fund Rankings: Tracking the Activity of Sovereign Wealth Funds, Pensions, Endowments and Other Public Funds*, SWFI—SOVEREIGN WEALTH FUND INST.

[144] IACOB N. KOCH-WESER & OWEN D. HAACKE, U.S.–CHINA ECON. & SEC.COMM'N, CHINA INVESTMENT CORPORATION: RECENT DEVELOPMENTS IN PERFORMANCE, STRATEGY AND GOVERNANCE 19–22 (2013).

[145] This is based on the data collected by American Enterprises Institute & the Heritage Foundation.

[146] Id.

[147] Id.

[148] KOCH-WESER & HAACKE, *supra* note 144, at 30.

Moreover, even though CIC had limited control rights over the companies in its portfolio, scholars have suggested that CIC can exert influence beyond its formal corporate rights.[149] This is because CIC's close connection with the Chinese government is often viewed as an important strategic asset for its portfolio companies, especially at times when the companies were contemplating expansion into the Chinese market or wanting to form partnership with other Chinese SOEs.[150] For instance, after CIC's investment in GDF Suez in 2011, the two firms agreed to a plan of strategic cooperation in the Asia-Pacific region.[151] GDF Suez subsequently entered into several high-profile cooperation projects with leading Chinese state-owned energy firms.[152] Thus, to determine a SWF's actual influence over a portfolio company, competition regulators cannot solely rely on a SWF's formal corporate rights. Indeed, if Chinese SWFs continue to invest in highly concentrated markets, there is a risk that this would create anticompetitive concerns similar to those generated by US institutional shareholders. Formalistic application of the EUMR framework in these circumstances is unbefitting to say the least, as it eschews the anticompetitive effects of state ownership.

2.2.2 Indirect Acquisition of Minority Interest

The policy debate on Chinese state capitalism has so far been preoccupied by Chinese SOEs. However, as Milhaupt and Zheng noted in an insightful article, '[D]rawing a stark distinction among Chinese firms based on the ownership of enterprise (SOE versus POE) to frame Chinese state capitalism . . . misperceives the reality of that country's institutional environment.'[153] Chinese state capitalism manifests in highly diverse forms of ownership. Despite several rounds of privatization, many Chinese SOEs have not totally sold off their state assets and have instead became firms with mixed ownership structures.[154] The mixed ownership enterprises (MOEs) have a substantial presence in the Chinese economy. According to an annual industrial survey, MOEs accounted for 20 per cent of the total number of industrial firms from 2004 to 2010.[155] Many economists have estimated that MOEs make up about 40 per cent of the Chinese economy in terms of assets and industrial value added.[156]

---

[149] Jing, *supra* note 142, at 79–80.
[150] Id. at 81; Dewenter et al., *supra* note 140, at 274.
[151] Jing, *supra* note 142, at 85.
[152] Id.
[153] Curtis J. Milhaupt & Wentong Zheng, *Beyond Ownership: State Capitalism and the Chinese Firm*, 103 GEO. L.J. 665, 668 (2015).
[154] Marshall W. Meyer & Changqi Wu, *Making Ownership Matter: Prospects for China's Mixed Ownership Economy*, PAULSON INST. 6 (Sept. 2014).
[155] Id.
[156] Id.

As such, the fine line between SOEs and POEs will become increasingly blurred in China. At the Third Plenum of the 18th Party Central Committee in 2013, the Chinese government endorsed the principles of the market economy and advocated mixed ownership reform, seeking to promote cross-holding and mutual fusion between public and private capital.[157] Since 2014, the Chinese government at all levels has started adopting guidelines and plans to convert SOEs into MOEs.[158] This reform intends to impose further market discipline on SOEs, thereby improving their financial performance and productivity.[159] Evidently, since the state's financial interest in MOEs has been diluted, the state's control over these firms are weaker. The Chinese state, however, is not an ordinary investor; it is not only an investor but also a financier and a regulator. The state's power and influence over a MOE, therefore, could surpass that of a common minority shareholder.

A recent Chinese investment highlights such a risk. In 2016, Fujian Grand Chip Investment Fund (FGC) attempted to acquire Aixtron, a German semi-conductor equipment maker.[160] FGC is 49 per cent held by Xiamen Bohao, another fund controlled by the Xiamen municipal government, with the other 51 per cent held by Liu Zhengdong, an ordinary Chinese citizen.[161] According to the New York Times, FGC possibly leveraged its web of intricate relationships to facilitate the attempted acquisition.[162] The story unfolded as follows.

In 2015, San'an Optoelectronics, based in the same province as FGC and an important customer of Aixtron, suddenly cancelled a large order at the very last minute, causing Aixtron's stock prices to crash. This sparked speculation that FGC had orchestrated the abrupt price crash with San'an. The Times reporters were able to identify some commonality of interest between Bohao and San'an, including a pre-existing financial relationship and a common shareholder by a state-run investment fund based in Xiamen. Moreover, Sino IC Leasing, in which San'an has a 5 per cent interest,[163] helped FGC finance the deal.[164] Further, a national state-investment fund holding an 11 per cent interest in San'an was also an owner of Sino IC Leasing. While it is plausible that there was

---

[157] *Decision of the Central Committee of the Communist Party of China on Some Major Issues Concerning Comprehensively Deepening the Reform*, CHINA.ORG.CN (16 Jan. 2014).

[158] Meyer & Wu, *supra* note 154, at 1–2.

[159] Id. at 2.

[160] Paul Mozur, *Germany Withdraws Approval for Chinese Takeover of Aixtron*, N.Y. TIMES (24 Oct. 2016).

[161] Paul Mozur & Jack Ewing, *Rush of Chinese Investment in Europe's High-Tech Firms is Raising Eyebrows*, N.Y. TIMES (16 Sept. 2016).

[162] Id.

[163] *Aixtron Investor Presentation: First Half 2016 Results*, AIXTRON 16 (11 Aug. 2016).

[164] Larry G. Franceski et al., *President Obama Blocks Proposed Chinese Acquisition of Controlling Interest in German Chip Maker*, NORTON ROSE FULLBRIGHT (Dec. 2016).

nothing untoward about these links between a large customer and a potential acquirer of Aixtron, the intricate relationships raise serious doubts about the actual independence of these companies. The multiple layers of common ownership by various local and national state funds provided the structural link between Bohao, a minority shareholder of the acquirer, and San'an, a large customer of the target. Yet, because these SOEs only held minority interests in the parties involved, their involvement likely fell outside EU antitrust scrutiny. This transaction also highlights the risk of coordination among Chinese SOEs. Since 2014, the Chinese government has been aggressively promoting the development of a robust domestic semiconductor capability with the goal of becoming a leader in the industry by 2030.[165] Massive national and local state funds were raised to finance the investment and acquisitions in this sector. The Aixtron transaction is one example of a state-sponsored overseas acquisitions. For instance, in addition to support from the National State-investment fund, FGC also received funding from the China Development Bank in Xiamen and the Agricultural Bank in Shanghai.[166] While this may suggest that the Chinese government assisted the acquisition behind the scenes, it is extremely hard to bring forth evidence of explicit communication between these funds. It is also difficult to obtain sufficient evidence to show that the government has in fact coordinated their activities.

The Aixtron deal also exemplifies the difficulties antitrust regulators would face in handling a similar transaction. One difficulty would be manoeuvring through the opacity of the SOE's investment in a transaction. On first impression, FGC is majority controlled by Zhengdong Liu, a Chinese businessman; however, there has been much suspicion in the West about whether Liu does indeed control the 51 per cent of FGC he owns on paper.[167] Liu kept a very low profile during the acquisition, and his resume shows that he has mostly invested his capital in the mining business; it is not entirely clear why he would want to expand his investment into the semiconductor industry. A number of Chinese news reports suggested that the real supporter behind

---

[165] *China's 13th Five-Year Plan: Opportunities & Challenges for the U.S. Semiconductor Industry: Hearing on China's 13th Five-Year Plan Before the US–China Econ. & Sec. Review Comm'n* (2016) (written testimony of Jimmy Goodrich, Vice President of Global Policy, Semiconductor Industry Association).

[166] Jost Wübbeke et al., *Made in China 2025: The Making of a High-Tech Superpower and Consequences for Industrial Countries*, MERCATOR INST. FOR CHINA STUD. 53 (2016).

[167] *See* David Böcking, *Chinesischer Aixtron-Investor: Herr Liu versteht die deutsche Angst nicht* [*Chinese Aixtron Investor: Mister Liu Does Not Understand the German Fear*], SPIEGEL ONLINE (10 Apr. 2016, 4:00 P.M.).

Mr. Liu is the Huaxin Fund, another state-owned fund in the semiconductor industry.[168]

Notably, these competition issues raised by Chinese entities were addressed by the US and German governments on national security grounds. The US government had long been vigilant about China's aggressive expansion into the semiconductor industry.[169] As Aixtron held some assets in the United States, the deal was blocked by the US government on national security grounds.[170] The German government also withdrew its approval for the transaction, citing national security concerns. As elaborated below, a national security review can serve as an important complement to an antitrust review in addressing the potential anticompetitive issues arising from Chinese state ownership.[171]

3 Enhancing Foreign Investment Review

The EUMR is not the only legal tool that can be used to address the Commission's concerns about Chinese acquisitions in Europe. From a competition law perspective, what makes regulators uneasy is the possibility that the Chinese state will acquire a critical block of ownership in Europe, allowing it to accumulate significant market power in a particular product market. Such an acquisition generates antitrust concerns and also poses a threat to national security, especially when the acquisition would allow a single state to monopolize the supply of a strategic product or service. Notably, the line between strategic and non-strategic sectors is becoming increasingly blurred. In the United States, the Committee on Foreign Investment (CFIUS) has investigated Chinese foreign acquisitions of meat processing firms and cinema chains.[172]

There are several obvious advantages of using foreign investment review to address anticompetitive concerns of coordination by SOEs belonging to the same state. To start with, it allows the regulator to conduct its investigation in a more comprehensive and flexible manner without compromising future jurisdiction over important potential cases involving SOEs. As noted earlier, a rigid

---

[168] *San'an Guang Dian Huo Can Yu Shougou Aisiqiang* （三安光电或参与收购爱思强）[*San'An Might Participate in Acquiring Aixtron*], ZHONGGUO DIANZI BAO （中国电子报）[CHINA ELECTRONIC NEWS] (26 May 2016).

[169] David Lawder, *U.S. Commerce Chief Warns Against China Semiconductor Investment Binge*, REUTERS (3 Nov. 2016).

[170] Shawn Donnan, *Obama Blocks Chinese Takeover of Tech Group Aixtron*, FIN. TIMES (2 Dec. 2016).

[171] Guy Chazan, *Germany Withdraws Approval for Chinese Takeover of Tech Group*, FIN. TIMES (24 Oct. 2016).

[172] *Shuanghui International Receives CFIUS Clearance for Its Purchase of Smithfield Foods*, SULLIVAN & CROMWELL LLP (10 Sept. 2013).

application of an undertaking to SOEs could lead to unintended consequences. Given that many Chinese SOEs actively invest in European countries or export their products to European markets, the Commission would presumably have an interest in intervening during such cases. For instance, if Chinese coal producers collude when they sell to the European market, the Commission should step in to protect the welfare of the consumers in Europe. But the position held by the Commission in *EDF/CGN* could jeopardize such legal action because the Chinese coal producers may defend themselves on the basis of single firm conduct.

What the Commission should not underestimate is China's crucial role in the global supply chain, and its production capacity to adapt quickly to a crisis could give it significant market power, even in the short term. Consider the raging COVID-19 pandemic. At the beginning of the outbreak, there was a surge in demand for face masks and other protective medical gear as ordinary citizens and medical professionals desperately sought to protect themselves. In fact, almost half of the world's masks were produced in China before the outbreak, and Chinese manufacturers have been able to boost their production capacity or switch production lines to start producing masks.[173] Sinopec, a state-owned oil and gas company, Chengdu Aircraft Industry Group, the manufacturer of China's stealth fighter jet, as well as smartphone makers such as Xiaomi and Oppo, just to name a few, are the latest Chinese companies to have entered the mask industry.[174] In particular, Sinopec has upped the production of raw materials such as polypropylene and polyvinyl chloride, which are important raw materials for making N95 respirators and surgical masks. Now, think about a scenario wherein Chinese manufacturers of these raw materials collude to raise prices. If the Commission follows the suggestions of some European scholars who have been advocating that all Chinese firms, regardless of ownership structure, should be viewed as one single entity, then such a scenario would be out of the Commission's reach as it would be deemed as part of the internal activity of the so-called China, Inc.

In addition, using a foreign investment review helps maintain the logical coherence of the Commission's legal position. A cogent interpretation of Recital 22 requires the Commission to focus on de facto, rather than de jure control when analysing SOEs. However, the Commission seems to be applying a double standard by relying on de jure control in cases involving Chinese SOEs

---

[173] Daniel Ren, *China Boost Face Mask Production Capacity by 450 Percent in a Month, Threatening a Glut Scenario*, SOUTH CHINA MORNING POST (16 Mar. 2020).
[174] Id.

and de facto control in cases regarding European SOEs. If the Commission insists on using a de jure approach to deal with Chinese SOEs, then it should treat all Chinese SOEs—regardless of the sectors in which they operate, regardless of whether they are owned by the local or central government, and regardless of whether they actually compete with each other—as one single entity. Such a conclusion is in glaring contradiction of the economic reality in China today. Practically speaking, the de jure approach would also create an undue burden for businesses, resulting in many superfluous and unnecessary merger notifications.

Furthermore, experts in charge of foreign investment reviews are in a superior position compared to antitrust regulators to assess a state's motives and its complex political as well as economic institutions to determine the state's actual influence over its SOEs. This would allow regulators to capture cases in which Chinese SOEs employ non-controlling subsidiaries as vehicles to acquire European assets. More importantly, the concern that the Chinese state can strategically coordinate its SOEs to monopolize a certain product or service market does not relate just to economics but also to politics. As the Aixtron transaction illustrates, competition regulators may not be able to rely on what they see on the surface to determine the ultimate controlling entity of an acquirer. An SOE can exert influence using various means and even an entity that appears to be privately controlled or privately owned may actually be controlled by an SOE.

In short, foreign investment review, which adopts a case-by-case approach, is more capable of adapting to a constantly changing political and economic environment. Yet despite these advantages, there is currently no centralized foreign investment control mechanism at the EU level. Indeed, the European Union endorses free trade, and it only allows its Member States to retain the right to impose restrictions on foreign investment based on public security considerations, as long as those restrictions do not result in arbitrary discrimination or appear as disguised restriction on trade.[175] At present only fourteen of the twenty-seven EU Member States have a national security review mechanism.[176] Member States including France, Germany, and Italy have established investment reviews to address security concerns, whereas Belgium, the Czech Republic, Iceland, and Ireland have no investment measures related to public order and essential security considerations. Some policy-makers are

[175] TFEU, *supra* note 12, art. 346.
[176] *See* List of Screening Mechanisms Notified by Member States (15 Apr. 2020), https://trade.ec.europa.eu/doclib/docs/2019/june/tradoc_157946.pdf.

therefore worried that the current patchwork of FDI rules at the EU Member State level risks sparking a race to the bottom, as some Member State authorities may rush to attract Chinese capital and abandon any attempts to screen the deals for security concerns.[177]

In practice, such fears may seem exaggerated. Recent acquisitions by Chinese companies in the strategic sectors have been subject to much scrutiny. For instance, when the EDF wanted to partner with CGN to build several nuclear power plants in Britain, the British government subjected the transaction to several rounds of intensive review. The deal eventually received the green light from the British government, with the imposition of certain remedies addressing potential national security concerns. Midea, a Chinese electronics company, had to obtain clearance from both Germany's Directorate of Defense Trade Control and CFIUS when it acquired Kuka, a German robot company. In 2016 alone, two Chinese investments fell through in Europe due to national security concerns. In the first deal, the city of Antwerp blocked State Grid's attempted acquisition of Eandis, a power distribution company based in Belgium. The Belgian authority allegedly received intelligence from the Belgian State Security Service warning them of links between State Grid, the Party, and the People's Liberation Army.[178] This caused a stir resulting in Belgian Minister for energy to rescind his support for the deal. This case is particularly noteworthy as it shows that even though Belgium has not established a formal national security review regime, the Belgian government can still block a deal on the grounds of alternative regulatory concerns.

Similarly, in the face of growing protectionist backlash against Chinese investment, the German government withdrew its approval for the acquisition of Aixtron in October 2016. According to existing German law, the German Economic Ministry has the authority to review any deals in which non-EU investors acquire at least 25 per cent of the voting rights of a German company and will block the deal if it 'poses a threat to Germany's public order or security'.[179] The concept of 'public order or security' is malleable and can be interpreted to cover a large number of industry sectors. In July 2017, Germany tightened its FDI screening by introducing, for the first time ever, a catalogue of industry sectors that were deemed critical infrastructures and security-related

---

[177] Sophie Meunier, *Political Impact of Chinese Foreign Direct Investment in the European Union on Transatlantic Relations* 7 (European Parliament Briefing Paper, 2012); François Godement et al., *The Scramble for Europe*, EUR. COUNCIL ON FOREIGN REL. 1 (July 2011).

[178] Michael Torfs, *'Mysterious Letter' Warns against 'Chinese Danger' Involving State Grid Deal*, FLANDERS NEWS (27 Sep. 2016).

[179] Chazan, *supra* note 171.

technologies.[180] Subsequently, Germany prohibited several Chinese attempts to acquire German companies, including a minority acquisition of 20 per cent interest in 50Hertz, one of Germany's electricity transmission system operators.[181]

Notably, as many multinational companies operate on a global scale, Chinese acquisitions of European assets are not only vetted by target countries in the European Union but also in other affected jurisdiction in which business operations might take place or where the assets are situated such as the United States. A good example is the previously mentioned Aixtron deal where CFIUS asserted US jurisdiction over the transaction on the grounds that of Aixtron had assets in the United States. In another 2016 deal, a consortium of Chinese investors failed to acquire Opera Software, a Norwegian browser company, because it did not obtain the requisite approval from CFIUS.

As illustrated above, foreign investment control has provided a much more searching and flexible way for EU Member States to regulate Chinese investment in Europe. But this may not apply to half of the EU Member States that currently have no foreign investment review. Moreover, the interests of the European Union and some of its Member States might not entirely align, and a situation can arise in which a Member State might welcome Chinese investment but the European Union will not. The rift between the European Union and some of its Member States has been enlarged in recent years as the former is gradually changing its policy from perceiving China as a potential partner to it being an economic and political adversary. It is thus no wonder that some policy-makers are calling on the Commission to forge a more coherent response to China by taking on a greater leadership role.[182]

The Commission has been doing exactly that by aggressively expanding its FDI review authority through various regulatory measures. On 10 April 2019, the Commission announced that its new EU framework for the screening of FDI entered into force.[183] This new framework sets minimum requirements for Member States to maintain or adopt a foreign investment screening mechanism that aims to enhance cooperation and information sharing between the Commission and Member States. However, the new framework does not require Member States to implement this foreign investment screening

[180] Frank Bickenback & Wan-Hsin Liu, *Chinese Foreign Direct Investment in Europe—Challenges for EU FDI Policy*, CESIFO FORUM, Vol. 19 (2018), at 17.

[181] Id.

[182] Julianne Smith & Torrey Taussig, *Europe Needs a China Strategy; Brussels Needs to Shape It*, BROOKINGS (10 Feb. 2020).

[183] European Commission, *EU Foreign Investment Screening Regulation Enters into Force* (April 10, 2019).

mechanism, nor does it empower the Commission to block foreign investments. Its main purpose is to create a hub that facilitates information exchange between the Commission and the Member States. During the COVID-19 pandemic, the Commission exploited the healthcare crisis as an opportunity to nudge Member States into being more vigilant about foreign investment, particularly when transactions involve critical assets and technology in healthcare.[184]

The Commission's most ambitious move came in June 2020 when it released a White Paper delineating a new regulatory tool that empowers the regulatory body itself to intervene directly in state-backed acquisitions. The new rule, which appears to be inspired by a Dutch proposal, intends to close a loophole in the existing EU merger framework.[185] It requires foreign firms planning to acquire a material stake in an EU company to notify the Commission and disclose any state subsidies go over a certain threshold.[186] This proposal attempts to address two potential loopholes in the EU merger review when dealing with Chinese acquisitions. First, it applies to all foreign firms that have received subsidies from their governments, regardless of whether the firm is state-owned or not. This appears to tackle the thorny issue of the blurred lines between SOEs and POEs in China. After all, the Chinese government is able to exert influence over a POE through various regulatory channels including the provisions of subsidies. Second, it applies to all foreign acquisitions that may confer material influence over an EU company. This will address the potential antitrust issue arising from minority acquisitions, which currently does not require notification to the Commission.

However, the proposed regulation is also riddled with legal risks and uncertainties. The thresholds set in the White Paper appear to be very low, thus new merger control rules are likely to capture a large number of transactions involving Chinese parties. Inevitably, this would increase the cost for Chinese SOEs to make acquisitions in Europe, potentially creating conflicts with the Member States' vetting procedures. Second, it is not clear how the Commission plans on enforcing these rules, as there are various ways a Chinese acquiring party can disguise or even conceal their state subsidies. Above all, the new

---

[184] Communication from the Commission, *Guidance to the Member States concerning Foreign Direct Investment and Free Movement of Capital from Third Countries, and the Protection of Europe's Strategic Assets, ahead of the application of Regulation* (EU) 2019/452 (25 Mar. 2020).

[185] Sam Fleming & Javier Espinoza, *Brussels Urged to Rein in State-Backed Foreign Rivals*, FIN. TIMES (4 Dec. 2019).

[186] European Commission, *White Paper on Levelling the Playing Field As Regards Foreign Subsidies*, COM (2020) 253 final, Brussels (17 June 2020).

measures seem to deviate from the EU's fundamental policy of endorsing free trade and could prompt retaliatory measures from China. Despite these uncertainties, it is clear that this new proposal, if adopted, will significantly expand the Commission's existing authority to scrutinize mergers and accord it greater regulatory leverage over Chinese acquisitions.

Summary

In this chapter, I have explained another facet of Chinese antitrust exceptionalism by revealing the paradoxical outcome when the Commission tried to apply its existing merger review framework to scrutinize Chinese SOEs. Even after decades of market reform, China remains a state-led economy with the Party maintaining omnipresent and pervading control over its SOEs. This, however, is only one side of the story. The various rounds of market reform created a new and invigorated private sector to compete fiercely with SOEs in the liberalized sectors. The Chinese state, even with its sheer size, its vast and intricate bureaucracy, along with its highly decentralized economic system, has limited capacity to exert control over SOEs and has a utility function different from that of a private commercial entity.

The Commission's latest regulatory response to Chinese acquisitions illustrates its misconceptions. When reviewing merger transactions involving Chinese SOEs, the Commission has focused on the possibility that the Chinese state can influence its SOEs. This assessment misses the point. If a state retains voting power in its SOEs it will always be possible for it to influence SOEs' commercial decisions. The same goes for all SOEs, irrespective of which to state they belong. The real question is not if a state *can have* control over SOEs but whether it *does* have such control. Indeed, in previous cases pertaining to European SOEs, the Commission focused on de facto control by the state but, with Chinese SOE cases, the Commission has transitioned to de jure control. In this regard, the Commission appears to be applying a burdensome double standard when it comes to Chinese SOEs.

Thus far, the Commission, in the process of scrutinizing Chines SOE transactions, has become fixated on defining the scope of China, Inc. The problem, however, is that there is no clear distinction between ownership and control for Chinese firms. A bright-line approach will, therefore, result in both overinclusive and underinclusive outcomes. From an economic standpoint, the extent to which coordination by the Chinese state has decreased competition is a quantitative question, rather than a qualitative one. As such, a thoughtful response to acquisitions by Chinese SOEs requires the regulator to shift its focus from defining the boundaries of an undertaking to understanding the effects of Chinese state ownership. This is no easy feat. In light of the current regulatory dilemma, it not surprising that both the Commission and some Member States are tightening their foreign investment review in their vetting of acquisitions from China.

4

US Scrutiny over China's Trade Dominance

In the early months of 2020, fears of potential disruption to global drug supply loomed in the United States when a large number of Chinese factories were forced to shut down in the wake of the coronavirus outbreak.[1] As Rosemary Gibson and Janardan Singh revealed in their popular book 'China Rx', the United States has become overly dependent on China for the supply of essential and critical ingredients required to produce medicinal drugs.[2] According to the US Food and Drug Administration, China is the second-largest exporter of drugs and biologics to the United States.[3] Almost 97 per cent of the antibiotics and more than 90 per cent of the vitamin C consumed in the United States are now manufactured in China.[4] Additionally, 80 per cent of the active pharmaceutical ingredients (API), the basic components used in the manufacturing of drugs in the United States, are imported from China and India. Meanwhile, India, the largest market for generics, sources almost 80 per cent of its APIs from China.[5] Some have warned that if China shuts down its exports of medicines and key ingredients to make drugs, US hospitals and clinics would fall apart within months, or even days.[6]

In fact, before the coronavirus outbreak, policy-makers in Washington had been aware that this over-reliance on China creates a vulnerability. On 31 July 2019, the US–China Economic and Security Review Commission hosted a hearing on the topic 'exploring the growing US reliance on China's biotech

---

[1] Laurie McGinley & Carolyn Y. Johnson, *Coronavirus Raised Fears of U.S. Drug Supply Disruptions*, WASHINGTON POST (27 Feb. 2020). Many of the footnote references in this book are online materials and they can be easily accessible online.

[2] ROSEMARY GIBSON & JANARDAN PRASAD SINGH, CHINA RX: EXPOSING THE RISKS OF AMERICA'S DEPENDENCE ON CHINA FOR MEDICINE (2018).

[3] U.S.–China Economic & Security Review Commission, Hearing on Exploring the Growing U.S. Reliance on China's Biotech and Pharmaceutical Products, Written Testimony of Mark Abdoo (31 July 2019).

[4] Yanzhong Huang, *The Coronavirus Outbreak Could Disrupt the U.S. Drug Supply*, COUNCIL ON FOREIGN RELATIONS (5 Mar. 2020).

[5] 2019 Report to Congress of the U.S.–China Economic & Security Review Commission (Nov. 2019), at 250.

[6] U.S. China Economic & Security Review Commission, Hearing on Exploring the Growing U.S. Reliance on China's Biotech and Pharmaceutical Products, Written Testimony of Rosemary Gibson (31 July 2019) (hereinafter Written Testimony of Rosemary Gibson).

Chinese Antitrust Exceptionalism. Angela Huyue Zhang, Oxford University Press (2021). © Angela Huyue Zhang.
DOI: 10.1093/oso/9780198826569.003.0005

and pharmaceutical products'.[7] During the hearing, Gibson pointed out that Chinese exporters have colluded to engage in predatory pricing of generic drugs to drive their foreign rivals, including US manufacturers, out of business. After they gain the monopoly positions, these exporters then raised prices to exploit US consumers.[8] She warned of the displacement of the US healthcare industry and the risks to US national health security in the event that China withholds all medical supplies.[9] Her concern is not completely unwarranted. During the US–China trade war in 2019, Li Daokui, a prominent Chinese economist, implied that China could curtail the export of antibiotics and other pharmaceutical supplies to the United States as a countermeasure against the US's attempt to bar chip sales to Huawei.[10]

Thus far, there have been no signs that Li's threat will become reality. Indeed, if the Chinese government restricts exports of pharmaceutical supplies or compels price hikes of essential supplies with Chinese exporters, this would raise a whole slew of legal issues under US antitrust law. Can the Chinese government be held liable for antitrust violations? What about Chinese exporters who follow through on the government's directives? Can companies elude antitrust liabilities by citing compulsion from the Chinese government? These questions do not solely serve as academic inquiries. As of March 2020, a number of lawsuits have been filed against China in US federal courts, with plaintiffs alleging that the Chinese government's mishandling of the outbreak caused irrevocable damage to US citizens and businesses.[11] One complaint lodged by the attorney general of Mississippi alleged, among other things, that the Chinese government's hoarding supplies of personal protective equipment (PPE) constitutes a violation of Mississippi antitrust law.[12]

Putting aside the factual issue of whether the Chinese government actually engaged in hoarding or price fixing, Mississippi's claim seems to stand on flimsy legal grounds. As Jacques deLise, an expert on Chinese law, points out, the Chinese misdeeds at issue are 'overwhelmingly regulatory', and thus would be entitled to immunity under the Foreign Sovereign Immunities Act.[13]

---

[7] U.S.–China Economic & Security Review Commission, Hearing on Exploring the Growing U.S. Reliance on China's Biotech and Pharmaceutical Products (31 July 2019); *see also* Yanzhong Huang, *U.S. Dependence on Pharmaceutical Products from China*, COUNCIL ON FOREIGN RELATIONS (14 Aug. 2019).

[8] Written Testimony of Rosemary Gibson, *supra* note 6.

[9] Id.

[10] Didi Tang, *China Threats to Halt US Antibiotics Supply*, TIMES (11 Mar. 2019).

[11] Angela Huyue Zhang, *Coronavirus-related US Lawsuits against China Risk a Further Worsening of Relations, and Could Backfire*, SOUTH CHINA MORNING POST (11 May 2020).

[12] The State of Mississippi v. The People's Republic of China et al., Southern District of Mississippi, Civil Action No. 1:20-cv-168-LG-RHW (2020).

[13] Jacques deLise, *Pursuing Politics Through Legal Means: U.S. Efforts to Hold China Responsible for Covid-19*, FOREIGN POLICY RESEARCH INSTITUTE (12 May 2020).

Broadly speaking, the United States confers immunity to foreign sovereigns based on the doctrine of reciprocity. If the United States permits lawsuits against other sovereign nations, this could prompt other countries to take reciprocal measures, exposing US citizens and businesses to legal risks abroad. But the Foreign Sovereign Immunities Act itself also delineates a few exceptions and restricts how sovereign immunity can be used. While the entitlement of immunity cannot be availed for commercial activities, it would be difficult for plaintiffs to meet the burden of proof that 'such activity be conducted in or cause a "direct effect" in the United States'.[14] Even though Mississippi's complaint against the Chinese government is likely to be dismissed on the ground of sovereign immunity, Chinese exporters of PPEs cannot escape the risk of antitrust liabilities entirely if they are targeted in a suit. A recent US Supreme Court decision involving a number of vitamin C manufacturers from China highlights such a predicament.[15]

The case dates back as early as 2005, when a group of US purchasers of Chinese-manufactured vitamin C alleged that the China's swift rise to dominance in the global vitamin C market had been facilitated by collusion among the Chinese manufacturers, the defendants in the case.[16] The Chinese defendants did not deny the allegations but moved to dismiss the suit on the basis that they should be exempt from antitrust liability since they had been compelled by the Chinese government to fix prices and limit output. In an unprecedented move, the Ministry of Commerce (MOFCOM) submitted an amicus brief in support of the Chinese defendants, acknowledging the fact the Chinese government had compelled the cartel's activities. MOFCOM claimed that the trade association that assisted the formation of the export cartel was an entity operating under the government's direct and active supervision. However, after lengthy pre-trial discovery, the New York district court refused to defer to MOFCOM's interpretation of Chinese law. The Second Circuit then reversed the decision of the district court and afforded conclusive weight to the statements made by the Chinese government.[17] The plaintiffs subsequently appealed the case to the Supreme Court. On 14 June 2018, the Supreme Court issued its opinion in which it held that although US courts should accord respectful consideration to a foreign government's submissions, they are not bound by such submissions.[18]

---

[14] Id.

[15] Animal Sci. Prods., Inc. v. Hebei Welcome Pharm. Co., 138 S. Ct. 1865 (2018).

[16] *In re* Vitamin C Antitrust Litig., 584 F. Supp. 2d 546, 548-50 (E.D.N.Y. 2008).

[17] *In re* Vitamin C Antitrust Litig. (*Vitamin C III*), 837 F.3d 175, 194 (2d Cir. 2016).

[18] Animal Sci. Prods., Inc. v. Hebei Welcome Pharm. Co., 138 S. Ct. 1865, 1869 (2018).

Certainly, the Vitamin C case is not the first time that foreign exporters have invoked sovereign compulsion as a defence in export cartel cases. In fact, the extent to which US courts should enforce antitrust laws against state-led export cartels has been the subject of intense debate among academics, courts, and policy-makers for decades.[19] In export cartel cases, defendants in such cartel cases have often argued that their conduct was compelled by foreign governments, and these cases have therefore turned on fact-specific inquiries into the reach and meaning of foreign laws and foreign sovereign involvement in the cartels.[20] The underlying rationale for such a defence is comity, a foundational doctrine applied by US courts to recognize an individual's act under foreign law out of respect for foreign sovereigns.[21] Although comity has been frequently invoked in cases involving conflict of laws with foreign nations, courts and commentators have bemoaned its ambiguity and inconsistent application.[22] Thus far, courts have tried in vain to set a benchmark for determining whether a foreign sovereign's involvement has reached a level that constitutes compulsion.[23]

In *Vitamin C*, the Supreme Court appears to have decided the case by solely focusing on whether to treat the statements by a foreign sovereign as conclusive. In doing so, it adopted a legalistic and formalistic approach by relying heavily on a provision in the Federal Rules of Civil Procedure. But I will propose an alternative interpretation: the underlying driver of the Supreme Court's decision was not law but politics. Indeed, the Supreme Court proactively solicited the opinion of the executive branch before hearing the case and its final ruling was perfectly aligned with the opinions and suggestions proposed by the US government. It is clear that the Supreme Court and the Executive spoke with one voice. What explains the high level of deference the Court accorded to the executive branch? More generally, how should courts apply the comity analysis when faced with abstruse factual evidence in future export cartel cases involving Chinese firms?

---

[19] See Jane Lee, Note, *Vitamin 'C' is for Compulsion: Delimiting the Foreign Sovereign Compulsion Defense*, 50 Va. J. Int'l L. 757, 759 (2010); Marek Martyniszyn, *Foreign State's Entanglement in Anticompetitive Conduct*, 40 World Competition 299, 306–07 (2017); Spencer Weber Waller, *The Twilight of Comity*, 38 Colum. J. Transnat'l L. 563, 564 (2000).

[20] Lee, *supra* note 19, at 759.

[21] See *In re* Vitamin C Antitrust Litig. (*Vitamin C III*), 837 F.3d 175, 183-86 (2d Cir. 2016); Joel R. Paul, *The Transformation of International Comity*, 71 Law & Contemp. Probs. 19, 19 (2008).

[22] See Donald Earl Childress III, *Comity as Conflict: Resituating International Comity as Conflict of Laws*, 44 U.C. Davis L. Rev. 11, 13 (2010); William S. Dodge, *International Comity in American Law*, 115 Colum. L. Rev. 2071, 2072 (2015); Louise Weinberg, *Against Comity*, 80 Geo. L.J. 53, 53 (1991).

[23] See Benjamin G. Bradshaw et al., *Foreign Sovereignty and U.S. Antitrust Enforcement: Is 'The State Made Me Do It' A Viable Defense*, 26 Antitrust 19, 20 (2012); Lee, *supra* note 19, at 790.

As revealed by the Vitamin C case, state-led export cartel cases often involve intricate and intertwined relationships between trade and antitrust issues. In fact, many Chinese exporters like those in *Vitamin C* have encountered a dilemma when selling overseas: if they compete fiercely and sell at reduced prices, they could be subject to antidumping duties levied by the importing country. But if they coordinate and raise prices together, they could be charged with antitrust violations. Similar to the dilemma faced by Chinese state-owned enterprises (SOEs) in Chapter 3, this facet of the Chinese antitrust exceptionalism is deeply rooted in the China's highly decentralized economic structure and its state-led governance model, resulting in problems of chronic overcapacity.

From the standpoint of the US government, the optimal strategy to deal with Chinese export cartels hinges not only on antitrust issues but also its own stance on trade issues. In previous cases, courts have often overlooked the complex dynamics between trade and antitrust. They have instead focused only on the antitrust issue, particularly on the factual evidence of foreign sovereign involvement in the export cartel. However, as is often the case, facts are very difficult to obtain and verify, and there has been a lack of consensus among courts about the extent to which a foreign sovereign's involvement in a cartel would rise to the level of compulsion.

Moreover, the judicial focus on facts alone tends to obscure the fundamental question of whether important US interests justify US courts' deference to foreign interests. In fact, comity analysis needs to take place in the specific context of state-led export cartels, where antitrust law issues are intertwined with trade policy and domestic politics of both the exporting and importing countries. Thus, whether a US court should accept the comity defence depends on the precise circumstances of the particular case, taking into consideration the interests of all players involved and the strategic nature of their decision-making. Since the executive branch is in the best position to consider and balance the competing interests, it makes sense for US courts to accord a high level of deference to the Executive.

This chapter is organized as follows. I will start by explaining why the anti-dumping policy of importing countries is often the impetus behind the organization of export cartels by foreign sovereigns. Then I will move on to discuss how the US executive branch has weighed trade and antitrust remedies in dealing with export cartels and, in fact, even encouraged the creation of Japanese export cartels to facilitate trade policy in the 1980s. Furthermore, to demonstrate the challenges faced by courts in handling export cartel cases, I will begin by introducing the background of the Vitamin C case, the opinions of all three levels of the federal courts, and related trade and antitrust cases.

I will then elaborate on why judicial focus on facts alone can be misguided and contend that courts should instead accord a high degree of deference to the executive branch when factual evidence proves to be ambiguous.

1. The Impetus for Export Cartels

Although cartels are consistently outlawed in established competition law regimes, virtually all jurisdictions tolerate export cartels. The Webb–Pomerene Act, in particular, expressly allows export cartels that operate exclusively in foreign markets.[24] Under the Export Trading Company Act of 1982, US firms can apply in advance for certifications to exempt their export cartels from antitrust laws in the United States.[25] The incentive for exporting countries to exempt national export cartels is obvious: consumer welfare loss is borne by consumers from importing countries, while the producers from the exporting countries reap the gains of monopoly rents.[26] Since export cartels pose a classic externality problem for the open economy, the benefits of international cooperation in this area are substantial. However, the effort of industrialized states to reach such an agreement has been rendered futile and, hitherto, the World Trade Organization (WTO) does not have a mandate to address export cartels.[27]

In cases concerning state-led export cartels, antitrust issues are often entangled with trade policy issues. While exporters are generally immune from antitrust liabilities in their home states, they could be subject to anti-dumping rules in the importing country. Unlike antitrust law, which protect consumer interests by encouraging low pricing, anti-dumping law condemns low pricing in order to shield domestic industries from foreign competition.[28] More specifically, anti-dumping law prohibits imports sold at less than fair value if the imports would materially injure a domestic industry.[29] Thus, anti-dumping not only develops friction between trading partners but also strains domestic

---

[24] 15 U.S.C. §§ 61–66 (1982); *see also* John F. McDernid, *The Antitrust Commission and the Webb-Pomerene Act: A Critical Assessment*, 37 WASH. & LEE L. REV. 105 (1980) (elaborating on the exemption).

[25] 15 U.S.C. § 6a (1994).

[26] Alan O. Sykes, *Externalities in Open Economy Antitrust and Their Implications for International Competition Policy*, 23 HARV. J.L. & PUB. POL'Y 89, 92 (1999).

[27] *See generally* Eleanor M. Fox, *International Antitrust and the Doha Dome*, 43 VA J. INT'L L. 911 (2003); Andrew T. Guzman, *Antitrust and International Regulatory Federalism*, 76 N.Y.U. L. REV. 1142 (2001); D. Daniel Sokol, *Monopolists Without Borders: The Institutional Challenge of International Antitrust in a Global Gilded Age*, 4 BERKELEY BUS. L.J. 37 (2007).

[28] Eleanor M. Fox, *Competition Law and the Agenda for the WTO: Forging the Links of Competition and Trade*, 4 PAC. RIM L. & POL'Y J. 1, 24 (1995).

[29] *See, e.g.*, Wentong Zheng, *Trade Law's Response to the Rise of China*, 34 BERKELEY J. INT'L L. 109, 115 (2016).

antitrust policy. As such, the conflict observed between a foreign exporting country's trade policy and US antitrust law is deeply rooted in the internal dissonance between US antitrust law and its domestic anti-dumping measures. Indeed, when a foreign government creates a single-country export cartel, profit maximization may be only one of the driving factors. A foreign government might react to the anti-dumping measures of the importing country by imposing export restraints or encouraging domestic firms to agree among themselves to restrict output or raise prices.

The Chinese vitamin C industry is an ideal example. Anti-dumping is one area China must carefully navigate after joining the world trading system.[30] Since China's entry into the WTO in 2001, China has become one of the most important players in world trade, but the exponential growth in Chinese exports has also dealt a blow to the world trading system, causing massive job losses for countries that import its goods. Meanwhile, the problem of excess capacity is a perennial challenge for the Chinese economy.[31] Since the mid-1990s, China has suffered from overcapacity in sixty-one of China's ninety-four major categories of industrial products and the capacity utilization rate has been below 50 per cent in thirty-five of them.[32] A natural consequence of the excess capacity is 'excessive competition'.[33] The intense price competition among Chinese exporters has sparked accusations from foreign importing countries that Chinese companies are dumping their goods into their markets. This has led to a spate of foreign anti-dumping actions against Chinese exporters.[34] From 2002 to June 2011, China was the subject of twenty-one WTO complaints, making it a major target of duties.[35]

To tackle the problem of overcapacity, the Chinese government has implemented a number of industrial policy measures.[36] Most of these measures have taken the form of 'industrial self-discipline', whereby major companies in a specific industry reach agreements to limit competition in order to stabilize the

---

[30] Chad P. Brown, *China's WTO Entry: Antidumping, Safeguards, and Dispute Settlement*, in CHINA'S GROWING ROLE IN FREE TRADE 281, 286–87 (Robert C. Feenstra & Shang-Jin Wei eds., 2010).

[31] Wentong Zheng, *Transplanting Antitrust in China: Economic Transition, Market Structure, and State Control*, 32 U. PA. J. INT'L L. 643, 675–77 (2010).

[32] Id.

[33] Bruce M. Owen et al., *China's Competition Policy Reforms: The Anti-Monopoly Law and Beyond*, 75 ANTITRUST L.J. 231, 247–49 (2008).

[34] Dingding Tina Wang, *When Antitrust Met WTO: Why U.S. Courts Should Consider U.S.–China WTO Disputes in Deciding Antitrust Cases Involving Chinese Exporters*, 1121 COLUM. L. REV. 1096, 1100–01 (2012).

[35] Id. at 1111.

[36] *See Fagaiwei: Wu Da Cuoshi Ezhi Weishengsu C Channeng Guosheng*（发改委：五大措施遏制维生素C产能过剩）[*Development and Reform Commission: Five Measures to Curb Excess Capacity of Vitamin C*], CHINA NEWS NET (中国新闻网) (30 Dec. 2009); *see also* Owen et al., *supra* note 33, at 249.

economy.[37] Trade associations, many of which were converted from government ministries, play a pivotal role in facilitating such cartels.[38]

In 2003, the Chinese government imposed a requirement that obliged exporters of thirty-six goods to submit their export contracts to their respective trade associations for approval before export.[39] According to MOFCOM, the main reason for imposing this new requirement was to 'make active efforts to avoid anti-dumping sanctions imposed by foreign countries on China's exports'.[40] Vitamin C also happens to be one of these goods.[41] According to the judicial record of the Vitamin C case, China's share of vitamin exports to the United States had risen from 60 per cent in 1997 to 80 per cent in 2002.[42] The defendants in *Vitamin C* controlled more than 60 per cent of the global market share in 2001. At the time, there was growing angst within the Chinese government that Western countries would soon adopt anti-dumping measures against Chinese vitamin C products. The Chinese government was thus presented with a dilemma: if it regulated the exports of Chinese products, it risked both exposing Chinese exporters to antitrust suits for price fixing in the United States and violating the General Agreement on Tariffs and Trade (GATT) commitments by instituting such export restraints. If, on the other hand, the Chinese government elected not to regulate the exports, there would be excessive competition among domestic exporters, thus subjecting Chinese exporters to potential anti-dumping allegations from the United States.

As the Vitamin C case ultimately revealed, the Chinese government decided to take action by coordinating the export of vitamin C. However, the potential trade violations that China could have been mired in may explain why the Chinese government did not impose any mandatory rules or regulations. Rather, MOFCOM relegated some of its regulatory authority to a chamber of commerce with a vague legal status. This appears to be a contrivance to conceal the government's role in coordinating the export cartels. And while the chamber publicly promoted itself as an independent non-governmental organization, in the amicus brief defending the vitamin C producers, the MOFCOM described the chamber as an instrument through which it oversaw and regulated the export business.

---

[37] *See* Owen et al., *supra* note 33, at 248–49; *see also* Zheng, *supra* note 31, at 687–91.
[38] *See* Owen et al., *supra* note 33, at 249.
[39] Id.
[40] *In re* Vitamin C Antitrust Litig. (*Vitamin C III*), 837 F.3d 175, 181 (2d Cir. 2016).
[41] *See Fagaiwei*, *supra* note 36.
[42] *In re* Vitamin C Antitrust Litig. (*Vitamin C II*), 810 F. Supp. 2d 522, 525 (E.D.N.Y. 2011).

Indubitably, China is not the first country to use export cartels to mitigate the problem of overcapacity. In the late 1970s, the Japanese government adopted a programme of adjustment assistance to protect its distressed industries. One primary tool of adjustment—in use since 1953—is the cartelization of such industries.[43] During this period, Japanese exports were highly cartelized. In 1977, there were eighty-six officially registered export cartels, accounting for 20–30 per cent of all Japanese exports.[44] By the mid-1980s, the Japanese government had established sixty-four separate cartel systems authorized by forty-six distinct cartel exemption statutes.[45] Like the Chinese government, the Japanese government believed that cartels were an effective way to eliminate excess capacity by allowing troubled companies to collaborate to find a mutually benefiting solution.[46]

But the problem of overcapacity is more serious and pervasive in China than it was in Japan in 1980s. In fact, overcapacity exposes the 'Achilles' heel' of China's macroeconomic predicament and its inherent weaknesses. As discussed in Chapter 3, while political power is concentrated in Beijing, the task of economic and fiscal governance has mostly been delegated to local governments. In reality, these local governments engage in fierce competition to achieve high GDP growth. They offer generous financial subsidies such as tax breaks and land to lure new manufacturing businesses and also provide implicit lending guarantees to help firms obtain cheap loans from state-owned banks.[47] As such, China's overcapacity issue is deeply entrenched in China's decentralized economic structure where different provinces vie for greater investment that will boost local employment and increase tax revenue in their regions, without taking the country's overcapacity situation into consideration. The state-led governance model further exacerbates the problem, as scholars have found that the issue of overcapacity is more severe among Chinese SOEs.[48] Concerned about unemployment and political instability, local governments continue to support a large number of so-called zombie firms which are companies that cannot survive without government support. This rampant phenomenon of zombie

[43] Akinori Uesugi, *Japan's Cartel System and Its Impact on International Trade*, 27 HARV. INT'L L.J. 389, 389–90 (1986).

[44] *See* Marek Martyniszyn, *Export Cartel: Is it Legal to Target Your Neighbour?: Analysis in Light of Recent Case Law*, 15 J. INT'L ECON. L. 181, 217 (2012).

[45] Uesugi, *supra* note 43, at 401.

[46] Id. at 391.

[47] European Union Chamber of Commerce in China, *Overcapacity in China: An Impediment to Party's Reform Agenda* 10 (2016).

[48] Guangjun Shen & Binkai Chen, *Zombie Firms and Overcapacity in Chinese Manufacturing*, 44 CHINA ECONOMIC REV. 327 (2017).

firms beset many Chinese industries and turn into a ticking time bomb for the Chinese economy.[49]

The problem of overcapacity has worsened since the global financial recession in 2008, when the Chinese government reacted quickly by introducing a massive fiscal stimulus package with unprecedently large lending programmes.[50] These lending programmes have poured funds into questionable projects and investments, further expanding the already enormous production capacity of Chinese SOEs.[51] Even though the Chinese central government has repeatedly issued policies and guidelines to rein in the excess capacity in various industry sectors, the actual implementation of these policies has been far from satisfactory.[52]

Furthermore, the fierce competition among Chinese producers has resulted in extremely low export prices directly increasing trade tensions with China's trading partners, especially in industries such as steel, aluminium, paper, and chemicals.[53] These tensions were further escalated after the launch of Made in China 2025, an industrial policy seeking to upgrade industrial manufacturing capabilities and shift gears to high-end production as well as invest in innovative technologies. Critics predict that this policy will be most likely to lead to greater overcapacity issues, as the Chinese government heavily subsidizes advanced industries by providing generous funding support.[54] One example can be found in the industry of solar panels. Since 2008, the manufacturing capacity of solar panels in China has grown ten-fold driving down global prices by 75 per cent.[55]

As the anti-dumping measures imposed by importing country often become the impetus for China to organize export cartels, the United States needs to consider carefully whether to launch antitrust actions against such cartels in the first place since such action could potentially conflict with domestic trade policy. These complex political dynamics behind state-led export cartels were particularly evident in the US policy towards Japanese export cartels in the 1980s.

---

[49] Shuaihua Wallace Cheng, *Overcapacity a Time Bomb for China's Economy*, SOUTH CHINA MORNING POST (28 Sep. 2015).

[50] Christine Wong, *The Fiscal Stimulus Programme and Public Governance Issues in China*, 11 OECD JOURNAL ON BUDGETING (2011).

[51] European Union Chamber of Commerce in China, *supra* note 47, at 8.

[52] Id. at 38–40.

[53] Id. at 36. *See also* Jorg Wuttke, *The Dark Side of China's Economic Rise*, 8 GLOBAL POLICY 62, 65 (2017).

[54] Id. *See also* Stephen Ezell, *China-Induced Global Overcapacity an Increasing Threat to High Tech Industries*, Information Technology & Innovation Foundation (27 Feb. 2018).

[55] Usha C.V. Haley & George T. Haley, *How Chinese Subsidies Changed the World*, HARV. BUSINESS REV. (25 Apr. 2013).

2. The Politics behind Export Cartels

The United States has considered both antitrust and trade remedies when dealing with export cartels, especially in its litigation with China. In fact, the US government has employed antitrust law as a strategic tool for trade policy, as illustrated by its response to the Japanese export cartel cases in the 1980s.

2.1 Weighing Trade and Antitrust

When dealing with export cartels, the United States generally has two options: it can seek succour via a multilateral treaty network such as the WTO or through direct diplomatic negotiations with the foreign sovereign, or, alternatively, it can bring antitrust actions against the foreign producers. The former is arguably the more efficient mechanism for dispute resolution. First, although antitrust litigation in the United States can be initiated by both public and private entities, it can produce inefficient results. Private enforcement of antitrust litigation is likely to involve piecemeal, decentralized, and uncoordinated efforts that aim to maximize plaintiffs' gains from litigation rather than increase the social welfare of the United States. Second, antitrust cases often involve lengthy discovery, heavily straining judicial resources. In comparison, the management of trade cases is coordinated and centralized by the US executive branch, and these cases are usually resolved more quickly through the WTO proceedings than through antitrust lawsuits.

At the same time, trade and antitrust remedies are mutually exclusive and at constant interplay. The success of a WTO proceeding hinges on evidential proof of China's imposition of export restraints, whereas the success of an antitrust proceeding relies on proving the absence of any government restraint (i.e. that the cartel is voluntary). Consequently, the United States cannot have it both ways as the use of one remedy will cut the use of the other. As discussed in Chapter 3, the European Commission (the Commission) faces an analogous dilemma with 'China Inc.': if the Commission eventually decides that all Chinese SOEs should be treated as a single entity, then this position could jeopardize its jurisdiction in future cartel and merger cases between Chinese SOEs. In the Vitamin C case, the United States did not directly challenge China's trading practices. Instead, as will be discussed below, the US government filed a complaint with the WTO in 2009 alleging that the Chinese government had introduced export restraints on a number of raw materials. In its WTO case, the US Trade Representative used MOFCOM's amicus brief in the vitamin C litigation as evidence of the latter's trade violations. Therefore, a US court holding that the vitamin C cartel was voluntary would contradict the position of the US Trade Representative and risk undermining the US case at the WTO. As it turned out, the United States won the raw materials case in the WTO proceeding even though the appellate panel voided the findings about MOFCOM's amicus brief later, deciding the case based on other evidence.[56] With the trade claims settled, the US courts did not have to worry about the spillover effects of this antitrust decision on US trade claims.

Furthermore, as China abandoned its export restraints on vitamin C products in 2008, the United States no longer had an interest in pursuing China via trade remedies. Nor did the United States have any incentive to raise vitamin C prices to protect domestic producers from foreign competition, as the market had already been dominated by Chinese producers and the US manufacturers no longer produce vitamin C.[57] Nevertheless, domestic antitrust litigation is not free from controversy as US courts' refusal to grant immunity to Chinese vitamin manufacturers could have grave implications for foreign relations.

After the district court in *Vitamin C* declined to defer to the MOFCOM statements, the Chinese government delivered several official statements to the US government and US courts, reiterating that the US government should respect comity.[58] In 2013, Shang Ming, the Director General of the Anti-Monopoly Bureau of MOFCOM, expressed 'deep dissatisfaction' with the district court's ruling, which he believed 'show[ed] disrespect for China'.[59] Shang Ming denounced the verdict as 'unfair', 'inappropriate', and 'wrong', and reportedly stated that if it stands, 'the international community will have concerns, and eventually [creating] disputes [that] may in turn hurt the interests of the United States'. These comments relayed a message to the United States that a refusal to defer to MOFCOM's statements could lead to further disputes between the two nations and the worsening of Sino-US relations.

Indeed, the Second Circuit seemed to have believed that rejecting blind deference could provoke requital and lead to adverse outcomes for the United States.[60] Thus, by choosing to defer to the Chinese government, the appellate court waived the need to adopt an intensive, fact-specific approach. Deference

---

[56] *See* Appellate Body Report, China-Measures Related to the Exportation of Various Raw Materials, ¶¶ 226–35, 362–63, WT/DS394/AB/R, WT/DS395/AB/R, WT/DS398/AB/R (30 Jan. 2011).

[57] Annie Harrison-Dunn, *Made in China: DSM Talks Vitamin C Price Pressures*, Nutra Ingrediants.Com (18 Feb. 2016), https://www.nutraingredients.com/Article/2016/02/17/Made-in-China-DSM-talks-vitamin-C-price-pressures.

[58] *In re* Vitamin C Antitrust Litig. (*Vitamin C III*), 837 F.3d 175, 193–94 (2d Cir. 2016).

[59] Client Memorandum, Davis Polk, Chinese Vitamin C Producers Price-Fixing Verdict Raises Questions of Comity and Conflict with Executive Branch Views (27 Mar. 2013).

[60] *Vitamin C III*, 837 F.3d at 193–94.

to the Chinese government's interpretation of its own law was a shortcut taken by the court to reach its preferred outcome. The US government though held a different view. In its amicus brief submitted to the US Supreme Court, the Solicitor General and the US Department of Justice argued that 'unlike a statement from the [e]xecutive [b]ranch, a foreign sovereign's objection to a suit does not, in itself, necessarily indicate that the case will harm U.S. foreign relations'.[61] This suggests that the US executive branch did not believe that MOFCOM's objection to the previous vitamin C decisions would materialize as a credible threat to Sino-US relations.

In the late 1990s, US federal agencies launched a crackdown on a large global vitamin cartel, ending a decade-long conspiracy among major vitamin producers, showcasing that the United States had endorsed a vigorous antitrust policy in the vitamin industry.[62] In light of its previous law enforcement efforts, it is not surprising that the US executive branch criticized the Second Circuit for giving 'inadequate weight to the interests of the U.S. victims of the alleged price-fixing cartel and to the interests of the United States in enforcement of its antitrust law'.[63]

As the analysis here reveals, the executive branch's plea to the Supreme Court to not grant conclusive deference to MOFCOM's statements was firmly rooted in the specific circumstances of the Vitamin C case. As trade remedies were not desirable nor beneficial in the Vitamin C case, it was natural for the United States to lean on antitrust remedies. But if the Executive had decided that it was in the United States' best interest to resolve the conflict via the trade route then it would have been best to refrain from suing the Chinese manufacturers on the basis of antitrust violations. In fact, it would have made more sense for the US federal courts to stay the antitrust action, pending the resolution of the trade dispute, as was done in *Resco Products* as elucidated below.[64] Under such conditions, the executive branch would have greater incentive to nudge the court towards giving immunity to the Chinese exporters, regardless of whether the Chinese government had filed an amicus brief in the litigation proceedings. Thus, contrary to the Second Circuit's decision in the vitamin C litigation, a foreign government's appearance in court is neither necessary nor sufficient for affording a comity-based defence to the foreign exporters, since such a defence

---

[61] *See* Brief for the United States as Amicus Curiae Supporting Petitioners, Petition for Writ of Certiorari at 20, *In re* Vitamin C Antitrust Litig. (*Vitamin C III*), 837 F.3d 175 (2d Cir. 2016) (No. 16-1220) [hereinafter United States' Amicus Brief in *Vitamin C*].

[62] *See* David Barboza, *Tearing Down the Façade of 'Vitamins Inc.'*, N.Y. Times (10 Oct. 1999).

[63] *See* United States' Amicus Brief in *Vitamin C*, *supra* note 61, at 20.

[64] Resco Prod., Inc. v. Bosai Minerals Grp., No. CIV.A. 06-235, 2010 WL 2331069, at *3, 6 (W.D. Pa. June 4, 2010).

ultimately turns on the specific circumstances of a case. As the US response to the Japanese export cartel in the 1980s will illustrate, under certain circumstances, the executive branch may even play host to foreign export cartels into the United States to address intractable trade problems.

2.2 Using Antitrust as a Tool for Trade Policy

Since the 1960s, the US executive branch has negotiated a number of voluntary restraint agreements as a means of resolving certain complicated trade issues, which had the effect of encouraging foreign export cartels in its market.[65] In fact, such tactics were widely used in the 1980s, amidst the trade war between Japan and the United States.

In the 1980s, the US automobile industry struggled to compete with low-priced Japanese imports.[66] Japanese auto manufacturers rapidly expanded into the US market, gaining nearly 24 per cent of the market share by early 1981. Meanwhile, the three largest US automakers all experienced financial hardships, witnessing a drastic decline in production and sales. The unemployment in the auto industry soared; over 300,000 auto workers became jobless, as did another 500,000 working in the auto supply industries. The economic threat posed by the rising tide of Japanese imports led to intensive lobbying from the US auto manufacturers and their unions, who petitioned for relief from Japanese imports.

However, the US International Trade Commission (ITC), which serves as an advisory body to the President and Congress on trade issues, denied the industry's petition. In a close call (three to two), the majority found that although foreign imports had significantly injured the domestic industry, they were not deemed the primary cause of the industry's problems. The commission instead attributed the industry's failures to other factors, such as the economic recession and shift in consumer demand for smaller cars. Congress, contrarily, threatened to impose a legislative quota on Japanese auto imports, a move that would have violated the United States' obligations under GATT. President Reagan, who had publicly endorsed free trade and the free market, succumbed to pressures from Congress to protect domestic industries

---

[65] Spencer Weber Waller, *The Ambivalence of United States Antitrust Policy Towards Single-Country Export Cartel*, 10 Nw. J. Int'l L. & Bus. 98, 106–09 (1999).
[66] Michael William Lochmann, *The Japanese Voluntary Restraint on Automobile Exports: An Abandonment of Free Trade Principles of GATT and the Free Market Principles of United States Antitrust Laws*, 27 Harv. Int'l L. J. 99, 100–04 (1986).

from Japanese competition at the expense of US consumers. But without a positive ITC decision, President Reagan lacked the statutory authority to enforce trade restraints. The Reagan Administration then arrived at an awkward solution: to convince the Japanese government to limit their exports voluntarily. This solution would satisfy the domestic political behest of Congress without violating the GATT obligations. The Japanese government found itself in a dilemma. It could either choose to impose export restraints and extract larger sums of profit from US consumers or it could opt for inaction and let the Japanese manufacturers continue expanding into the US market, in which case Congress would be likely to respond by imposing stringent quotas on Japanese imports. The former option was perceptibly more desirable, except with voluntary export restraints (VER), Japan risked contravening obligations under GATT and could also face antitrust lawsuits in the United States.[67] But as it was the US government that requested Japan to follow through on the VER, the United States would not attempt to challenge Japan under GATT. Thus, the only remaining concern for the Japanese government was the prospect of future antitrust violations. During rounds of discussion, the Japanese government sought assurance from the Reagan Administration that its VER system would not amount to violations of US antitrust law.[68] The then-US Attorney General, William French Smith, in response to a letter from the Japanese Ambassador in May 1981, replied that the Department of Justice was confident that the VER system would be 'viewed as having been compelled by the Japanese government' and thus 'would not give rise to violations of United States antitrust laws.'[69] Moreover, Smith gave assurances that the Department of Justice believed that US courts' interpretation of the antitrust laws would be likely to persist in exempting the VER system from antitrust infringements. To reach an agreement, Japan required affirmation from the Reagan Administration that the US government would grant immunity and that US courts would follow accordingly. The letter from the Department of Justice to the Japanese government served this exact purpose; without this formal commitment, the two countries would not have been able to reach a cooperative outcome.

Under the auspices of the Reagan Administration, the Japanese auto VER lasted almost four years from 1981 until 1985.[70] In part due to the restrictions of Japanese imports, the United States auto industry saw a dramatic recovery

---

[67] Id. at 130.
[68] Id. at 104–07.
[69] Id. at 107 n. 65.
[70] Lochmann, *supra* note 66, at 108–12.

and quickly returned to profitability. As imports shrank, US auto manufacturers also regained their market share resulting in significantly increased production in the United States. This generated all-time record profits for the domestic auto industry. As the VER restricted the number of imports and reduced the competition among domestic and foreign auto manufacturers, both domestic and foreign automakers were able to raise their prices substantially, but the successful revival of the auto industry also came at a price for US consumers. The outcome did not maximize total social welfare of the United States but it was arguably the Reagan Administration's best response, given the political and economic circumstances at the time.

This analysis demonstrates that when the interests of the exporting country and the importing country are aligned, the issue of whether the exporting country actually compelled cartel behaviour becomes irrelevant. In terms of game theory, the optimal strategy for the United States depends on the payoffs received as well as on the strategy of the exporting country responsible for making the first move in this game. The strategy of the exporting country in turn depends on its own foreseeable payoffs, which can vary according to the existing trade policies of the United States along with many other factors. These include the probability of being hit with antitrust violations in the United States, the expected antitrust litigation cost, and the trade loss should the United States administer sanctions. Thus, the optimal tactic for the United States is by no means static: instead it is a complicated assessment of various factors ranging from antitrust and trade to domestic politics. As a sequential game, it requires players to contemplate the future consequences of their current moves in the present day before settling on their course of action. Thus, the comity analysis needs to anticipate these changing circumstances in politics and accommodate such flexibility.

2.3 The Fluid Executive Stance

The United States' encouragement of the Japanese automobile cartel in the 1980s was not the first time that it had used antitrust as a strategic tool for trade policy. In the 1960s, in anticipation of hostile congressional action that would lead to stringent quotas for steel imports, the US executive negotiated directly with European steel producers and concluded a series of voluntary restraint agreements.[71] The executive branch bypassed its governmental counterparts

---

[71] Waller, *supra* note 65, at 107.

and directly encouraged the European producers to form export cartels. The government's action was subsequently challenged in court in *Consumers Union of United States, Inc. v. Rogers*.[72] The plaintiff argued that the agreements constituted a violation of the Sherman Act and that the existing congressional trade legislation pre-empted the President's power in the field. And while the district court upheld the steel agreements, it noted that the President had no authority to grant immunity to foreign exporters participating in the voluntary agreement.[73]

The US executive branch learned its lesson from Consumers Union's complaint and modified its approach towards addressing trade crises. This explains why the Reagan Administration recommended the Japanese government to impose VER on Japanese automobiles.[74] Thereafter, the US government issued similar assurances to the Japanese government in connection with the imposition of a VER on semiconductors.[75] President Reagan reintroduced these tactics when negotiating with a number of exporting countries on steel imports, effectuating a trade agreement with Australia in 1985 by allowing the latter to enforce restraints on its steel exports.[76] In 2005, the United States and China signed an agreement in which China promised to place a VER on Chinese textiles and apparel goods in order to avert steep US import duties following a surge of related Chinese imports to the United States.[77]

The executive branch's preference for utilizing export cartels as a means to accomplish policy objectives has also been reflected in private antitrust litigation on some occasions. In *Matsushita Electric*, two US television manufacturers filed a case against Japanese television manufacturers for fashioning an export cartel to force US competitors out of the market.[78] The defendants argued that their conduct should be immune from antitrust liability because the Ministry of International Trade and Industry (MITI) had 'mandated agreements fixing minimum export prices' in order to avoid anti-dumping liability and retaliatory trade barriers against Japanese goods. In a statement submitted

---

[72] Consumers Union of U.S., Inc. v. Rogers, 352 F. Supp. 1319, 1322–23 (D.D.C. 1973).

[73] Id. at 1323.

[74] Waller, *supra* note 65, at 108.

[75] Id.

[76] Brief for the United States as Amicus Curiae Supporting Petitioners at 19 & n. 17, Matsushita Elec. Indus. Corp. v. Zenith Radio Corp., 475 U.S. 574 (1986) (No. 83-2004), 1985 WL 669667 [hereinafter United States' Amicus Brief in *Matsushita Electric*] (citing Letter from J. Paul McGrath, Assistant Att'y Gen., to Kenneth McDonald, Austl. Charge d'Affaires (18 Jan. 1985)).

[77] See Brown, *supra* note 30, at 311 & n. 27.

[78] *In re* Japanese Elec. Prods. Antitrust Litig., 723 F.2d 238, 251 (1983), *rev'd sub nom.* Matsushita Elec. Indus. Corp. v. Zenith Radio Corp., 475 U.S. 574 (1986).

to court, the MITI admitted that Japanese cartel had been developed under its direction.[79] Moreover, the agency claimed that it would penalize firms for failing to comply with its directives, using its authority to allocate foreign exchange under certain foreign trade control laws.[80] The US Solicitor General and the Department of Justice acknowledged this position and urged the court to give the MITI's statements conclusive weight.[81]

In its amicus brief, the executive branch strongly endorsed a view of conclusive deference to the Japanese government:

> [C]laims of compulsion are most appropriately entertained when the foreign government, either directly or through the State Department, informs the court that the conduct at issue was compelled. It is in such instances the depth of the foreign government's concern and the possibility of diplomatic friction following from further court proceedings will be most clearly expressed . . . Once a foreign government presents a statement dealing with subjects within its area of sovereign authority, however, American courts are obligated to accept that statement at face value; the government's assertions concerning the existence and meaning of its domestic law generally should be deemed 'conclusive.'[82]

The US government advocating to accord deference to a foreign government's statements in *Matsushita Electric* contrasts sharply with its staunch objection to doing so in the Vitamin C case. While this legal inconsistency and logical incoherence may seem puzzling, it becomes comprehensible once the underlying political and economic circumstances are clarified. The executive branch explicitly discerned these forces at play in *Matsushita Electric*: 'in a system of international trade where the United States can be found negotiating for certain export restraints, failure to recognize a limited sovereign compulsion exception to the Sherman Act necessarily would "interfere with delicate foreign relations conducted by the political branches"'.[83]

Yet the Third Circuit plainly ignored the executive branch's request and was caught up in the complicated factual inquiry of whether compulsion existed in this case, ultimately refusing to grant immunity to the Japanese producers.

---

[79] Brief for the Government of Japan as Amicus Curiae in Support of Petitioners at 4, Matsushita Elec. Indus. Corp. v. Zenith Radio Corp., 475 U.S. 574 (1986) (No. 83-2004).

[80] Id. at 14a.

[81] United States' Amicus Brief in *Matsushita Electric, supra* note 76, at 22.

[82] Id. at 23.

[83] Id. at 19–20.

The court overlooked the fact that the Japanese imposition of export restraints was not a static decision; rather, it was a dynamic decision involving the trade policy and domestic politics of the United States. The United States did not act in a vacuum; its judicial decision-making would affect the Japanese government's future actions. Thus, by simply focusing on the antitrust case at hand, the court missed the bigger picture of the dynamic relationship between the United States and Japan.

Indeed, the US government has taken a fluid stance with regards to export cartels. When a trade remedy is no longer seen favourably, the executive branch tries to persuade US courts to avoid granting conclusive deference to a foreign government's statement, as in the Vitamin C case. Meanwhile, when the executive branch prioritizes the protection of domestic industries from foreign competition, it tries to coax US courts to treat a foreign government's statement as conclusive, as in *Matsushita Electric*. This shows that the basis of the executive branch's actions did not stem from the law but rather arose out of the contemporary political climate. Ultimately, the decision on which approach to pursue came down to the assessment of costs and benefits of using trade or antitrust remedies, which are mutually exclusive when dealing with a conflict.

3. The Vitamin C Saga

After exploring the political dynamics behind export cartels, I now turn to the vitamin C litigation, which spanned over a decade and made it all the way to the US Supreme Court. The radically different approaches adopted by the different courts involved in the case provides a perfect illustration of the difficulties US courts faced in dealing with export cartels.

In January 2005, a group of US purchasers filed claims against Chinese manufacturers of vitamin C, accusing them of fixing prices and limiting the quantity of sales to the United States.[84] The cases were subsequently consolidated in a New York federal court. The plaintiffs asserted that the defendants had colluded with the Chamber of Commerce of Medicines and Health Products Importers and Exporters (the Chamber), agreeing to limit the production of vitamin C and increase its prices to create a supply shortage in the international market.[85] The defendants did not deny the price-fixing accusations.[86]

---

[84] *In re* Vitamin C Antitrust Litig. (*Vitamin C III*), 837 F.3d 175, 179 (2d Cir. 2016).
[85] Id. at 180.
[86] *In re* Vitamin C Antitrust Litig., 584 F. Supp. 2d 546, 550 (E.D.N.Y. 2008).

However, they contended that they had acted pursuant to Chinese regulations regarding export pricing and that the Chamber was a government-supervised entity through which the Chinese government had compelled the collusion. The defendants then moved to dismiss the claims on account of three defences founded on comity: the act of state doctrine, under which courts should refrain from judging the acts of a foreign state; the foreign sovereign compulsion defence, under which courts should abstain from exercising jurisdiction in cases in which the defendants' conduct is coerced by the government; and the international comity doctrine, under which courts should resist exercising jurisdiction in cases that might influence the working diplomatic relationships between nations.

3.1 The District Court's Decision

At the heart of the district court's analysis in applying the above comity-based doctrines is the factual inquiry of 'whether the Chinese government required defendants to fix prices in violation of the Sherman Act'.[87] That is, was the defendants' behaviour *actually* compelled by a foreign sovereign? In an unusual move, MOFCOM delivered an amicus brief in 2006 in support of the Chinese defendants and further accrediting the challenged conduct to a government approved regulatory pricing scheme.[88] As the highest central ministry in charge of overseeing international trade in China, MOFCOM's appearance in a US court was unprecedented.[89]

In its submission, MOFCOM declared that it had created the Chamber in order to enforce its authority to cut prices and limit the production of vitamin C.[90] MOFCOM explained that the Chamber was a government-supervised entity, unlike the trade associations in the United States. The ministry further claimed that the penalty for non-compliance with the Chamber's mandate is severe: the Chamber could provide 'warning, open criticism and even revocation of . . . membership', and could even advise the relevant government department to suspend or cancel the producers' export rights. The district court asserted that MOFCOM's statements were entitled to substantial deference,

---

[87] Id. at 552.

[88] *In re* Vitamin C Antitrust Litig., 584 F. Supp. 2d at 552.

[89] Id. It is common practice, however, for other foreign states to submit amicus curiae briefs in antitrust cases before the US courts. *See* Marek Martyniszyn, *Foreign States' Amicus Curiae Participation in U.S. Antitrust Cases*, 61 ANTITRUST BULL. 611 (2016).

[90] *In re* Vitamin C Antitrust Litig., 584 F. Supp. 2d at 552–53.

but it found conflicting evidence concerning the compulsion by the Chinese government.[91] The court pointed to the Chamber's statements on its website which portrayed the exporters as coming to a 'self-regulated' agreement to restrict the prices and quantity of exports voluntarily.[92] The court then denied the defendants' motion to dismiss in order to allow further factual investigation into the issue of compulsion.[93]

In 2009, MOFCOM provided a new statement to the district court, clarifying that '[s]elf-discipline does not mean complete voluntariness or self-conduct' and that such language needs to be read in the context of China's regulatory culture.[94] Nonetheless, the district court accepted the plain language of the Chamber's documents and refused to defer to MOFCOM's interpretation.[95] After lengthy and detailed discovery, the court found that the Chinese government merely encouraged cartel behaviour as a policy preference, and that MOFCOM's conduct did not amount to the level of compulsion, there was no such obligation for the vitamin C manufacturers to fix prices.[96] The court also held that even if manufacturers had been partially forced, the defendants went beyond the requirements of the Chinese government and set prices higher than necessary to achieve the government's goals.[97] The case then went to trial and the jury subsequently decided that the Chinese defendants had violated US antitrust law awarding to the plaintiff USD 54.1 million in damages.[98]

3.2 The WTO Case and Other Chinese Export Cartels

As the antitrust case against the Chinese vitamin C producers was progressing through the US district court, China was dealt another blow on the trade front. In 2009, the United States launched a WTO suit against China for breaching its WTO commitments when it imposed export restraints on certain raw materials.[99] Although the WTO proceedings implicated different export goods and another trade association, the US Trade Representative used MOFCOM's

---

[91] Id. at 557.

[92] Id. at 554–55.

[93] Id. at 559.

[94] *In re* Vitamin C Antitrust Litig. (*Vitamin C II*), 810 F. Supp. 2d 522, 532–33 (citing statement of the Ministry of Commerce of the People's Republic of China).

[95] Id. at 542.

[96] Id. at 525, 550, 552.

[97] Id. at 560–61, 566.

[98] *In re* Vitamin C Antitrust Litig. (*Vitamin C III*), 837 F.3d 175, 178 (2d Cir. 2016).

[99] Request for the Establishment of a Panel by the United States, *China—Measures Related to the Exportation of Various Raw Materials*, WTO Doc. WT/DS394/7 (9 Nov. 2009).

statements in the Vitamin C case as evidence that the Chinese government imposed 'minimum export price requirements'.[100] The United States argued that such export restraints violated China's WTO obligations under the GATT, as well as its Accession Protocol.[101] These arguments were upheld by the WTO panel, which in July 2011 pronounced that China had flouted its WTO commitment after instituting export restraints.[102]

During the Vitamin C trial, the district court took into the account the WTO proceedings that coincided with the case, but paid little heed to the position of the US Trade Representative. The district court emphasized that vitamin C was not an export at issue in the WTO proceeding and the executive branch had not requested the court to accord MOFCOM's statements heightened deference.[103] While considering the findings of the WTO panel, the district court held that the panel's conclusion did 'not alter [its] interpretation of Chinese law' because the WTO findings did not demonstrate any contradictory attestation as China never denied the existence of the price restraints nor did the WTO touch on whether the trade association membership had been voluntary or not.[104] The district court also observed that the WTO panel failed to address the deficiencies with MOFCOM's filings when deferring to its 2009 statements.[105]

When the Vitamin C case was pending in front of the district court, several Chinese manufacturers of magnesite and bauxite were met with similar antitrust litigation for conducting export cartels in the United States.[106] Analogous to the Vitamin C case, the defendants in two cases did not deny the charges but sought to dismiss the lawsuits on the basis of various doctrines addressing actions by foreign governments.[107] In the Resco Products case, the allegations of which were conspiring to fix prices of bauxite, the court stayed the proceedings pending the resolution of the US-initiated WTO proceedings over China's

---

[100] First Written Submission of the United States of America, China—Measures Related to the Exportation of Various Raw Materials, ¶¶ 207, 208, 216, 229, 352, WT/DS394, WT/DS395, WT/DS398 1 June 2010) [hereinafter US First Written Submission].

[101] Id. ¶¶ 10–17.

[102] See Panel Report, China—Measures Related to the Exportation of Various Raw Materials, ¶¶ 7.185, WT/DS394/R, WT/DS395/R, WT/DS398/R (5 July 2011) [hereinafter Panel Report]. However, on appeal from the parties, the WTO's Appellate Body vacated some of the panel's rulings on the grounds of due process, thus voiding the panel's findings that the Chinese government had imposed export price restraints. See Appellate Body Report, supra note 56.

[103] In re Vitamin C Antitrust Litig. (Vitamin C II), 810 F. Supp. 2d 522, 551–60 (E.D.N.Y. 2011).

[104] Id. at 555–60.

[105] Id. at 559–60 & 559 n.49.

[106] Animal Sci. Prods., Inc. v. China Nat. Metals & Minerals Imp. & Exp. Corp., 702 F. Supp. 2d 320 (D.N.J. 2010), vacated sub nom. Animal Sci. Prods., Inc. v. China Minmetals Corp., 654 F.3d 462, (3d Cir. 2011); Resco Prods., Inc. v. Bosai Minerals Grp., No. 06-235, 2010 WL 2331069, at *3 (W.D. Pa. 4 June 2010).

[107] Resco Prods., 2010 WL 2331069, at *3. See also Animal Sci. Prods., 702 F. Supp. 2d at 429–37; Wang, supra note 34, at 1121–24.

export constraints for bauxite.[108] The court found that factual and legal inquiries between the pending case and the WTO proceedings were strikingly similar, exhibiting considerable deference to separation of powers and sovereignty considerations.[109] In *Animal Science*, a case concerning putative price inflation of magnesite, the New Jersey district court afforded 'a nearly binding-degree of deference' to MOFCOM's statements.[110] The court also actively scoured through evidence from other proceedings bearing on the compulsion defence raised by the defendants, including *Resco Products* and *Vitamin C*.[111] In the end, the court was swayed by the totality of the evidence, which indicated that the offending trade association was an appendage of the government, and that the Chinese government had indeed coerced the defendants' conduct.[112]

Thus, the district court's decision in *Vitamin C* represents a clear departure from the more deferential approach taken by the courts in the raw material cases, giving rise to confusion about the standards courts apply when deciding how to take into account comity-related defence. The New York district court's decision in the Vitamin C case generated a great deal of controversy, as many commentators criticized the court for its failure to consider the decision's implications on US trade policy.[113]

3.3 The Second Circuit's Decision

On appeal, the Second Circuit applied a ten-factor balancing test to evaluate whether the district court should refrain from exercising its jurisdiction on international comity grounds.[114] Citing the US Supreme Court's ruling in *Hartford Fire Insurance Co. v. California*, the Second Circuit primarily focused on the first factor, that is, the degree of conflict between the US and foreign law.[115] Instead of centring its analysis around a factual inquiry into the existence of compulsion by the Chinese government, the Second Circuit gave conclusive deference to the official statements by MOFCOM.[116] The Second

---

[108] *Resco Prods.*, 2010 WL 2331069, at *3, *6.
[109] Id. at *6.
[110] *Animal Sci. Prods.*, 702 F. Supp. 2d at 426.
[111] Id. at 403–18.
[112] Id. at 437.
[113] *See* Michael N. Sohn & Jesse Solomon, *Lingering Questions on Foreign Sovereignty and Separation of Powers After the Vitamin C Price-Fixing Verdict*, 28 ANTITRUST 78, 83 (2013). *See generally* Wang, *supra* note 34.
[114] *In re* Vitamin C Antitrust Litig. (*Vitamin C III*), 837 F.3d 175, 184–85 (2d Cir. 2016).
[115] Id. at 192–95.
[116] Id. at 186–94.

Circuit asserted that it was unable to identify a single case 'where a foreign sovereign appeared before a U.S. tribunal and the U.S. tribunal adopted a reading of that sovereign's law contrary to that sovereign's interpretation of them'.[117] The appellate court continued: 'Not extending deference in these circumstances disregards and unravels the tradition of according respect to a foreign government's explication of its own laws, the same respect and treatment that we would expect our government to receive in comparable matters before a foreign court.'[118] In a footnote, the court also made reference to counterfactual circumstances: had the Chinese government not chosen to appear in the litigation proceedings, the district court's fact-specific approach would have been entirely appropriate.[119] Thus, it appears that the Chinese government's exceptional appearance in this case played a decisive role in influencing the outcome.

Notably, the Second Circuit's decision also encompassed a lengthy recitation of the adverse consequences that would arise out of from the district court's disregard of MOFCOM's statements.[120] Thus, it appears that the Chinese government's response was an important component of the court's comity analysis. Ultimately, the Second Circuit reversed the decision of the lower court.

3.4 The Supreme Court Decision

In April 2017, the plaintiffs filed a petition for certiorari to the Supreme Court, asking the Court to clarify, among others, two important issues.[121] The first issue identified concerned the level of deference given to a foreign government's interpretation of its own law, specifically, whether a US court should give conclusive deference to a foreign government's interpretation of its own law if representatives of the government appeared in court.[122] The second issue revolved around the long-standing split among circuit courts regarding how to apply the international comity doctrine. In this case, the Second Circuit applied the balancing test adopted by the Ninth and Third Circuits, selecting

---

[117] Id.
[118] Id.
[119] Id. at 191 n.10.
[120] Id. at 193–94.
[121] Petition for Writ of Certiorari, Animal Sci. Prods. v. Hebei Welcome Pharm. Co., 138 S. Ct. 1865 (2018) (No. 16-1220), 2017 WL 1353281 [hereinafter Petition for Certiorari]; see also Reply to Brief in Opposition, Animal Sci. Prods., Inc. v. Hebei Welcome Pharmaceutical Co., 138 S. Ct. 1865 (2018) (No. 16-1220), 2017 WL 2610072 [hereinafter Reply to Brief in Opposition].
[122] Petition for Writ of Certiorari, supra note 121, at 29–34; see also Reply to Brief in Opposition, supra note 121, at 11–12.

this test over different variations employed in other circuits.[123] On 26 June 2017, the Supreme Court invited Acting Solicitor General Jeffery Wall to file a brief expressing the views of the United States in the Vitamin C case.[124] The US Solicitor General and the Department of Justice subsequently submitted their amicus brief to the Supreme Court in November 2017, arguing that the Second Circuit had erred by treating MOFCOM's statements as conclusive.[125]

In its brief, the US government relied heavily on Federal Rule of Civil Procedure 44.1, adopted in 1966 to assist courts in determining issues relating to foreign law. The government highlighted two aspects of Rule 44.1. First, the determination of foreign law is a 'question of law' for the courts rather than a question of fact. Second, the Court may consider any relevant material or sources in determining foreign law. This accords federal courts great flexibility. In addition, the US government argued that federal courts should not treat foreign governments' characterizations as conclusive in all circumstances. The executive branch enumerated a list of factors that courts should consider when weighing a foreign government's statements, including 'the statement's clarity, thoroughness, and support; its context and purpose; the authority of the entity making it; its consistency with past statements; and any other corroborating or contradictory evidence'. The brief then noted that the Second Circuit disregarded other relevant materials, including China's testimony to the WTO that it had given up export administration of vitamin C. Further to this, the brief disagreed with the Second Circuit's interpretation of previous case law, arguing that not 'every submission by a foreign government is entitled to the same weight'. Last but not least, the brief disputed the Second Circuit's trepidations about reciprocity, stating that the United States has never argued before foreign courts that they are bound to accept its characterizations of US law.

The final decision of the US Supreme Court conformed with what was proposed by the executive branch. In fact, the reasoning and arguments in the Court's final ruling were remarkably similar to those advised in the government's amicus brief, and in some places it seems to have been copied verbatim.[126] The strong resemblance between the Supreme Court's decision and the amicus brief shows that the Court adopted a highly deferential approach to the executive branch when deciding this case. This represents a fundamental shift from previous case law, in which courts had a tendency to focus

[123] Reply to Brief in Opposition, *supra* note 121, at 12.

[124] Shepard Goldfein & James Keyte, *Vitamin C Litigation: Window into Trump White House International Relations?* N.Y.L.J. (18 July 2017).

[125] *See* United States' Amicus Brief in *Vitamin C, supra* note 61, at 9.

[126] Animal Sci. Prods., Inc. v. Hebei Welcome Pharm. Co., 138 S. Ct. 1865, 1867–75 (2018).

on the factual issue of whether a foreign sovereign had compelled cartel conduct. As illustrated below, facts are often muddled and difficult to ascertain. Even when a foreign government has appeared in US courts to offer interpretation of its own law, courts still struggle to define a threshold that would determine whether the foreign sovereign's involvement constituted compulsion.

4. Judicial Challenges with Export Cartels

Against the backdrop of the Vitamin C case, I will explain why the focus on factual evidence of a foreign sovereign's involvement in export cartels has posed a perennial challenge for US courts deciding such cases. To cope with such challenges, I propose a legal framework of comity analysis for courts to respond optimally to export cartel cases, particularly when the facts are uncertain and difficult to discern.

4.1 Judicial Frustrations with Facts

In export cartel cases, a focal point of the litigation is the issue of whether foreign sovereign compulsion exists. This problem frequently creates a significant challenge for courts, since the information gap between the exporting country and the importing country is often very wide. Cartels are often contrived secretly and it is difficult to obtain evidence of the cartel's formation. Moreover, as export cartels are organized extraterritorially, it is more difficult for the importing countries to detect their existence. When defendants attempt to invoke a comity-related defence, US courts and agencies face the additional burden of understanding foreign laws and legal practices. The Second Circuit highlighted some of these challenges in its opinion on the Vitamin C case. For instance, the court observed that Chinese law is less transparent than that of the United States and other countries.[127] Moreover, the court also pointed out that the Chinese legal system is distinct from the US system, and that it maintains a vast regime of administrative regulation. It found that the plain language of the Chinese government's directive may not reflect Chinese law accurately, especially considering the need for translation and the understanding of the term of arts in the Chinese system. When the foreign government has not imposed any

---

[127] *In re* Vitamin C Antitrust Litig. (*Vitamin C III*), 837 F.3d 175, 190 (2d Cir. 2016) (quoting *In re* Vitamin C Antitrust Litig., 584 F. Supp. 2d 546, 559 (E.D.N.Y. 2008)).

mandatory law, there is further ambiguity as to whether the government has actually compelled the action.

In practice, there have been two means through which courts have tried to fill the information gap. One way is through trial discovery. However, factual evidence is often ambiguous due to the covert nature of the cartels, and sometimes the foreign state's deliberate attempt to disguise its imposition of export restraints to avoid potential trade violations. When foreign sovereigns appear in court to provide their own characterization of their law, judges also differ significantly in deciding the degree of deference to afford such foreign statements.

Trial discovery is the essential means for a fact-specific approach. But trial discovery is a costly and lengthy process. Moreover, ambiguities abound as to the authority of the government's directive and the severity of the sanctions. As Spencer Weber Waller acutely observed: '[t]he interaction between governments and private firms can be understood as a spectrum, ranging from sanctions to purely voluntary requests with no sanctions at all'.[128] In practice, US courts have been unclear about the required threshold for a foreign sovereign's involvement in the cartels and have taken divergent approaches to deciding these cases.[129]

The complex factual circumstances of the Chinese Vitamin C case offer a good illustration of the difficulties faced by courts in trying to uncover the conditions of compulsion. There is no doubt that the Chamber was closely involved and facilitated the formation of the cartel, but it is not entirely clear whether the government had compelled the cartel. The MOFCOM asserted that the Chamber was government-supervised and that the appointment of its staff was government controlled.[130] It described the Chamber as 'the instrumentality through which the Ministry oversees and regulates the business of importing and exporting medicinal products in China'. However, plaintiffs challenged the Ministry's position, arguing that the Chamber was merely an independent non-governmental organization. To buttress their claims, the plaintiffs submitted proof of the Chinese government's previous public statements extolling the independence of the Chamber.

Another vexing issue is the difficulty courts have in drawing the line between voluntary and compulsory conduct. For instance, upon learning that the EU contemplated taking anti-dumping actions against Chinese producers of

---

[128] See Spencer Weber Waller, *Redefining the Foreign Compulsion Defense in U.S. Antitrust Law: The Japanese Auto Restraints and Beyond*, 14 LAW & POL'Y INT'L BUS. 747, 795 (1982).

[129] See Bradshaw et al., *supra* note 23.

[130] *In re* Vitamin C Antitrust Litig. (*Vitamin C II*), 810 F. Supp. 2d 522, 551 n.37 (E.D.N.Y. 2011).

vitamin C in the autumn of 2011, the MOFCOM specifically instructed the Chamber to organize firms to take active steps to avoid running into potential anti-dumping challenges. The Chamber subsequently coordinated a meeting with the defendants. However, there was no indication in the meeting minutes that the Chamber had compelled these defendants to abide by a minimum export price. To the contrary, according to the court's findings, the minutes suggested that the agreement among them was voluntary.

There was further confusion as to whether the Chamber was able to enforce the price scheme successfully, as claimed by MOFCOM in its brief submitted to the district court, given the lack of clear penalties and sanctions for non-compliance. The district court pointed out several ambiguities in MOFCOM's official statements that raised doubts about the government's level of compulsion. The briefings and discovery unveiled that the firms were entitled to export vitamin C even if they were not members of the Chamber's subcommittee. During a meeting convened by the Chamber, a representative from the MOFCOM admitted that the government's regulation of the vitamin C industry 'ha[d] not been very successful'.[131] In addition to 'maximizing their profits', he urged the companies to also 'consider the interest of the state as a whole'.[132] There was also evidence showing that those manufacturers who deviated from the agreed minimum price did not incur any punishment.

Additionally, courts were puzzled as to whether the parties actually went above the quoted price. The district court found that while the Chamber had been entrusted with the responsibility to coordinate export prices in order to avert anti-dumping actions and below-cost pricing, the firms themselves enjoyed significant discretion in determining their profit margins, and in practice the Ministry did not intervene. Therefore, the court believed that any form of compulsion was limited to avoiding anti-dumping and below-cost pricing sanctions. The district court noted that the Chinese government had asserted in the WTO proceedings that it had repealed the price restraint system and ceased the imposition of penalties from 28 May 2008. The Chinese government also stated in the proceedings that it had abandoned the 'export administration' of vitamin C as of 1 January 2002. This was contradictory to the MOFCOM's position throughout vitamin C litigation. All these factual inconsistencies ultimately led the district court's refusal to defer to MOFCOM's statements. In its denial of summary judgment, the court described MOFCOM's 2009 statement

---

[131] Id. at 534.
[132] Id.

as 'a carefully crafted and phrased litigation position'.[133] The district court even portrayed MOFCOM's assertion of compulsion as 'a post-hoc attempt to shield defendants' conduct from antitrust scrutiny'.[134]

As illustrated in the Vitamin C case , the challenge of using the fact-specific approach in Chinese export cartel cases lies in the inherent difficulty of identifying the extent of state control over domestic companies.[135] This is similar to the Commission's quandary in Chapter 3 over the boundary of the 'China Inc.' On the one hand, even if a state imposes a mandatory export restraint on its own companies, it may fail to coordinate an export cartel. After all, firms participating in a cartel may have incentives to cheat in order to line their pockets. Thus, the effectiveness of the state's policing system directly impacts the success of the state-led cartel. On the other hand, the state is no ordinary legal actor. Even if the state does not issue any binding administrative law or order, it can threaten to penalize a firm if the firm does not voluntarily comply with the state's request. In other words, the state could have de facto control over the firms, even without clear de jure control. In the Vitamin C case, neither the MOFCOM nor any other government department imposed a mandatory requirement on the Chinese manufacturers to coordinate their prices, but the Chinese government may have been able to obtain de facto control over these exporters via other administrative means. However, the extent of such de facto control is very difficult for a court to discern through discovery.

4.2 The Shortcut of Deference

The other means by which US courts can close the information gap is to rely on the foreign sovereign's interpretation of its own law. The simplest way for the exporting country to convey information to the United States is through direct communication. But in a strategic game, a player may be concerned that the other is mendacious or hesitant to take their word for it. If the exporting country and the United States have perfectly aligned interests, then direct communication can be successful. If the exporting country confesses to coercing export cartel conduct, then the United States should grant immunity to the exporters. Conversely, if the exporting country denies any act of compulsion,

---

[133] Id.
[134] Id.
[135] See Curtis J. Milhaupt & Wentong Zheng, *Beyond Ownership: State Capitalism and Chinese Firms*, 103 GEO. L.J. 665 (2015). *See generally* Angela Huyue Zhang, *The Antitrust Paradox of China Inc.*, 50 N.Y.U. J. INT'L L. & POL. 159 (2017).

the United States should deny immunity to the exporters accordingly. In most circumstances, however, the exporting country and the United States will not have perfectly aligned interests; they may have only partially aligned interests or even completely conflicting interests. Moreover, in the game between the exporting country and the United States, the former may have an incentive to protect domestic manufacturers that have solicited government statements in the hope of receiving immunity from antitrust liabilities. This is especially true if the direct communication coming from the exporting country has zero or negligible direct cost, also known as 'cheap talk' in economics.[136] The United States is aware of the incentives that foreign governments have to lie, and thus it will not fully trust the words of the exporting country.

At the same time, a foreign government that has imposed export restraints, either formally or informally, on domestic producers would have the incentive to admit that it has imposed export restraints and coordinated the export cartel. The Chinese Vitamin C case is an ideal example. Indubitably, an admission carries some cost for China; however, it can potentially also help Chinese exporters evade antitrust violations. The Chinese government and Chinese exporters are engaged in a repeated game. As the players will continuously interact with each other in the future, they will need to consider the impact of their current action on the future actions of other players. It also follows that if the Chinese government refuses to defend its domestic firms in US courts, it would lose its credibility among Chinese exporters. Knowing that the government would not bail them out from antitrust liabilities, the exporters would be less likely to comply with the government's instructions in the future. In order to maintain its credibility, the Chinese government is predisposed to defend Chinese manufacturers. This is not to say that the Chinese government does not have any incentive to shield its domestic manufacturers from antitrust liabilities regardless of whether it has imposed such restraints or not.[137] However, other things being equal, the Chinese government is strongly inclined to defend its own firms especially in cases of genuine state-led export cartels, as the failure to do so will hurt its credibility among domestic exporters.

Before the Supreme Court's final verdict in the Vitamin C case, the case law was unclear as to how much legal weight should be accorded to the characterization of foreign laws by national governments. In its decision on *United States v. Pink* in 1942, the Court examined a case regarding the extraterritorial reach of a decree nationalizing Russia's insurance business.[138] The Court viewed the

---

[136] *See generally* Joseph Farrell & Matthew Rabin, *Cheap Talk*, 10 J. ECON. PERSPS. 103 (1996).
[137] *See* Martyniszyn, *supra* note 19, at 307.
[138] United States v. Pink, 315 U.S. 203 (1942).

Russian government's declaration as conclusive evidence of the effects of the decree and did not stop to review other evidence.[139] Several courts, including the Third Circuit and the Fifth Circuit, applied *Pink* to declare that official declarations made by foreign governments must be accepted as 'conclusive'.[140] Likewise, the Department of Justice and the Federal Trade Commission held that such foreign statements are sufficient to establish compulsion, stating that 'the representation must contain enough detail to enable the Agencies to see precisely how the compulsion would be accomplished under foreign law'.[141]

On the other hand, many lower courts continued to maintain that such statements should not necessarily be accepted as conclusive. For instance, the Sixth Circuit[142] and D.C. Circuit[143] have performed independent analyses of the foreign law in question, irrespective of a foreign sovereign's contrary arguments.[144] The Eleventh Circuit held that although a foreign government's amicus brief is the most logical place to look for infallible and accurate information, it is not entitled to conclusive deference.[145] The Seventh Circuit has also previously applied a flexible standard of deference. With regards to *In re Oil Spill by the Amoco Cadiz*, the court deferred to a foreign sovereign's proffered interpretation of its own law only because the foreign government appeared before the federal court and its interpretation was both plausible as well as consistent with its stated views over many years of domestic and international litigation on the subject.[146] Similarly, in a prior decision relating to statements by the Indonesian government, the Second Circuit established that the government's amicus brief was entitled to substantial deference but did not take it as conclusive evidence of compulsion.[147] Notably, this ruling contrasts with its reasoning in the Vitamin C case, in which the Second Circuit firmly held that a US court is bound to defer to the statements of a foreign

---

[139] Id. at 218–20.

[140] D'Angelo v. Petroleos Mexicanos, 422 F. Supp. 1280, 1284 (D. Del. 1976), *aff'd*, 564 F.2d 89 (3d Cir. 1977); *see also* Delgado v. Shell Oil Co., 890 F. Supp. 1324, 1363 (S.D. Tex. 1995), *aff'd*, 231 F.3d 165 (5th Cir. 2000).

[141] U.S. Dep't of Justice & Fed. Trade Comm'n, Antitrust Guidelines for International Enforcement and Cooperation § 4.2.2 (13 Jan. 2017).

[142] Chavez v. Carranza, 559 F.3d 486, 495–96 (6th Cir. 2009) (rejecting the argument that the Sixth Circuit was bound to defer to the arguments filed in the Republic of El Salvador's amicus brief).

[143] McKesson HBOC, Inc. v. Islamic Republic of Iran, 271 F.3d 1101, 1108–09 (D.C. Cir. 2001), *cert. denied*, 537 U.S. 941 (2002), *vacated in part on other grounds*, 320 F.3d 280 (D.C. Cir. 2003).

[144] Reply to Brief in Opposition at 6, *In re* Vitamin C Litig., 584 F. Supp. 2d 546, 550 (E.D.N.Y. 2008) (No. 16-1220).

[145] United States v. McNab, 331 F.3d 1228, 1241 (11th Cir. 2003), *cert. denied*, 540 U.S. 1177 (2004).

[146] *In re* Oil Spill by the Amoco Cadiz, 954 F.2d 1279, 1312–13 (7th Cir. 1992).

[147] Karaha Bodas Co. v. Perusahaan Pertambangan Minyak Dan Gas Bumi Negara, 313 F.3d 70, 92 (2d Cir. 2002).

government when it 'directly participates in a U.S. court proceeding', and its interpretation is 'reasonable under the circumstances presented'.[148]

Even though the Supreme Court's decision in the Vitamin C case has clarified that US courts are not bound to treat such statements as conclusive, the question remains: when the factual evidence is ambiguous, how should courts set the benchmark to determine whether a foreign sovereign's involvement in the cartel amounts to the level of compulsion? As explained below, the judicial focus on facts tends to obscure the fundamental question of whether granting a comity-based defence to the foreign exporters is in fact in the best interest of the United States.

4.3 The Optimal Judicial Response

As illustrated by the US government's contrasting stance in regard to Japanese export cartels in the 1980s and in the recent Vitamin C case, the optimal response to export cartels is never fixed as a specific formula. Rather, it is contingent upon the changing political and economic conditions. Thus, US courts should be aware of the risks that their judgments in state-led export cartel cases can have for international relations, especially when the underlying factual circumstances are unclear. However, courts are not institutionally well equipped to make such a cost-benefit analysis. In her remarks at an antitrust conference, Judge Diane Wood, Chief Justice of the Seventh Circuit, acknowledged that it is extremely difficult to ask a court to administer comity as the court's hands are often tied.[149] This implies that US courts should generally defer to the position of the executive branch, which possesses the foreign relations expertise and is in the best position to balance competing interests.

Indeed, in cases involving foreign relations, US courts have traditionally accorded a high level of deference to the executive branch, which is in a superior position to determine strategies for the United States in such cases.[150] Prominent legal scholars including Eric Posner and Cass Sunstein have proposed extending the *Chevron* deference doctrine to executive actions concerning international affairs.[151] In a seminal article, they argue that US courts

---

[148] *In re* Vitamin C Antitrust Litig. (*Vitamin C III*), 837 F.3d 175, 189 (2d Cir. 2016).

[149] Chief Justice Diane P. Wood, *Keynote Speech: What's the Role of Comity in the International Antitrust Enforcement?*, in CONCURRENCES REVIEW & GW LAW, EXTRATERRITORIALITY OF ANTITRUST LAW IN THE UNITED STATES AND ABROAD: A HOT ISSUE 4 (28 Sep. 2015).

[150] *See* Eric A. Posner & Cass R. Sunstein, *Chevronizing Foreign Relations Law*, 116 YALE L.J. 1170, 1202 (2007); *see also* Daniel Abebe & Eric Posner, *The Flaws of Foreign Affairs Legalism*, 51 VA. J. INT'L L. 507, 508 (2011).

[151] *See* Posner & Sunstein, *supra* note 150, at 1204–05.

should only defer to foreign sovereigns' interests after a careful assessment of the consequences. More specifically, they observe that the cost of deference is the loss of US control over certain regulatory activities. In the context of export cartels, granting immunity to foreign producers on the basis of comity implies that the United States cedes control over antitrust regulations, compromising the interests of US consumers. On the other hand, Posner and Sunstein also suggest that the benefits of deference include reciprocal gains from the foreign government's deference to US regulations and the reduction of potential tension with the foreign country. In the context of export cartels, there may be other benefits, such as the governments bailing out failing domestic producers and sheltering them from foreign competition, as illustrated in the Japanese export cartel cases.

This approach of deferring to the executive branch would greatly simplify the current case law, which has focused too narrowly on the foreign sovereign compulsion issue. As shown in the Japanese export cartel cases, a foreign sovereign's involvement in the cartels may not even be relevant. Under certain political and economic circumstances, it might be in the best interests of the United States to encourage export cartels. In fact, the US government concluded a number of VER agreements directly with foreign steel producers in the 1960s, bypassing their governmental counterparts. The appearance of the foreign sovereign in a US court is not necessarily decisive either, as seen in the Vitamin C case. The deference analysis ultimately is influenced by the government's determination of whether the harm on foreign relations resulting from the refusal to defer to the foreign government will outweigh the damage done to domestic consumers if foreign producers are exempt from antitrust litigation.

In practice, with cases involving Chinese state-led export cartels, the executive branch may have already meted out actions against China or Chinese exporters, either through trade or antitrust. Therefore, US courts' optimal response should not be static; rather, they must take into consideration the specific steps the executive branch has undertaken to handle export cartels. More specifically, I propose the following legal framework of comity analysis when courts are presented inconsistent and ambiguous factual evidence in Chinese export cartel cases.

Scenario 1. Has the executive branch brought actions against Chinese exporters for antitrust violations? The executive branch is in a superior position to weigh the costs and benefits of its actions on foreign relations. Therefore, its decision to initiate an antitrust lawsuit sends a clear signal that the challenged conduct is more harmful to the United States than the corresponding damage caused to foreign relations from the antitrust lawsuit.[152] If a US court endorses a comity-based defence under these circumstances, this would conflict directly with the position of the executive branch and undermine the government's efforts to protect domestic consumer welfare.

Scenario 2. Has the executive branch negotiated the imposition of export restraints with China to accommodate the desires of the United States? If so, US courts should refrain from reaching a ruling that might undermine the efforts of the US executive branch. Under unique political circumstances, the United States could negotiate for VER agreements in the hope of avoiding more drastic legislative responses to foreign exports. China may be reluctant to coordinate with the US government unless the latter provides adequate assurances that the comity defence can be availed, and China would not be liable under US antitrust law. In this situation, a comity-based defence such as foreign sovereign compulsion becomes of critical importance for the United States and China to facilitate the establishment of VER agreements.

Scenario 3. Has the US government tried to persuade China to abandon export restraints via diplomatic means or through other multilateral treaty networks such as the WTO? As diplomacy and trade measures are nimbler and more efficient than antitrust litigation in resolving conflicts between exporting and importing countries, US courts should refrain from making decisions that might impede such efforts. Indeed, in *Resco Products*, the US district court suspended the antitrust suit to await the resolution of such disputes through diplomatic means or trade remedies.

Scenario 4. If the executive branch has not taken any action through either trade or antitrust, US courts are then advised to solicit opinions from the executive branch. In the Vitamin C case, the Second Circuit chose to defer to MOFCOM's statements for fear of developing new tensions with the Chinese government. The Second Circuit however, had attempted to make such a judgment on international relations on its own. As the executive branch's amicus brief to the Supreme Court revealed, in this particular case, the executive branch did not appear to deem that the harms of not deferring to the Chinese government outweighed US interests in the prosecution of antitrust violations. In this respect, the Supreme Court made precisely the right move by proactively seeking the opinion of the executive branch before making its final decision.

---

[152] United States' Amicus Brief in *Matsushita Electric, supra* note 76, at 23.

As discussed earlier in this chapter, the US government did not seem interested in imposing trade restraints on Chinese vitamin C products as US companies no longer compete with the Chinese manufacturers in the vitamin C market. In fact, tariffs placed on vitamin C imports from China could actually hurt US producers as their dietary supplement products include vitamin C as one of its ingredients.[153] But the US position on Chinese pharmaceutical imports could change. The outbreak of COVID-19 and its consequent disruption to the global supply chains have caused the US government to reconsider its heavy reliance on China for essential medical supplies.[154] If the US government decides to scale up the manufacturing capacities of US-based facilities producing vitamin C and other essential drugs in order to reduce its dependence on Chinese imports, then the US government could even decide that it is worth sacrificing the interests of its consumers to protect national health security. Notably, the supply shortage during the COVID-19 pandemic has led to increased scrutiny by the United States over its reliance on China for not only medical supplies but also other general essential products. This echoed calls from the Trump Administration, which has long been pushing US companies to bring manufacturing back from overseas. But this is much easier said than done, and experts have expressed reservations about such a proposal.[155] As a consequence, the US stance on Chinese export cartels can be highly fluid, depending on future US trade policy.

The legal framework I propose above, however, is designed with the assumption that the United States cannot simultaneously pursue trade and antitrust remedies, as these are mutually exclusive remedies that would undercut each other under the multilateral trading framework of the WTO. However, with the United States crippling the appellate functions of the WTO and instead resorting primarily to bilateral negotiation to deal with China, the US government may be less concerned about the possible spillover effects of the antitrust proceeding on its trade claims and vice versa. Amid the escalating Sino-US tensions and the US government's new initiatives to uproot global supply chains based in China, there is a heightened risk that Chinese exporters might be subject to more challenges on both trade and antitrust fronts in the years to come.

---

[153] Hank Schultz, *Tariffs Will Benefit Competitors, Drive Manufacturing Offshore, NPA to Testify Today* (21 Aug. 2018).

[154] Huang, *supra* note 4.

[155] Willy C. Shih, *Bringing Manufacturing Back to the U.S. is Easier Said than Done*, HARV. BUSINESS REV. (15 April 2020).

Summary

For many US citizens, the COVID-19 pandemic is a wake-up call regarding the country's heavy reliance on China for medical supplies.[156] Thus far, the US government has yet to formulate a clear strategy in dealing with the systematic risks posed by China's central role in the global supply chains. The Vitamin C case is one of the latest examples where Chinese exporters were accused of having orchestrated a cartel to raise prices exploiting US consumers. Although the Chinese government was allegedly involved in directing the cartel, US courts struggled to determine the scope of its involvement and whether it equated to compulsion. When MOFCOM came to the rescue by boldly admitting its compulsion of these exporters to fix prices, it further raised comity-related questions about deference to a foreign sovereign.

In this chapter, I have explained the complicated dynamics between antitrust and trade issues prevalent in Chinese export cartel cases by delving into China's macroeconomic landscape and the difficulties besetting it. Chronic overcapacity, a persistent issue emanating from China's highly decentralized economic structure and its state-led governance model, has been the main impetus for the government's organization of export cartels. This inherent structural problem in the Chinese economy exposes Chinese exporters to a catch-22 dilemma. If they compete fiercely and price low, they could be subject to antidumping duties, but if they coordinate with each other to raise prices, they could be subject to antitrust challenges.

US courts, however, have struggled to deal with this facet of the Chinese antitrust exceptionalism. Much of the US judicial response to state-led export cartels has been more or less static, and judges have often failed to appreciate the dynamic features of these cases. Judges have also tended to fixate on the factual issue of compulsion, thereby giving inadequate consideration to other dimensions, such as trade and politics. But whether a US court should abstain from exercising its jurisdiction and defer to the interests of the foreign sovereign should depend on the specific circumstances of the particular case, taking into account the interests of all players involved, while recognizing the strategic nature of their decision-making. Since the executive branch is in the best position to reconcile competing interests, this explains why the US Supreme Court decided to accord a high level of deference to the executive branch in

---

[156] Uri Friedman, *China Hawks Are Calling the Coronavirus a 'Wake-Up Call'*, THE ATLANTIC (11 Mar. 2020).

the Vitamin C case. Inevitably, this deferential approach means that the outcome of such cases will turn not only on law but also politics. With the near collapse of the WTO and rising US–China tensions, there is a heightened risk that Chinese exporters could be subject to more trade and antitrust challenges in the years to come.

PART III

REGULATORY INTERDEPENDENCE

In this Part, I will return to the analysis of China's antitrust law, albeit in a different context, showing that there exists a close interdependence between the regulatory moves of the United States and those of China. In addition to launching a trade war against China, the United States is aggressively claiming extraterritorial jurisdiction over Chinese technology companies and executives, and China is now emulating this practice by wielding its antitrust law to demonstrate its own extraterritorial regulatory capacity.

PART III

REGULATORY INTERDEPENDENCE

5

Weaponizing Antitrust During
the Sino-US Tech War

In Chapters 1 and 2, I illustrated how Chinese antitrust agencies, in their relentless drive to expand their policy control, have applied the Anti-Monopoly
Law (AML) not just as part of Chinese competition policy but also as a tool
for price control and market stabilization. In this chapter, I will demonstrate
an additional function of the AML: its use as an instrument of trade and foreign policy. In the following discussion, I will present this specific facet of the
Chinese antitrust exceptionalism and the versatility of the law by situating my
analysis within the context of the Sino-US tech rivalry.

Since the eruption of the Sino-US trade war in 2018, President Donald
Trump has accused China of unfair trade practices, forced technology
transfer, and intellectual property theft. China, on the other hand, believes
that America started the trade war to curtail its rise as an economic superpower. The Trump Administration then proceeded to impose tariffs on hundreds of billions of dollars' worth of Chinese goods and China retaliated in
kind. As the Sino-US trade dispute continues to dominate global headlines,
another contemporaneous threat to Chinese companies exists: America's aggressive prosecution of Chinese technology companies and individuals for
violations of US laws, which has transformed into an important component
of the Sino-US tech war.

In March 2017, the US Department of Commerce levied a USD 1.19 billion
fine on ZTE, a Chinese technology company specializing in telecommunication, for violating US trade sanctions after exporting US-made technology to
Iran and North Korea. This is the largest US fine ever imposed for the violation of export control sanctions. Subsequently, the Department of Commerce
found that ZTE breached its compliance commitments by giving bonuses to
some of the employees involved in the violations. After this information surfaced, the Department of Commerce prohibited ZTE from importing components originating from US suppliers for a period of seven years. With almost
30 per cent of the components in ZTE's products originating from the United

Chinese Antitrust Exceptionalism. Angela Huyue Zhang, Oxford University Press (2021). © Angela Huyue Zhang.
DOI: 10.1093/oso/9780198826569.003.0006

States, the crippling technology ban endangered ZTE's business. The firm was forced to suspend major operations in early May 2018.

These harsh sanctions placed on ZTE were only the beginning of the tech war and were followed by a series of aggressive prosecutions of leading Chinese technology firms. On 1 December 2018, the Canadian police detained Meng Wanzhou, the chief financial officer (CFO) of Huawei, a Chinese information and communications giant, at Vancouver Airport, upon receiving an extradition request from the US government. The arrest of Meng angered the Chinese government, which spewed harsh rhetoric aimed at the Canadian government. As revealed in a subsequent court proceeding, a New York court issued an arrest warrant for Meng in August 2018 based on allegations that Meng intentionally concealed attempts made by Huawei subsidiaries to sell equipment to Iran in violation of US sanctions. The US Department of Justice then unveiled sweeping indictments against Meng for defrauding several banks in order to skirt US sanctions against Iran.[1] In separate indictments, Huawei and a few of its subsidiaries were also charged for orchestrating an elaborate decade-long scheme to evade US sanctions on Iran, stealing trade secrets from T-mobile and obstructing a criminal investigation.[2] Taken together, these imputations portray Huawei as a deeply corrupt company that had disregarded US laws.

While the United States may have had valid legal justification to pursue ZTE and Huawei,[3] these cases have also coincided with an aggressive US campaign aimed at Chinese technology companies. For some time now, the United States has been urging its allies in Europe and Asia to bar Huawei from building 5G computer and phone networks in their countries. In June 2018, the White House issued a report entitled 'How China's Economic Aggression Threatens the Technologies and Intellectual Property of the United States and the World'.[4] The report denounced China, accusing her of engaging in technology and intellectual property theft through economic espionage, evasion of US export control laws, and counterfeiting and piracy, in addition to coercive and intrusive regulatory gambits to force technology transfer, among other things. Given the sweeping power and discretion of the US authorities, speculations abounded that Huawei and ZTE were being exploited by the Trump Administration as

---

[1] U.S. Dep't of Justice Press Release, *Chinese Telecommunications Conglomerate Huawei and Huawei CFO Wanzhou Meng Charged with Financial Fraud* (28 Jan. 2019). Many of the footnote references in this book are online materials and they can be easily accessible online.

[2] David E. Sanger et al., *Huawei and Top Executive Face Criminal Charges in the U.S.*, N.Y. TIMES (28 Jan. 2019).

[3] Julian Ku, *The Detention of Huawei's CFO is Legally Justified. Why Doesn't the U.S. Say So?* LAWFARE BLOG (12 Dec. 2018).

[4] White House, *How China's Economic Aggression Threatens the Technologies and Intellectual Property of the United States and the World* (June 2018).

potential bargaining chips in exchange for favourable terms during trade ne-gotiations.[5] President Trump's statements about his intention to intervene in these cases sent a clear signal that his administration was willing to utilize law enforcement as a tool for geopolitical purposes.

With the US exertion of extraterritorial jurisdiction over Huawei and ZTE generating heated discussions in China, Chinese policy-makers and scholars are now advocating for strong countermeasures to retaliate against US aggres-sion.[6] While China has yet to adopt any sanction-specific measures, the AML has emerged as a powerful weapon that can be used in China's regulatory re-sponse. China is not the first country to employ its antitrust regulations as a strategic tool to advance trade policy. In Chapter 4, we see how the US govern-ment promised to grant antitrust immunity to Japanese exporters in the 1980s in order to persuade the Japanese government to impose voluntary export restraints. These export restraints raised the prices of Japanese exports, thus shielding US domestic manufacturers from Japanese competition. However, unlike the US government, whose antitrust enforcement was deactivated to assure the Japanese government, the Chinese government is doing the exact opposite by enhancing the sanctioning power of the AML and invigorating its antitrust enforcement. In fact, the Chinese government has regarded the AML as a potent economic weapon that can be readily and easily implemented as a component of its tit-for-tat strategy against the United States during the trade war.

As President Xi Jinping reportedly told a group of chief executives of American and European multinationals at a gathering in June 2018: 'In the West you have the notion that if somebody hits you on the left cheek, you turn the other check. In our culture we punch back.'[7] So what is the rationale be-hind China's decision to return America's fire? How does China use its anti-trust law to exert influence? Is there a limit of China's regulatory response? In this chapter, I will attempt to answer these questions by applying game theory analysis of conflict and cooperation. I draw heavily upon the insights from Thomas Schelling, a renowned economist who won the Nobel prize in 2005 for applying game theory to the study of war and peace.[8]

---

[5] Julia Horowitz, *Companies Become Bargaining Chips in US–China Turmoil*, CNN (27 May 2018); Editorial, Donald Trump Makes Huawei CFO Meng Wanzhou A Bargaining Chip, FIN. TIMES (13 Dec. 2018).

[6] Wencai Zhao, *Long-Arm Jurisdiction Exposes U.S. Law of the Jungle Mentality*, XINHUA (9 June 2016); Guoyou Song, *U.S. Long-Arm Jurisdiction Must Be Combatted*, GLOBAL TIMES (16 Jan. 2019).

[7] Lingling Wei & Yoko Kubota, *China's Xi Tell CEOs that He'll Strike Back at the U.S.*, WALL ST. J. (25 June 2018).

[8] THOMAS SCHELLING, THE STRATEGY OF CONFLICT (1960).

Schelling is a pioneer who revolutionized how we should think about conflict resolution. In contrast to realists in international relations theory who stress the material foundations of power, Schelling perceives most conflicts as a strategic bargaining situation.[9] Essentially, such bargaining is a process of influence through which actors attempt to resolve a conflict. Schelling was also the first to propose that the bargaining process can be explicit or tacit.[10] The ongoing Sino-US trade negotiation involving formal diplomatic exchanges between the two countries is an example of an explicit bargain. Worth noting is that a bargain is tacit when there is no explicit negotiation between the countries, or when there exists some communication but the negotiation remains incomplete.[11] In such circumstances, it is the actions, rather than rhetoric, that constitute the main medium of communication.[12] To put this into perspective, when the United States imposed sanctions on Chinese technology companies and used such cases as bargaining chips during trade talks, there was no formal diplomatic dialogue between the countries on the subject of dispute resolution. After all, the handling of sanctions is ostensibly a matter for the US government and its judicial branch and is an internal affair. This, however, does not mean that China cannot exert influence. In the event that China responds aggressively and threatens to retaliate in kind, the US government and courts will not ignore such grievances completely, something that could then affect their next move. The interdependent actions of the two countries can therefore be viewed as a tacit bargain.

In his seminal work, *The Strategy of Conflict*, Schelling often makes interesting analogies between the criminal underworld and international relations. Just like the criminal underworld, the international system lacks a central authority such as an enforceable legal system that can resolve conflicts arising between countries embroiled in a dispute.[13] That said, repeated interactions between the countries could act as an enforcement mechanism. If a country expects that it will repeatedly engage with the other in the near future, this forethought could cast a long shadow over the present negotiations and affect the countries' strategic moves today.[14]

Indeed, in response to America's waywardness in applying its sanctions laws as an instrument of trade and foreign policy, China has settled on a rather

---

[9] Id. at 5.

[10] Id.

[11] Id. at 53.

[12] George W. Downs & David M. Rocke, *Tacit Bargaining and Arms Control*, 39 WORLD POLITICS 297, 297 (1987).

[13] *See* Schelling, *supra* note 8, at 12; *see also* ROBERT AXELROD, THE EVOLUTION OF COOPERATION 4 (1984).

[14] AXELROD, *supra* note 13, at 12.

unyielding approach. The Chinese antitrust authority has been flexing its regulatory muscles by holding up multi-billion-dollar merger transactions between large multinationals, amending provisions in the AML to allow for high monetary fines and potential criminal liabilities, and threatening to impose heavy antitrust sanctions on firms that boycott or refuse to supply key components to Chinese technology companies. As such, the line between national security and antitrust policy, once belonging to separate spheres, is becoming increasingly blurred amid the growing Sino-US trade tension.

The rest of my discussion will proceed as follows. I will first explain how the United States, particularly the Trump Administration, has adopted an aggressive legal strategy against Chinese technology companies. The US executive branch, in particular, uses its wide discretion in prosecuting companies as an instrument of trade and foreign policy. I then move on to describe China's tit-for-tat strategy of invoking a number of regulatory weapons to retaliate against US aggression. As illustrated by China's withholding of the merger approval of Qualcomm's attempted acquisition of NXP, an American–Dutch semiconductor manufacturer, antitrust law has been wielded as a powerful economic weapon in China's regulatory response. Moreover, China is in the process of revising its AML to strengthen its punitive power still further. The AML could therefore serve as an even more potent economic weapon in the future. Finally, I touch on the limits of China's countermeasures. Much like other countries that have tried to counter US sanctions, China faces significant economic constraints in weaponizing its law against US businesses. Attacking US businesses with antitrust law will harm China's reputation and undermine its long-term strategy of attracting more foreign investment. I therefore predict that the AML will, at its fullest extent, only be applied to fight a limited war with the United States rather than being turned into a weapon of mass retaliation.

1. US Coercive Strategies

The United States prides itself as a country where the rule of law is respected and followed. However, the US system of checks and balances is discounted on matters involving international affairs. The US judicial branch tends to give high deference to the executive branch in cases concerning national security, giving the latter broad discretion in prosecuting foreign businesses and executives. This also gives rise to temptation for the Trump Administration to employ its prosecutorial discretion strategically for geopolitical purposes.

1.1 The Long Arm of US Law

For many, the arrest of Meng Wanzhou, the CFO of Huawei, came as a surprise. It is very unusual to arrest a top executive for violating US sanctions.[15] But her arrest was not predicated on the violation of economic sanctions but rather bank fraud. In fact, the implicating evidence that led to the fraud charges against Meng and Huawei had been obtained from HSBC, the bank that represented Huawei at the time of misconduct.[16] In 2013, Meng delivered a presentation to HSBC bankers to assure them that Huawei was not carrying out any business with Iran. During the probe into Huawei, HSBC disclosed the very presentation submitted by Meng denying any links with Iran to the Department of Justice along with all Huawei's transactions in Iran. HSBC's readiness to cooperate with the US government was partly driven by its fear of breaching more US sanctions laws. In 2012, the bank was fined USD 1.9 billion for failing to prevent money laundering lapses in countries such as Iran. However, by claiming that it had been misled by Huawei, the HSBC could distance itself from the crime and US officials could elect not to prosecute the bank. Even though HSBC was defrauded, it suffered no losses. To the contrary: HSBC most likely profited from its business dealings with Huawei. Thus, the Department of Justice in fact applied an innovative no-loss bank fraud theory to Huawei and its executives.[17] Using bank fraud charges significantly expands the prosecutorial discretion of the US federal government, since the statute of limitation for bank fraud is ten years, twice as long as the five-year penalty for sanctions violations. As such, it allows prosecutors to cast a much wider net over foreign entities that dupe banks into processing transactions in the United States.

Notably, both the ZTE and Huawei cases involved contravening US sanctions against Iran. Even though the Chinese companies' alleged transactions with Iran occurred outside the United States, the US authority was able to enforce its law extraterritorially, exercising the so-called long-arm jurisdiction.[18] Such extraterritorial reach of the US sanctions laws is often founded

---

[15] David E. Sanger et al., *Huawei and Top Executive Face Criminal Charges in the U.S.*, N.Y. TIMES (28 Jan. 2019); Jeffery D. Sachs, *The War On Huawei*, PROJECT SYNDICATE (11 Dec. 2018).

[16] Matthew Goldstein et al., *How A National Security Investigation of Huawei Set Off An International Incident*, N.Y. TIMES (14 Dec. 2018).

[17] Brian Frey, *Huawei Indictments Signalled U.S. Government Commitment to Prosecuting Chinese companies*, BIGLAWBUSINESS.COM (13 Feb. 2019).

[18] Bruce Zagaris, *The Merging of the Anti-Money Laundering and Counter-Terrorism Financial Enforcement Regimes after September 11*, 22 BERKELEY J. INT'L L. 123 (2001); *see also* Meredith Rathbone et al., *Sanctions, Sanctions Everywhere: Forging A Path Through Complex Transnational Sanctions Law*, 44 GEO. J. INT'L L. 1055 (2013).

on weak links with the United States, for example, the use of the US financial clearing system.[19] In fact, US authorities have applied sanctions laws to
transactions overseas even when these dealings had nothing to do with the
United States whatsoever.[20] As Henry Farrell and Abraham Newman describe in their influential article 'Weaponized Interdependence', the politics
of sanctions has been transformed by globalization.[21] Countries that previously imposed sanctions restricting access to their internal market can now
exclude another country from the global network by leveraging control over
key hubs in global networks.[22] These networks include the dollar clearing
system, the SWIFT financial network, or Google and its Android operating
system.[23] Since the attack on 11 September, the United States has started
weaponizing this economic interdependence.[24] For example, the vast majority of global foreign exchange transactions involve the US dollar. As such,
depriving access to dollars would be fatal to any financial institution involved
in international payments. This strategy has successfully allowed the United
States, often with the help of its European allies, to isolate enemy states such
as Iran and North Korea.

At the same time, America's weaponization of its unique position as an
important hub within the global network has sparked a great deal of controversy.[25] In fact, there has been suspicion that US counter-terrorist financing
measures have been used to weaken foreign business rivals. A case in point
is the disproportionately high penalty on BNP Paribas in 2014.[26] The French
bank was alleged to have facilitated payments for Iran, Sudan, and Cuba contravening US sanctions and it received a fine amounting to USD 8.9 billion, more
than the profit it made in the previous year. The bank was banned from dollar
clearing for the year, forcing it to reroute transactions via other banks. BNP
Paribas is just one in a long list of European banks that have received heavy
penalties for US sanctions violations, with other prominent targets including
the HSBC, Standard Chartered Bank, ING Bank, Barclays, Credit Suisse, and

---

[19] *See* Rathbone et al., *supra* note 18, at 1111.
[20] Id. at 1113.
[21] Henry Farrell & Abraham L. Newman, *Weaponized Interdependence: How Global Economic Networks Shape State Coercion*, 44 INT'L SECURITY 42 (2019).
[22] Id.
[23] Id. at 47.
[24] Suzanne Katzenstein, *Dollar Unilateralism: The New Frontline of National Security*, 90 IND. L. J. 293, 293 (2014). *See also* Joanna Diane Caytas, *Weaponizing Finance: U.S. and European Options, Tools and Policies*, 23 COLM. J. EUR. L. 441, 442.
[25] *See* Caytas, *supra* note 24, at 458–60.
[26] Capital Punishment, THE ECONOMIST (5 July 2014).

Lloyds TSB.[27] Strikingly, all these sanction cases against European banks were resolved with settlements.

Furthermore, the decisions of the US Department of the Treasury's Office of Foreign Assets Control (OFAC), responsible for administrating trade restrictions against sanctioned countries, are rarely challenged. The OFAC is regarded as a subject-matter expert and judges generally defer to its decisions rather than second-guessing its rulings on specific issues. In fact, a federal court usually only overturns an administrative decision if it is found to be 'arbitrary, capricious, an abuse of discretion, or otherwise not in accordance with law'.[28] This sets the bar quite high, especially because access to the administration's evidence can be restricted due to national security or foreign policy concerns. The combination of the exceedingly high evidentiary standard and the secrecy around the entire administrative process therefore makes it extremely difficult to challenge OFAC. Thus, the sweeping prosecutorial power of OFAC and the lack of due process have raised serious reservations about the legitimacy of the US measures and prosecutions.[29] Scholars are warning that use of financial tools by the United States, which originated as emergency measures for the purpose of preserving vital national interests, could be abused for the convenience of putting forward auxiliary law enforcement and political objectives.[30]

In addition to sanctions laws, the United States can exert long-arm jurisdiction on foreign entities and their executives through other laws related to export control, national security reviews of foreign investment, and anti-corruption and securities regulation. Increasing evidence has shown that US aggressive enforcement of the Foreign Corruption Practice Act (FCPA) against foreign firms could confer a competitive advantage on US firms.[31] Empirical evidence further reveals that foreign corporations have received disproportionally larger penalties under the FCPA, after controlling for other variables that affect the size of the penalty.[32] Among the ten largest monetary penalties imposed under the FCPA, nine were levied on foreign companies. As in sanction cases, most of these FCPA cases were settled and are, in general, rarely

---

[27] See Alacra, *Enforcement Actions for U.S. Sanctions Violations Offer Lessons for Compliance*, Issue 3, https://www.alacra.com/alacra/help/alacracomplianceprimer3.pdf.

[28] See Administrative Procedure Act, 5 U.S.C. § 706(2)A (1966); *see also* Vanessa Baehr-Jones, *Mission Possible: How Intelligence Evidence Rules Can Save UN Terrorist Sanctions*, 2 HARV. NAT'L SECURITY J. 447, 467 (2011); Caytas, *supra* note 24, at 459 and its accompanying footnotes.

[29] See Human Rights Watch, *In the Name of Security: Counterterrorism Laws Worldwide Since September 11* (2012); *see also* Caytas, *supra* note 24, at 459.

[30] See also Caytas, *supra* note 24, at 445.

[31] Rebecca Perlman & Alan Sykes, *The Political Economy of the Foreign Corrupt Practice Act*, 9 J. LEGAL ANALYSIS 153, 176 (2018).

[32] Stephen J. Choi & Kevin E. Davis, *Foreign Affairs and Enforcement of the Foreign Corrupt Practices Act*, 11 J. EMPIRICAL LEGAL STUD. 409 (2014).

challenged in court. On 1 November 2018, the Department of Justice announced a new 'China Initiative', designed to target a host of regulatory and criminal violations pertaining to China.[33] One of the many goals of the China Initiative is to identify FCPA cases 'involving Chinese companies that compete with American businesses'. This represents a paradigm policy shift for the Department of Justice, which previously denied any assertions that its enforcement directed at companies from a particular country.[34] In light of the China Initiative, practitioners have cautioned that Chinese companies operating outside of China, especially those involved in the 'Belt and Road initiative', could become potential targets of future FCPA enforcement.[35] This gives rise to further concern that the Department of Justice is becoming an instrument of foreign policy taking aim at the geopolitical adversaries of the United States.[36]

When US laws afford the administration such wide prosecutorial discretion, businesses and executives then become open targets and are vulnerable to regulatory attack. Without rigorous judicial checks, there is a danger that such administrative discretion could be strategically employed to promote commercial and geopolitical interests, as shown in Trump's brinkmanship during the technological war with China.

1.2 Trump's Brinkmanship

On 13 May 2018, President Trump tweeted that he and President Xi Jinping of China would be 'working together to give massive Chinese phone company, ZTE, a way to get back into business, fast'.[37] After receiving a storm of criticisms for his tweet, President Trump defending his endeavours to save ZTE by further tweeting that the company 'buys a big percentage of individual parts from U.S. companies' and that it is 'also reflective of the larger trade deal we are negotiating with China and my personal relationship with President Xi'.[38] On 7 June 2018, the Department of Commerce rescinded the sanctions against ZTE. In return, ZTE paid out another USD 1 billion fine, placed USD

---

[33] Department of Justice, Information About the *Department of Justice's China Initiative and Compilation of China-related Prosecutions Since 2018* (22 June 2020).

[34] Jodi Wu et al., *A Shift in U.S. FCPA Policy—Should Chinese Companies Be Worried*, KIRKLAND & ELLIS (10 June 2019).

[35] Eric Carlson, *National Security: Are Chinese Companies Targeted for FCPA enforcement?* FCPABLOG. COM (8 Nov. 2018).

[36] K& L Gates LL.P, *DOJ v. China: Is DOJ Acting As An Instrument of Foreign Policy?* (3 Oct. 2019).

[37] Ana Swanson et al., *Trump Shifts from Trade War Threats to Concessions in Rebuff to Hardliners*, N.Y. TIMES (14 May 2018).

[38] Jessica Dye, *Trump Responds to Criticism of ZTE U-Turn*, FIN. TIMES (15 May 2018).

400 million of suspended penalty money in escrow, replaced its entire senior management, and agreed to embed a new team of compliance officers hand-picked by the Department. The dramatic turn in the ZTE case represents a significant departure from the presidential norm as US presidents rarely reverse decisions made by government agencies. Along similar lines, though President Trump said he had been unaware of US request to extradite Meng and case developments, on several occasions he hinted that he had the ability to retract the case against Meng as part of the trade deal with China. In fact, five days after the arrest of Meng in Vancouver, the US President informed a group of reporters: 'If I think it is good for what will be certainly the largest trade deal ever made—which is a very important thing—what's good for national security, I would certainly intervene if I thought it was necessary.'[39] Clearly, President Trump's statements suggest that national security can be traded for commercial interest.

While President Trump's statements are highly controversial, his action can in fact be rationalized as brinkmanship, a dangerous and delicate balancing act that consists of 'a deliberate and controlled loss of control'.[40] As game theorists state, brinkmanship is the strategy of exposing oneself and one's opponent to 'a gradually increasing risk of mutual harm'.[41] To make his threat credible, the strategist needs to lose control over the potential realization of the bad outcome, in other words he must be willing to risk a loss. At the same time, the strategist needs to control the probability of the disastrous outcome occurring. Thus, for the brinkmanship scheme to be successful, the strategist making the threat must have control over the loss of control such that the risk of a disastrous outcome is at a level acceptable to him.[42] The Cuban missile crisis of 1962 offers a prime example of brinkmanship.[43] In an attempt to compel the Soviet Union to withdraw its missiles from Cuba, the United States threatened a nuclear war. It drove the Soviet Union to the brink of disaster. In doing so, the United States risked becoming involved in a nuclear war but managed that risk in a controlled and deliberate manner.

President Trump has skilfully employed this kind of brinkmanship during the tech war. In his capacity as President, he sets the broad policy agenda

---

[39] Steve Holland et al., *Trump Says Would Intervene in Arrest of Chinese Executive*, REUTERS (12 Dec. 2018).
[40] Schelling, *supra* note 8, at 200.
[41] Avanish Dixit et al., *'We Haven't Got But One More Day', The Cuban Missile Crisis As A Dynamic Chicken Game* (3 Nov. 2019), https://papers.ssrn.com/sol3/papers.cfm?abstract_id=3406265, at 23.
[42] Id.
[43] Id.

that shapes prosecutorial priorities, one of which is to take a more aggressive stance against China. Once the policy agenda is determined, however, a President does not normally interpose himself in the investigation of specific cases. Even if President Trump could, in theory, give orders to the Department of Justice, he will face heavy criticism from the media and political opposition for interfering in the enforcement of law. Indeed, there is currently a heated, scholarly debate about whether the US president holds authority over the ultimate conduct and disposition of all criminal investigations.[44] Some commentators have argued that, from a historical perspective, the Department of Justice is independent of the President and its investigations and decisions are largely immune from presidential interference.[45] This is why the Trump Administration's dramatic reversal of the penalty imposed on ZTE generated so much controversy. In fact, a clear lack of coordination between President Trump and the Department of Justice was exhibited when the United States requested Meng Wanzhou's extradition. In an apparent coincidence, Meng was arrested on the day President Trump and President Xi Jinping met for dinner during the G-20 Summit in Buenos Aires, the same day Chinese delegates were expected to arrive in Washington to negotiate deals and finalize trade discussions.

Thus, Trump's delegation of the prosecutorial authority to the Department of Justice has made his threat more credible. He did not seem to be in full control of the situation. Instead, matters were apparently left to chance, rendering the outcome of Huawei and Meng's case unpredictable. In response to the extradition request, the Chinese government hit back with angry protests and arrested several Canadian citizens in an effort to prevent Canada from extraditing Meng. However, President Trump could not be seen to have lost control of the situation. For his brinkmanship to succeed, he needed to convince the Chinese government that if it yielded, it was in his power to de-escalate the crisis. Without this assurance, China would not consider cooperating with the United States to secure a trade deal as the crisis would deteriorate if neither party had a degree of control over events and the desired result. This, I believe, explains why President Trump sent clear messages to the Chinese government that he could intervene in the extradition order if he so pleased, in order to persuade the Chinese government to reach amicable deal with him.

---

[44] Bruce A. Green & Rebecca Roiphe, *May Federal Prosecutors Take Direction from the President?* 87 FORDHAM L. REV. 1817, 1819 (2019).

[45] *See* Bruce A. Green & Rebecca Roiphe, *Can The President Control The Department of Justice?* 70 ALABAMA L. REV. 1, 1 (2018).

2. China's Tit-for-Tat Strategy

In response to US hostility, China has chosen to retaliate tit-for-tat. Such a strategy simultaneously consists of a promise and a threat: if the United States does nothing, then neither will China; conversely, if the United States attacks, so will China. One of the most famous examples of this strategy is the 'live-and-let-live' system that emerged during the trench warfare in the First World War.[46] There, it was observed that cooperation is possible even amongst antagonists. Soldiers on the frontline defied orders from their higher command and refrained from shooting at the enemy as long as their opponents reciprocated.

To deter America's aggressive strategy of stifling Chinese leading technology companies, China has a few regulatory tools at its disposal. One of them is the AML which has emerged as a powerful economic weapon allowing the Chinese authority to exercise extraterritorial jurisdiction over foreign multinationals. The coercive capacity of the AML is expected to increase, given that a pending amendment to its powers would enhance its punitive capacities.

2.1 The Folk Theorem

To illustrate China's tit-for-tat strategy, consider the following hypothetical game between the United States and China.[47] In this game, the United States makes the first move, and it must decide whether it will maintain the status quo of accommodating the rise of China or take a more aggressive stance in order to deter China from acting in a way that would harm US interests. In this hypothetical game, if the United States keeps to the status quo, both countries will receive the same payoff score of 10. However, if the United States takes an aggressive approach, it will receive a score of 15 and China will obtain a score of 1. China must then decide whether to punish the United States, which will harm both itself and the United States. If China chooses to punish the United States, then both countries gain nothing. While the cooperative outcome yields the highest joint payoffs for the two countries, this equilibrium cannot be achieved in a one-shot game. If the game is only played once, then the United States' dominant strategy will be one of aggression in which it will receive the largest advantage. In this scenario, United States will obtain the maximum

---

[46] AXELROD, *supra* note 13, at 21.

[47] This example is inspired by the tit-for-tat example given by Robert J. Aumann, Nobel Prize winner in 2005 in his prize lecture *War And Peace*, PRIZE LECTURE (8 Dec. 2015).

payoff of 15. China will not be content but it is better off acquiescing and collecting a payoff of 1 instead of being left with zero gain. However, in reality, the United States and China are repeatedly and continuously interacting with each other in this relationship. Given that this game involves an infinite number of interactions, China will opt for a different strategy to fulfil its objectives. It will choose to punish the United States, in which case the United States will obtain nothing. In anticipation of being punished by China, the United States will modify its strategy to tolerate China's rise, as a result of which China will acquiesce, achieving a payoff of 10 for both players. The key to maintaining this equilibrium is the implicit threat of punishment, and peace is only possible if China has the capacity to retaliate against any US aggression. This logic applied during the Cold War. In his Nobel Peace Prize lecture, Robert Aumann said: 'In the long years of the cold war between the US and the Soviet Union, what prevented "hot" war was that bombers carrying nuclear weapons were in the air 24 hours a day, 365 days a year. Disarming would have led to a war.'[48]

But there is one important caveat: the discount rates for the two countries cannot be too high. For example, if the United States is very impatient, then it will still be worthwhile for it to attack Chinese technology companies. For instance, if America's discount rate is over 67 per cent, the entire punishment at its present value is worth less than 5, which is all that the United States can gain today by attacking China. Therefore, if we assume that the parties engaged in an infinitely repeated game are patient and far-sighted enough, the cooperative outcome is achievable in equilibrium. Repeated interaction acts as an enforcement mechanism for a cooperative outcome.[49] This is also known as the folk theorem because it was widely known among game theorists. A key insight of the folk theorem is that any player who does not carry out his punishment will be punished by the other player for its failure to do so.[50] This motivates players to carry out the punishments, making their threat more credible while keeping each other on edge.

Accordingly, there are three important lessons that can be drawn from this hypothetical scenario. First, China must strike back in the event of US aggression, otherwise it might be punished for its failure to do so and in turn face heightened US aggression in the future. This, indeed, echoes the official line from the highest echelon of China's Communist Party. Second, the Chinese threat must be large enough to deter US aggression. If, however, China appears

---

[48] Id. at 351.
[49] Id. at 354.
[50] Id. at 356.

to lack commitment to execute its threat, the United States may then decide that it is still better off attacking China today. For instance, if the costs and the risks associated with carrying out the punishment are very high, and China might back down, then the threat will appear less tenable to the United States. Third, China must react quickly so that the United States promptly senses the pains, since the Trump Administration appears impatient and near-sighted. Given China's limited capacity to strike back with its own tariff sanctions, China needs to sharpen its economic weapons in order to swiftly retaliate against US aggression.

In the past, China has leveraged its expansive market access for its reprisals against other countries. As described by Barry Naughton, a renowned China expert: "China has established almost a kind of tit-for-tat machinery so that carefully calibrated punishment can be meted out to counterparts".[51] The example Naughton provided was China's retaliation against South Korea. In July 2016, South Korea made a public announcement that it was installing an American anti-missile system to intercept missiles from North Korea. This move irked the Chinese government which perceived the deployment as a security threat and a way for the United States to extend its interests into Asia. In response, China imposed a number of economic sanctions on South Korea.

Lotte, a company that agreed to allow its golf course in South Korea to be converted into a missile base, was directly targeted in this particular backlash. In December 2016, Lotte was obliged to suspend the construction and development of a large theme park project in Shenyang after the local government claimed that the project had not followed administrative procedures properly. In early 2017, Lotte was also fined for its advertising practices, and it was also forced to shut down 80 per cent of its supermarkets in China due to fire code violations. South Korea endured many such casualties in the aftermath of the installation of the anti-missile system. The Chinese government later imposed a travel ban on South Korea, boycotted South Korean products, and refused to provide licence approvals to South Korean online games for a year. The two countries reached a détente in late 2017. However, it was not until May 2019 that the Shenyang government lifted sanctions. Notably, none of these economic sanctions on South Korean businesses were imposed formally or as part of a bilateral negotiation. They were part of a tacit bargain where the punishment was delivered under the guise of violations of Chinese laws. In other words, China weaponized its various administrative regulations to levy informal economic

---

[51] Barry Naughton, *Economic Policy under Trade War Conditions*, 57 CHINA LEADERSHIP MONITOR (29 Aug. 2018), at 2.

sanctions on South Korean businesses. These Chinese measures constituted a credible threat sufficient enough to cause South Korea to back down. After all, China is South Korea's primary export market, receiving almost a quarter of all South Korea's total exports.

In theory, China could take a similar retaliatory strategy against the United States. Foreign direct investment from the United States to China amounted to USD 284 billion between 1990 and 2019, so China possesses an immense capacity to damage American businesses.[52] Since the start of the trade war, US businesses have complained about the tighter scrutiny they undergo in Chinese customs clearance, as well as more stringent regulation of labour, advertising, and environment matters. For example, it has been reported that Chinese customs officials inspected 100 per cent of the imports of one US car manufacturer, as opposed to just 2 per cent in earlier years. US food importers are also subject to a longer quarantine period at airports, resulting in food spoiling or goods being sent back to the United States.

2.2 Antitrust as a New Economic Weapon

Still, none of the regulatory measures China has inflicted on US firms were administered on the basis of long-arm jurisdiction. To respond in kind, China would need to demonstrate that it can also regulate US business operations beyond its own borders. The AML, promulgated in 2007, has developed into an attractive tool during the tech war. First, the AML allows the Chinese government to exert extra-territorial jurisdiction over foreign businesses.[53] Based on the 'effects doctrine', a principle which originated in the United States, antitrust laws in many jurisdictions allow a country to exercise its jurisdiction over an individual or entity beyond its physical borders as long as the activities have effects within that country's territory.[54] For this reason, even if a merger transaction or a business practice is conducted overseas and has little nexus with China, China can exert its jurisdiction on the mere basis that the participating parties have sufficient sales in the Chinese market. As China has a vast and

---

[52] Rhodium Group, *US FDI in All Chinese Industries from 1990-December 2019*, THE US–CHINA INVESTMENT HUB.

[53] Art. 2, the AML.

[54] This 'effects doctrine' is first applied in an antitrust case decided by Judge Learned Hand in United States v. Aluminium Co. of America, 148 F. 2d 416, 443 (2d Cir., 1945). *See also* Koren Wong-Ervin & Andrew J. Heimert, *Extraterritoriality: Approaches Around the World and Model Analysis*, in CONCURRENCES BOOK HONORING ELEANOR FOX (2020).

lucrative consumer market that few multinational companies can afford to ignore, this gives the Chinese government significant leverage over foreign firms.

Second, antitrust sanctions are powerful and immediate. As discussed in Chapter 1, an inherent characteristic of Chinese antitrust laws is that they empower regulators to impose heavy sanctions on infringing firms. For instance, a multibillion-dollar merger between large multinational companies, which generally requires approvals from multiple jurisdictions, can be held up by China's intentional delay of antitrust approval. Similarly, a foreign firm operating in China can be slapped with hefty fines and harsh conduct remedies for its business practices in violation of the AML. Under the AML, the fining ceiling is elastic; it is typically based on a percentage (1–10 per cent) of the firm's revenue in the previous fiscal year. Therefore, an antitrust fine can amount to billions of dollars for a large multinational company. In addition to high fines, strict behavioural remedies can also be imposed on firms, significantly impacting on their business model. In 2015, the National Development and Reform Commission (NDRC) imposed a RMB 975 million fine on Qualcomm for abusing its dominant position in the Chinese market, along with a number of behavioural remedies. Despite receiving a strict penalty, Qualcomm was satisfied with such an outcome. As was discussed in Chapter 1, the NDRC could have pushed further at the time by requiring the firm to change how it charges licensing fees completely, which would have directly threatened Qualcomm's survival.

Third, using antitrust law will only send a noisy signal to the market about China's strategic leverage of the law to achieve its geopolitical purpose. Antitrust cases often rest on issues of economic effects, and the analyses can be highly technical and complex. In high-profile cases involving prominent business targets, well-known economists are often engaged to proffer evidence to support each side. And as noted in Chapter 1, the substantive issue of whether there is a legitimate legal basis for the Chinese authority to penalize a particular firm is often less observable to outsiders. Even if the parties concerned argue that politics has played a role and influenced their case, it is extremely difficult to verify such claims. Furthermore, as I illustrated in Chapter 2, the AML affords Chinese regulators wide discretionary power, and businesses rarely challenge the agency for fear of retribution and the imposition of reputational sanctions. As such, in spite of their complaints, businesses have more often than not acquiesced to the demands of the Chinese agency by publicly admitting their guilt. This thus sends a loud signal to the market that China is strategically employing the AML to inflict pain on particular foreign firms. The Chinese government can therefore achieve its policy objectives without explicitly flaunting existing international trade and investment rules. This strategy also causes less damage to China's reputation as it tries to maintain a friendly business environment for foreign businesses.

Since the eruption of the Sino-US. trade war, China has reportedly been withholding final approvals of many takeover transactions, using its administrative authority as leverage in the face of an aggressive US trade strategy. In fact, when the Trump Administration reversed its technology ban decision on ZTE, the Chinese government reportedly reciprocated by easing regulatory restrictions for US firms. On 17 May 2018, the State Administration and Market Regulation (SAMR) approved Bain Capital's USD 18 billion purchase of Toshiba's memory chip unit, a deal that had been held up by the Chinese government for so long that the parties were on the verge of giving up. However, Qualcomm's attempted USD 44 billion purchase of NXP Semiconductors did not have the same fortune. In October 2016, Qualcomm announced its intention to acquire NXP Semiconductors, a large semiconductor manufacturer. The deal was deemed critical for Qualcomm, which held a dominant position in the smartphone chips sector but was looking for growth and expansion into other areas. As both merging parties were multinational companies with a business presence in several jurisdictions, nine different jurisdictions including the United States, the European Union, and China were notified of the deal. By early 2018, Qualcomm had obtained regulatory clearances from eight jurisdictions, with China being the sole jurisdiction holding up the transaction. In the European Union, the major concern of the European Commission revolved around the ability and incentive of the merged entity to access NXP's technology, the interoperability of Qualcomm's baseband chipsets, and how NXP's chips would fare against rival products, as well as the significant combined intellectual property portfolios owned by the merged entity.[55] But none of these anticompetitive concerns proved fatal. To address the Commission's issues, the two companies offered significant behavioural remedies, ultimately leading to full clearance.

The clearance decisions in eight jurisdictions seem to have emboldened the merging parties. Up till late May 2018, Qualcomm was fairly optimistic about sealing a deal with the Chinese antitrust regulator. The Wall Street Journal even ran pre-emptive headlines like 'China Set to Approve Qualcomm-NXP Deal, A Sign of Easing Trade Tension'.[56] The Chinese regulator had reportedly expressed concerns about the potential for the merging parties to crowd

---

[55] European Commission, M. 8306 *Qualcomm/NXP* Semiconductors (2018).
[56] Kubota & Wei, *supra* note 7.

out domestic businesses in areas including mobile payments, largely on the rationale that NXP had retained its strong market position in those specific markets. However, a person privy to Qualcomm's interactions with the SAMR underscored that 'all the technical issues had been resolved', and 'from Qualcomm's perspective everything that needed to be done was done'.[57] When Qualcomm's executive met Wang Qishan, China's Vice President, in May 2018, along with other foreign business executives, Wang purportedly revealed that the deal stood a good chance of being approved by the Chinese regulator.[58]

Yet Qualcomm's hopes were dampened a few days later when President Trump decided to proceed with punitive tariffs on Chinese goods worth USD 50 billion. Subsequently, the Chinese antitrust regulator began sending undesirable signals by making statements such as 'your President embarrassed Liu He' and 'He offended the Chinese people'.[59] On 26 July 2018, Qualcomm terminated its proposed takeover of NXP. Richard Clemmer, Chief Executive of NXP, criticized the Chinese government for providing no explanations for withholding the deal, noting that there were no regulatory requirements that the deal had failed to meet and that Qualcomm and NXP had both agreed to offer remedies to address the regulator's concerns.[60]

There seems to be widespread consensus among foreign critics that the Chinese government used Qualcomm, in the same way that the Trump Administration exploited ZTE, as a bargaining chip in trade negotiations. Although both Qualcomm and NXP believed that Sino-US trade tensions contributed to the collapse of the deal, China denied that this factor played a role at all. Notably, the Chinese antitrust authority did not explicitly block the transaction but delaying the approval was sufficient to deter the merging companies from proceeding. This is not to suggest that political consideration will necessarily taint every antitrust decision in China, but even one extreme case is sufficient to demonstrate the potency of such administrative power; it simply depends on when and how the Chinese authority chooses to wield its discretionary authority. By tacitly holding up the Qualcomm merger, the Chinese authority demonstrated its coercive regulatory capability.

But the story does not end here. On 1 December 2018, during the dinner between President Trump and President Xi at the G-20 meeting in Buenos Aires, President Xi communicated that 'he is open to approving the previously

[57] Id.

[58] Id.

[59] Tom Mitchell et al., *China's Suffocation of Qualcomm-NXP Merger Signals New Era*, FIN. TIMES (26 July 2018).

[60] Don Clark, *NXP's Chief Criticizes China after Qualcomm Deal Collapses*, N.Y. TIMES (27 July 2018).

unapproved Qualcomm-NXP deal, should it again be presented to him'.[61] President Xi's statements in this context dispelled doubts that Qualcomm was held hostage by the Chinese government.

Having displayed its regulatory prowess by stalling mergers between foreign multinational companies, China is further enhancing the coercive capacity of its antitrust law. On 2 January 2020, the SAMR released a draft amendment of the AML for public consultation.[62] The proposed revision significantly increases the level of sanctions that could be imposed under the law. For instance, the maximum fine for merger control violations has been augmented from RMB 500,000 to up to 10 per cent of the annual turnover of the undertaking in the previous year, bringing China's fining power in line with other jurisdictions such as the United States and the European Union.[63] The new plan allows the SAMR to stop the clock and freeze its assessment in situations where it is waiting for a response from the parties or engaged in remedy negotiations.[64] Within the existing legal framework of the AML, the SAMR has up to 180 days to review a merger transaction. The proposed changes would afford the regulator more flexibility, permitting it to extend its review period.

Another striking modification is the explicit reference to criminal sanctions as they relate to anticompetitive conduct that amounts to a crime.[65] Although China has yet to amend its criminal law, this reference sends a clear indication that such an amendment is under way. Practitioners are keeping a close eye on this development as the introduction of criminal liabilities for criminal sanctions will be deemed a game changer for the sanctioning power of the AML. It should also be emphasized that, by introducing criminal liabilities into antitrust sanctions, China will be following the model of the United States, known for actively imposing criminal liabilities on individuals for antitrust violations. In the United States, criminal sanctions under the US Sherman Act can amount to USD 100 million for a corporation and USD 1 million for an individual, as well as a ten-year imprisonment sentence.[66] China has also significantly increased its penalties with respect to conduct violations. The penalty for concluding an

---

[61] White House, *Statement from the Press Secretary Regarding The President's Working Dinner with China* (1 Dec. 2018).

[62] State Administration & Market Regulation (SAMR), Shichang JianGuan Zongju Jiu FanlongduanFa XiudingCao'an GongkaiZhengqiu Yijian Gao GongkaiZhengqiu Yijian de Gonggao（市场监管总局就《<反垄断法>修订草案（公开征求意见稿）》公开征求意见的公告） SAMR Announcement Regarding the Public Consultation of the Draft Amendment of the Anti-Monopoly Law), 2 Jan. 2020 (hereinafter Draft AML).

[63] Art. 55, Draft AML.

[64] Art. 30, Draft AML.

[65] Art. 57, Draft AML.

[66] Federal Trade Commission, *The Antitrust Laws*, https://www.ftc.gov/tips-advice/competition-guidance/guide-antitrust-laws/antitrust-laws

anticompetitive agreement which has not been implemented has been raised from RMB 500,000 to RMB 50 million.[67] Meanwhile, the penalty for investigation obstruction by undertakings has been raised from RMB 1 million to 1 per cent of the turnover in the previous year, or RMB 5 million if it is difficult to calculate the turnover, and the penalty for investigation obstruction by individuals has similarly been elevated from RMB 100,000 to RMB 1 million.[68] Given the lack of checks and balances in Chinese antitrust enforcement, this considerable enhancement of the sanctioning power under the AML will no doubt afford the administrative enforcement agency even greater discretion in punishing companies under investigation.

3. Fighting a Limited War

China is hardly the first country to try to push back against the aggressive claims of extraterritorial jurisdiction made by the United States. When the United States applies sanctions laws to advance its own foreign policy interests, it has generated substantial opposition from the international community, and many countries have instituted regulatory measures to counter this influence. However, these measures have largely fallen short of achieving their intended purpose of protecting domestic businesses from US sanctions. China faces similar economic constraints as it contemplates imposing strict legal measures to fend off US aggression.

3.1 Weapons of Mass Retaliation

The United Nations General Assembly has repeatedly condemned 'unilateral extraterritorial coercive measures [used] as a means of political and economic compulsion'.[69] Many US trading partners have issued countermeasures designed to block the application of US sanctions within their jurisdictions.[70] In 1984, Canada passed the Foreign Extraterritorial Measure Act, devised to

---

[67] Art. 53, Draft AML.

[68] Art. 59, Draft AML.

[69] Elimination of Coercive Economic Measures as a Means of Political and Economic Compulsion, Resolutions of the United Nations General Assembly, A/RES/51/22 (6 Dec. 1996), A/RES/53/10 (3 Nov. 1998), A/RES/57/5 (1 Nov. 2002).

[70] Harry L. Clark & Lisa W. Wang, *Foreign Sanctions Countermeasures and Other Responses to U.S. Extraterritorial Sanctions*, DEWEY BALLANTINE LLP., Aug. 2007; *see also* Meredith Rathbone et al., *Sanctions, Sanctions Everywhere: Forging A Path Through Complex Transnational Sanctions Laws*, 44 GEO. J. INT'L L. 1055, at 1073–75.

thwart compliance by 'persons in Canada' with non-Canadian trade laws that adversely affect the trade interests of Canada. Mexico followed suit by enacting a similar law in 1986. In 1996, the European Union issued its own blocking statute 'Council Regulation 2271/96' as a countermeasure against the US embargo of Cuba. These blocking statutes generally prohibit compliance with US sanctions, negate effects of judgments and administrative orders that give weight to the sanctions, and allow a clawback claim for recovering damages incurred due to sanction violations. In addition, a long list of countries including the United Kingdom, Australia, South Africa, Belgium, Denmark, Finland, France, Germany, the Netherlands, and Sweden have statutes that could potentially be used to rebuff US extraterritorial sanctions.[71]

On 8 May 2019, President Trump announced the US withdrawal from the Joint Comprehensive Plan of Action agreement on Iran's nuclear deal and the re-imposition of sanctions. This put European entities at risk of violating secondary sanctions as European firms could be subject to sanctions for doing business with Iranian entities, regardless of whether they had nexus with the United States.[72] The US move sparked intense political opposition from the European Union, which alleged that current US sanctions were in violation of international law and declared that it would protect European businesses from the extraterritorial reach of US sanctions laws.[73] Shortly after the announcement, the European Union amended its Blocking Statutes to include the new Iran sanctions that had been re-imposed by the United States.

However, such countermeasures have severe limitations. Countries that have implemented blocking statutes can only invalidate the effects of US law in their domestic jurisdictions. Moreover, although businesses are promised protection in domestic jurisdictions, they are still subject to penalty for non-compliance with US sanctions in other overseas jurisdictions. This actually multiplies the compliance concerns for businesses as they are placed in the catch-22 situation of choosing between complying with the US law or with the foreign law. Likewise, favourable judgments in the European courts are unlikely to be enforceable in the United States.[74] More importantly, as we have seen in the ZTE and Huawei cases, the penalty for violating US sanctions not only includes hefty fines but also potential criminal liabilities for business executives. Thus, for

---

[71] Rathbone et al., *supra* note 18, at 1074.

[72] Markus Lieberknecht, *The Renaissance of the Blocking Statutes* (12 Dec. 2018), http://conflictoflaws. net/2018/the-renaissance-of-the-blocking-statute/.

[73] European Commission Press Release, *Updated Blocking Statutes in Support of Iran Nuclear Deal Enters into Force* (6 Aug. 2018).

[74] *See* Sascha Lohmann, *Extraterritorial U.S. Sanctions: Only Domestic Courts Can Effectively Curb the Enforcement of the U.S. Law Abroad*, SWP COMMENT 5 (Feb. 2019).

many global firms, succumbing to US pressure is difficult but rational choice of action. Given this delicate set of circumstances, many European firms have no choice but quietly to concede, complying with the US law and winding down operations in Iran without explicit reference to the US sanctions. As such, the enactment of the blocking statutes holds purely symbolic value.

In addition to the blocking statutes, US trading partners have also tried to contest US sanctions through international dispute settlement proceedings. In 1996, the European Union took issue with US sanctions against Cuba at the World Trade Organization (WTO). The case ended in political compromise in 1997.[75] Four years later, the European Union challenged Section 211, a piece of US sanctions law that prohibits US courts from considering or enforcing certain trademark claims of Cuban nationals.[76] The WTO ultimately ruled in favour of the European Union, finding that the US legislation contravenes the WTO national treatment and most-favoured nation requirements. The case resulted in a political settlement. Although the United States has retained Section 211 formally, it has in reality retracted the legislation and refrained from enforcing it.[77] The European Union, on the other hand, still retains the right to retaliate against the United States. The fact that both legal challenges resulted in a political compromise clearly demonstrates the weak enforcement power of the international dispute resolution mechanisms.

China is now similarly contemplating the introduction of countermeasures against US sanctions. Chinese scholars have been advocating for the adoption of blocking statutes to counter US long-arm jurisdiction, given how the events involving ZTE and Huawei transpired.[78] Song Guoyou, a scholar from Fudan University, suggested that China may consider adopting EU-style blocking statutes that would make Chinese companies immune to unilateral US sanctions against other countries. Song believes that Chinese companies and individuals suffering losses from these sanctions should be able to sue and claim compensation from the party inducing harm in a Chinese court. Thus far, China has yet to adopt any blocking statute, but it has threatened to impose an 'Unreliable Entity List', apparently inspired by the 'Entity List' issued by the US Department of Commerce.[79]

---

[75] Clark & Wang, *supra* note 70, at 3. *See also* Harry L. Clark, *Dealing with US Extraterritorial Sanction and US Countermeasures*, 20 U. Pa. J. Int'l Econ. L. 61, 87–89.

[76] Clark & Wang, *supra* note 70, at 20.

[77] Id. at 21.

[78] Song, *supra* note 6.

[79] The Bureau of Industry and Security of the US Department of Commerce has maintained a list of entities and individuals that are subject to specific licence requirements for the export, re-export, and/or transfer of specific items according to Export Administration Regulation.

On 31 May 2019, China's Ministry of Commerce (MOFCOM) announced that it would publicize a list of unreliable foreign companies and individuals that have seriously impaired Chinese companies by boycotting supplies to Chinese firms for non-commercial purposes.[80] According to MOFCOM, the four criteria for determining whether a foreign entity or individual will be listed as an 'unreliable entity' include: (1) whether there is evidence of boycotting, cutting off supplies, or specific discriminatory actions against Chinese companies; (2) whether actions taken are for non-commercial purposes, in violation of market rules or in breach of contractual obligations; (3) whether actions have caused significant harm to the Chinese companies and relevant industrial sectors; and (4) whether actions constitute a threat or potential threat to China's national security. The Unreliable Entity List is widely perceived as the Chinese government counteracting US sanctions targeting Chinese businesses, particularly sanctions placed on Huawei, by way of legislation. MOFCOM explained that this new regulatory regime will be established according to China's Foreign Trade Law,[81] the AML, and National Security Law.[82] On 19 September, 2020, MOFCOM released the Provisions on the Unreliable Entity List and the final provisions removed the AML as a statutory basis. Despite this removal, the inclusion of the AML as a statutory basis in the initial draft rules shows the unequivocal intention of the Chinese government to leverage its antitrust law as an instrument of trade policy.

Consider the following scenario: the US Department of Commerce refuses to grant export licences to US firms such as Intel, Google, and Qualcomm to transfer technology to Huawei. As a result of the new regulation, these companies are forced to cut off their supply to Huawei and can no longer honour their contractual commitments. Huawei then files complaints with the SAMR, which then began its investigation into the matter. These American technology firms could then be deemed to have violated Article 13 of the AML, which prohibits companies from colluding in order to restrict the purchasing of new technologies or equipment. As Professor Wang Xiaoye, a prominent Chinese

---

[80] Lester Ross & Kenneth Zhou, *China's Unreliable Entity List*, WILMER HALE (29 July 2019).

[81] Art. 7 of the Foreign Trade Law provides that if a foreign country or region adopts prohibitive trade measures on a discriminatory basis against China, China could take corresponding countermeasures against such country.

[82] Art. 59 of the National Security Law provides that the state shall establish a national security review and supervision system to conduct reviews on foreign investment, specific articles, key technologies, products, and services relating to network information technologies, infrastructure construction products, and other important transactions and activities that impact or may potentially impact national security.

antitrust scholar commented during an interview, such political boycotting should be deemed a violation of the AML.[83]

In addition to potential collusion charges, these US firms can also be held liable for 'abuse of dominance'. During an interview at a press conference, Wang Hejun, the director general of the MOFCOM's treaty and law department, explained that his department relied heavily on the concept of abuse of dominance while drafting the Unreliable Entity List.[84] Under Article 17 of the AML, a firm can be held accountable for abusing its dominant position by refusing to trade with counterparties or instituting discriminative prices or other transactional terms without justifiable reasons. The main premise of violating Article 17 of the AML is that the firm must already hold a dominant market position. But in China, there is a low standard of proof to demonstrate dominance as expressed in Article 19 of the AML. The article presumes a firm to be dominant if its market shares exceed 50 per cent, two firms to be collectively dominant when their joint market shares surpass 66 per cent, and three firms that hold market shares beyond 75 per cent. This collective dominance provision thus makes it easier for the Chinese authority to prosecute a cartel or a political boycott in this context, despite the absence of categorical evidence of collusion.

Pursuant to the new proposed AML, the SAMR could threaten to impose a fine of up to RMB 50 million on each of these US companies, even if the boycotting or refusal to deal remained only an unimplemented plan. If the conduct has already occurred, the SAMR could charge up to 10 per cent of the firms' turnover in the previous fiscal year, which could amount to billions of dollars in fines. Moreover, if China prescribes criminal liabilities for antitrust violations, the executives of US technology firms could fear the imposition of potential criminal sanctions and worry that they may be taken hostage, akin to Meng Wanzhou of Huawei.

In the hypothetical situation outlined above, US companies such as Intel, Google, and Qualcomm would be caught in a dilemma if they cut off supplies to Huawei in accordance with US restrictions. If faced with antitrust sanctions in China, these companies can defend themselves on the basis of foreign sovereign compulsion, arguing that they were forced by their own government to engage in anticompetitive behaviour. This bears close

---

[83] Guo Liqin（郭丽琴）, *Zhongmei Jingmao Cuoshang Jiangju Daijie*（中美经贸磋商僵局待解）*(The Impasse of the Sino-US Trade Negotiation Remains to Be Resolved)*, YıCAı (第一财经) [No. 1 FINANCE] (22 June 2019).

[84] Zhang Yang, *Unreliable Entity List Embraces Abuse of Dominance under Anti-Monopoly Law*, ANJIE LAW FIRM (4 July 2019).

resemblance to the defence presented by the Chinese vitamin C producers and challenged in US courts, as noted in Chapter 4. It remains to be seen whether the SAMR or the Chinese court will be willing to accommodate such a defence. However, as revealed in the Vitamin C case, the grant of immunity in such cases depends very much on the position of the executive branch which also seems the most apt body to rule on the optimal regulatory response in this situation. In China, given the lack of judicial independence and the political nature of such cases, it is highly likely that the courts will defer to the antitrust agency in such circumstances. Accordingly, should a Chinese antitrust authority pursue US technology companies on the basis of boycotting or refusal to deal, these companies would be unlikely to receive immunity even if they had been compelled by the US government to partake in anticompetitive conduct.

The scenario I have described above is hypothetical, but not far-fetched. In fact, Huawei already launched a complaint against Google with the SAMR, alleging that the US firm has been leveraging its dominance of its Android mobile operating system to harm competition.[85] At the same time, it is important to emphasize that a distinction should be made between a threat of force and its actual application. As noted by Thomas Schelling: 'What nuclear weapons have been used for, effectively, successfully, for sixty years has not been on the battlefield nor on population targets: they have been used for influence.'[86] Indeed, the existence of a threat creates costs for both players, the strategist initiating the threat and the opponent that is influenced by the threat. However, a successful threat is one that is not actually carried out.[87] China has demonstrated the coercive capacity of its AML by withholding approvals of large merger transactions. The purpose of fighting a limited war is to intimidate the enemy and to make pursuit of his limited objectives tolerably risky to him.[88] By strengthening the sanction powers of the AML, the Chinese government will hope that the threat of potential force can dissuade the US government from adversarial trade and legal strategies. This also reflects a commitment from China that in the absence of a US attack it will have no incentive to wage an all-out general war. But the mere threat of a limited war exposes the two countries to an increasing risk of such a war.

---

[85] Cheng Leng *et al.*, *Exclusive: China Preparing An Antitrust Investigation into Google-Sources*, Reuters (30 Sep. 2020).

[86] Thomas C. Schelling, *An Astonishing Sixty Years: The Legacy of Hiroshima*, Prize Lecture (8 Dec. 2005), at 374.

[87] Schelling, *supra* note 86, at 200.

[88] Id. at 191.

3.2 The Limits of Countermeasures

After the MOFCOM's announcement of the Unreliable Entity List, rumours spread that FedEx and the HSBC would soon be included on the list. In May 2019, the Chinese regulatory agencies launched a regulatory investigation into FedEx, a move that is widely believed to be a retaliation to President Trump's decision to outlaw Huawei from dealing with US companies. The Chinese investigation originated from Huawei's complaint that FedEx had diverted and rerouted several of its packages addressed to locations in China to the United States without authorization. The Global Times, a state-controlled English-language newspaper, revealed that FedEx had delayed over 100 packages sent from overseas to Huawei in China.[89] The newspaper also quoted an expert from the Chinese Academy of Social Science, who implied that the Chinese government would make public more details about the ongoing probe into FedEx as 'China wants to gain the initiative in negotiations with the US'.[90] HSBC, the bank that handed over important records to the Department of Justice which enabled the indictment of Meng Wanzhou for bank fraud, was lambasted by the state media for leaking confidential client information as well.[91]

In October 2019, the MOFCOM's spokesman revealed that it had finalized the legislation of the Unreliable Entity List and would enforce it when necessary. This is a clear indication that China is not actually enforcing the list or effecting the regulation but rather using it as a threat in an attempt to influence the United States. In other words, China is making its punishment probabilistic rather than certain, and there is a clear reason for this. While there is no apparent limit as to the cost of the threatened action, the player making the threat may be concerned about the risk of error.[92] There is a possibility that the threat may fail to achieve its purpose or that the threatened action may occur accidently. Therefore, it is in the interests of a strategist to use the minimal threat possible to achieve the purpose of deterrence.[93] In the absence of minimal threats, a large threat can be scaled down thereby making the fulfilment of the threat probabilistic.[94] That is, the strategist creates the probability that a mutually destructive outcome would occur in the event of the opponent's

---

[89] Tu Lei & Chen Qingqing, *China's Potential Unreliable Entity List Emerges*, GLOBAL TIMES (26 July 2019).

[90] Id.

[91] Shen Weiduo & Zhang Hongpei, *HSBC at A Crossroads As Huawei Issue Remains, Hong Kong Unrest Continues*, GLOBAL TIMES (13 Aug. 2019).

[92] AVINASH DIXIT ET AL., GAMES OF STRATEGY 560 (4th ed. 2015).

[93] Id.

[94] Id.

defiance. This is precisely what China is doing. From China's standpoint, the Unreliable Entity List is analogous to a weapon of mass destruction and used only as a last resort.

Meanwhile, Chinese technology companies like Huawei are actively exploring alternative strategies to ease the concerns of the US regulators. For instance, Ren Zhengfei, the chairman of Huawei, proposed to sell its 5G technology to a foreign rival.[95] Huawei's suggestion signals that the company is willing to become more hostage to the United States by surrendering its technology in the hopes of gaining trust from the US government. Huawei's friendly gesture, however, proved unsuccessful. On 13 February 2020, the Department of Justice unveiled a sixteen-count superseding indictment against Huawei and its subsidiaries along with its CFO, Meng Wanzhou.[96] The new charges in this case relate to the alleged decade-long effort by Huawei and its subsidiaries to misappropriate intellectual property from US counterparts. The prevailing conviction also includes new accusations regarding Huawei and its subsidiaries' involvement in businesses and technology projects in countries subject to US sanctions, such as Iran and North Korea.

Since early 2020, the Trump Administration has escalated its coercive measures aimed at suppressing Huawei. On 15 May 2020, the US Department of Commerce unveiled a new rule that would modify the existing foreign direct product rule, requiring chip factories worldwide to first obtain US licences in order to use American equipment to create chips for Huawei.[97] This new measure, expected to take effect in September 2020, threatens to cut off Huawei's access to US semiconductors entirely. In response, the Global Times reiterated that 'China will take forceful countermeasures to protect its legitimate rights'.[98] These countermeasures include re-activating the Unreliable Entity List, launching investigations on US technology companies such as Qualcomm, Cisco, and Apple for violations of antitrust law and Internet security law, and halting the purchase of Boeing planes.[99] Some have called such countermeasures towards large American firms comparable to a 'nuke bomb'.[100]

---

[95] *Piece Offering: Ren Zhengfei May Sell Huawei's 5G Technology to A Western Buyer*, THE ECONOMIST (12 Sep. 2019); *see also* Thomas L. Friedman, *Huawei Has A Plan to Help End Its War With Trump*, N.Y. TIMES (13 Sep. 2019).

[96] Department of Justice Press Release, *Chinese Telecommunications Conglomerate Huawei and Subsidiaries Charged in Racketeering Conspiracy and Conspiracy to Steal Trade Secrets* (13 Feb. 2020).

[97] Press Release, U.S. Department of Commerce, *Commerce Addresses Huawei's Efforts to Undermine Entity List, Restricts Products Designed and Produced with U.S. Technologies* (15 May 2020).

[98] China Readies Biggest Counterattack against US, GLOBAL TIMES (16 May 2020).

[99] Id.

[100] Benjamin Fearnow & Asher Stockler, *China Will 'Nuke Bom' Apple with Endless Investigations in Retaliation for Huawei Penalties, State Media Says*, NEWSWEEK.COM (16 May 2020).

However, China's regulatory threats have not deterred the United States, nor have its cooperative gestures persuaded the United States to move towards a more peaceful resolution. There are at least three factors that hinder a cooperative outcome. The first is the absence of a credible deterrence threat, that is, the country initiating the action lacks the commitment to carry out his threat. The second is the problem of asymmetric information. In reality there is often no sure way of knowing what the counterparty will do next nor is it easy to predict the payoffs, in other words the consequences that will follow from a particular move. Information asymmetry becomes particularly severe when the bargain is tacit since communication becomes much costlier in this context. A third factor is myopia: if countries in a dispute are very impatient, they may not value their future interactions as much as their interactions in the present. I will elaborate on each of these factors in the following discussion.

First and foremost, China's threat is not credible to the United States. The risks and costs for China to carry out its punishment are so high that it is doubtful that China would follow through on any threat. Similar to the blocking statutes, compliance with the Unreliable Entity List would create further regulatory burden for businesses operating in China, who will be placed in a catch-22 scenario with the dilemma of having to choose between violating Chinese or American laws. For example, the Anti-boycott Act of 2018 prohibits US firms from complying with the boycotting requirements of other countries, and thus a firm's compliance with the Chinese law may risk violating US law.[101]

Fundamentally, the Unreliable Entity List, which leverages China's market access as an economic sanction tool, is a double-edged sword. In fact, the more deterrence it creates, the more backlash it produces. Anxiety amongst US businesses has already been on the rise since the Chinese government's announced its intention to pursue this route. Many US companies are pondering whether this regulatory measure is a deliberate attempt by the Chinese government to obtain more bargaining leverage during the trade negotiations, or whether it is an actual effort to force businesses into the difficult position of giving up one for the other. The release of the Unreliable Entity List will send a bad signal to US companies because they could become the next target. This is different from the Chinese government's strategic intervention in merger cases such as *Qualcomm/NXP*. Outwardly, the Chinese government denied that politics had influenced the review process. And even though there is much anecdotal evidence suggesting that politics had in fact played a role, the collapse of the deal sent a noisy signal at best. But the application of the Unreliable Entity List has

---

[101] Clifford Chance, *U.S. Antiboycott Laws: They're Not For Everyone* (May 2019).

perfectly observable results. If a US company placed on the List is targeted for antitrust violations, it will be clear that the decision is a political one. The List will have a much wider and deeper negative impact on the confidence of US companies operating in China than the previous tactic of simply withholding approvals of certain merger transactions. In the worst-case scenario, it will induce many more US businesses to leave the Chinese market.

Such economic decoupling would be disastrous for the Sino-US relationship. Since the outbreak of the trade war, foreign investment, particularly US investment in China, has been a crucial countervailing force against the heightening trade tensions. Indeed, the closely integrated global supply chain has, to a great extent, aligned the interests of US multinationals and their Chinese counterparts. When the Department of Commerce contemplated a comprehensive proposal that would systematically block transactions between US firms and their Chinese counterparts, businesses in Silicon Valley were left scrambling to respond.[102] Qualcomm, a US company deriving over half of its revenue from the Chinese market, is a good case in point. The company supplies chips for all ZTE's phones in the United States and more than half the phones it sells overseas. It thus comes as no surprise that Qualcomm has quietly pressed the US government to ease the trade sanction ban on ZTE.[103] Qualcomm also lobbied the Trump Administration to roll back restrictions barring the sale of chips to Huawei, noting that the export ban will place the firm at a competitive disadvantage because Huawei can source its chips from other non-US firms.[104] Notably, foreign firms operating in China have also forged strong relationships with the Chinese government through the creation of massive employment opportunities for the country's large labour workforce. Apple Inc., a US company caught in the middle of the Sino-US spat, is one of many such firms. The firm relies heavily on supplies from Foxconn, which employs millions of workers in China.[105] Chinese applications developers have also earned billions of dollars on its platform.[106] If Apple is forced to leave the Chinese market, it will move its manufacturing base out of China, affecting the employment of hundreds of thousands of Chinese migrant workers. For this reason, analysts predict that

[102] Anna Swanson & David McCabe, *Trump Effort to Keep U.S. Tech Out of China Alarms American Firms*, N.Y. Times (16 Feb. 2020).

[103] Stephen Nellis & Alexandra Alper, *U.S. Chipmakers Quietly Lobby to Ease Huawei Ban*, Reuters (17 June 2019).

[104] Asa Fitch & Kate O'Keeffe, *Qualcomm Lobbies U.S. to Sell Chips for Huawei 5G Phones*, Wall St. J. (8 Aug. 2020).

[105] Tippe Mickle & Yoko Kubota, *Tim Cook and Apple Bet Everyone on China. Then Coronavirus Hit*, Wall St. J. (3 Mar. 2020).

[106] Arjun Kharpal, *Why Apple is Unlikely to Face Backlash from China Over New U.S. Rule on Huawei*, CNBC (19 May 2020).

Chinese antitrust authority will be unlikely to go after Apple over the Huawei export ban.[107]

Indeed, despite escalating Sino-US tensions, China has continually reduced the list of restricted areas of investment for foreign businesses over the past few years.[108] In April 2019, China adopted a new Foreign Investment Law that promises to provide a more level playing field for foreign and domestic enterprises.[109] In January 2020, the United States and China reached a Phase-I trade deal in which China pledged to expedite the removal of foreign investment restriction on securities and financial firms.[110] This would allow the Chinese government to attract greater foreign capital and assets, further helping to stabilize China's relationship with the United States and its allies. However, the more countermeasures tacitly or explicitly adopted by the Chinese government, the more volatility it will create for investments by foreign businesses. This economic reality of the Chinese economy therefore places a hard constraint on China's retaliatory regulatory response.

Moreover, the crisis situation created by the Trump Administration is replete with uncertainties. Neither the US nor the Chinese government can be assured of the payoffs for the other side. It is extremely hard for one government to estimate the value system of another and it is not easy for one government to be certain that the other government's intended actions will materialize. Indeed, the tension between the United States and China is multi-dimensional, and neither one of the governments can easily predict how the other will react to a particular move. But for cooperation-based tacit bargaining to be successful, decision-makers must do everything possible to minimize the bias with which they view a rival state's actions as well as their own natural inclination to avoid risk.[111] As observed by Downs and Rocke, a state is rarely sure enough about an opponent's response to make a large cooperative gesture, and the opponent is rarely trusting enough to respond enthusiastically to a small one.[112] As such, tacit bargaining is often a fragile, opaque process which ends in frustration or further escalation.[113]

---

[107] Id.

[108] *China Focus: China Opens More Sectors to Foreign Investment with New Negative Lists*, Xinhua (30 June 2019).

[109] Foreign Investment Law of the People's Republic of China (adopted at the Second Session of the 13th National People's Congress on 15 March 2019).

[110] The White House, *President Donald J. Trump Is Signing A Landmark Phase One Trade Agreement with China* (15 Jan. 2020).

[111] George W. Downs & David M. Rocke, *Tacit Bargaining and Arms Control*, 39 World Politics 297, 322 (1987).

[112] Id.

[113] Id.

Finally, the myopia of the Trump Administration plays a role here. The Trump Administration's aggressive use of sanctions laws over foreign entities and their executives has consequences. As the main leverage of the US sanctions law is owed to the US dollar's dominant role as the global currency, countries such as China, Russia, and those in the European Union are now trying to challenge the dollar's hegemony by nurturing their own international payment system circumventing its use. In recent years, many countries have conducted new monetary experimentation such as the de-dollarization of assets, trade workarounds using local currencies and swaps, new bank payment systems, and digital currencies.[114] However, the process of de-dollarization is long and imbued with ambiguity. In a similar vein, the US attempt to strangle Huawei with tighter export controls might backfire by pushing the US chip industry offshore. Industry experts have indicated that American toolmakers have considered moving their patents abroad to establish new operations from scratch in order to avoid increasingly stringent US export control rules.[115] However, the Trump Administration does not seem deterred by the erosion of the reputation of the almighty dollar or the shift of US production, especially when it focuses on the short-term gains while ignoring the long-term consequences.

Summary

In this chapter, I have explained one last facet of the Chinese antitrust exceptionalism by showing how the Chinese government has employed the AML as part of its tit-for-tat strategy against aggressive US sanctions. By holding up merger approvals of high-profile transactions involving US companies, and by threatening to penalize firms that boycott or refuse to deal with Chinese technology firms, the Chinese government is wielding the AML to administer targeted retaliation against the United States. With the pending revision of the AML, which will significantly increase the punishment power of the Chinese antitrust authority, the AML will likely play a more prominent role in China's geopolitical contestation with the United States. However, the Chinese government will find it difficult to overcome the economic constraints it faces in using antitrust law as an instrument of trade policy. China continues to be heavily dependent on US investment not only as a form of capital investment but also

---

[114] *America's Aggressive Use of the Sanctions Endangers Dollar's Reign*, THE ECONOMIST (18 Jan. 2020).
[115] *America's Latest Salvo Against Huawei Is Aimed At Chipmaking in China*, THE ECONOMIST (21 May 2020).

as a countervailing political force against aggressive US trade policy. I therefore predict that the AML will at best be used to fight a limited war with the United States rather than being turned into a weapon of mass retaliation.

Prominent scholars of Chinese laws have long debated the Chinese government's attitude towards the law in general. Some argue that China has retreated from legal reform, while others have stated that Chinese politics has in fact become more legally oriented, and then there are those who have witnessed both trends occurring simultaneously, albeit in different areas of governance.[116] Thus far, most of these legal arguments are quite inward-looking, focusing on the incentives of domestic constituents. However, with China's accelerated integration into the global economy, foreign governments have taken on more prominent roles and are actively shaping the developments of Chinese laws. The invigoration of Chinese antitrust law as a tit-for-tat strategy during the Sino-US tech war thus serves as a good illustration of the effects of foreign influence on Chinese law.

At this point, there is a great deal of uncertainty around how China's legal strategy will evolve. China's domestic regulatory moves are profoundly dependent on how the United States chooses to proceed, and the latter's decision in turn is contingent on what it perceives China's likely response will be. But one thing is clear: as the United States steps up its efforts to claim exterritorial jurisdiction over Chinese technology firms and executives, China will retaliate in kind by boosting its own extraterritorial regulatory capacity. The two sides are now locked in a dangerous battle of regulatory competition, leaving the occurence of a disastrous outcome to chance.

---

[116] Carl F. Minzner, *China's Turn Against Law*, 59 Am' J. Comparative L. 935 (2011) (observing the trend that the Chinese authorities are de-emphasizing the role of formal law and court adjudication substantively and relying on political rather than legal levers in their effort to remake the Chinese judiciary); Taisu Zhang & Tom Ginsburg, *China's Turn Towards Law*, 59 Va J. Int'l L. 278 (2019) (arguing that the Chinese government invests in legality because of the need to tackle principal–agent problems arising from the Chinese bureaucratic state, and there is an increasing desire among the Chinese population for legitimacy and legality); Hualing Fu, *Editorial: Duality and China's Struggle for Legal Autonomy*, 1 China Perspectives 3, 3 (2019) (observing a duality in the Chinese legal system: a private law system that has become professionalized and semi-autonomous in parallel to the highly politicized and unpredictable prerogative system).

Hostage and Peace

I like the notion that East and West have exchanged hostages on a massive scale and that as long as they are unprotected, civilization depends on the avoidance of military aggression that could escalate to nuclear war.

— Thomas C. Schelling[1]

There is an overwhelming consensus within the antitrust community that modern day antitrust analysis is firmly grounded in economics. This book has shown that other factors are also essential, particularly when addressing issues related to China. Antitrust first originated as policies designed to correct market failures in Western democracies, but in the hands of the Chinese government, antitrust has become a multi-functional regulatory tool. In relentless attempts to expand their bureaucratic turf, Chinese administrative agencies have deployed the Anti-Monopoly Law (AML) not only to tackle monopolies but also to control and stabilize prices. In the latest phase of the Sino-US tech war, the Chinese government even weaponized its antitrust laws as part of its tit-for-tat strategy against aggressive US sanctions imposed on Chinese technology companies and individuals. At the same time, Chinese antitrust agencies are seldom challenged in court and companies under investigation have exhibited unusual levels of cooperation with the government. As it turns out, Chinese agencies use the vast discretion available to them to entice firms to yield to their demands and penalize those who refuse to cooperate. Furthermore, in order to quickly establish its reputation as a tough enforcer, the National Development and Reform Commission (NDRC), one of the three former antitrust units, repeatedly leveraged state media to strategically shame uncooperative firms. It is no surprise then, that the international community is

---

[1] Thomas C. Schelling, *What Went Wrong with Arms Control?* 64 FOREIGN AFFAIRS 219, 233 (1985). Many of the footnote references in this book are online materials and they can be easily accessible online.

Chinese Antitrust Exceptionalism. Angela Huyue Zhang, Oxford University Press (2021). © Angela Huyue Zhang. DOI: 10.1093/oso/9780198826569.003.0007

often bewildered and frustrated by China's peculiar uses of antitrust law and its occasional abusive enforcement tactics.

Chinese antitrust exceptionalism is manifested not just in the way China regulates but also in the way it is regulated. Over the past decade, the overseas expansion of Chinese companies, particularly those backed by the state, has created significant challenges for Western antitrust enforcers. Baffled by the inextricable relationship between the Chinese government and Chinese state-owned enterprises (SOEs), EU competition regulators are starting to view Chinese SOEs as part of a massive China, Inc. Meanwhile, Chinese exporters have tried to evade accusations of cartel formation by claiming that they had been compelled by the Chinese government to collude. When reviewing these cartel cases, US judges, like their European counterparts, have struggled to discern the extent to which Chinese firms are independent from the state. In both cases, the elusiveness of the state influence over Chinese firms has made EU and US regulators increasingly jittery. But when these regulators tried to apply their existing antitrust legal framework to scrutinize the 'China Inc', they realized that such a legalistic approach could lead to a paradoxical outcome jeopardizing their jurisdiction over other cases involving Chinese firms. Now faced with this regulatory dilemma, the European Union and its Member States are in a hurry to revamp their foreign investment control rules, with the latest regulatory proposal aimed at tackling Chinese state-backed acquisitions. The US judges presiding over these cases, on the other hand, adopted a highly deferential approach to the Executive, affording the latter more flexibility in formulating strategies to deal with Chinese export cartels.

My depiction of this side of China's globalization story, therefore, is not a buoyant one. Indeed, the friction between China and the global antitrust regulatory order offers us a lens through which we can closely observe the systemic issues dividing China and the Western liberal democracies. This echoes a growing consensus view by many US intellectuals that US engagement with China over the past five decades has done little to resolve the fundamental differences between the two regimes.[2] Some observers went even further, stating that 'globalization has created a Chinese monster'.[3] In their opinion, China has not just gone global without instituting democratic reform, but has instead emerged as more totalitarian.[4] Even Janos Kornai, a Hungarian economist

---

[2] Orville Schell, *The Death of Engagement*, WIRE CHINA (7 June 2020); Jerome A. Cohen, *Was Helping China Build Its Post-1978 Legal System A Mistake?* 61 VIR. J. INT' L. ONLINE 1 (2020).

[3] Emile Simpson, *Globalization Has Created A Chinese Monster*, FOREIGN POLICY (26 Feb. 2018).

[4] *See generally* ELIZABETH C. ECONOMY, THE THIRD REVOLUTION: XI JINPING AND THE NEW CHINESE STATE (2018).

among a group of leading Western economists who once advised China on market reform, rued his contributions.[5] Kornai accused Western scholars of contributing to China's globalization without fully understanding its dire consequences, in the same way Dr Frankenstein created his monster. He urged the Western community to contain the 'Chinese monster' before it was too late. This policy of containment as advocated by Kornai is in line with much of the current Western political discourse and evident in the Trump Administration's increasingly tougher stance on China.[6]

But is this really the best strategy? Clearly, the recent US measures to isolate China through restrictive deals with major US trading partners is damaging the global economy. The hefty US tariffs imposed on Chinese goods have dealt a blow to the Chinese economy and brought about significant harm to US consumers and exporters. The US government's travel ban on Chinese nationals in its attempt to supress the COVID-19 pandemic has proven futile as well. At the time of writing, the number of confirmed COVID-19 cases in the United States has far surpassed that of China. Just like many countries around the globe that have sought out advice and resources from China to combat the pandemic, the United States also needs to cooperate with China, which has the capacity to produce face masks as well as the other protective gear that America so desperately needs. The coronavirus has forced us to accept the reality that China is now deeply embedded in the highly interconnected global system and it is simply too costly and unrealistic to disengage China. In fact, the current degree of global interdependence is exactly what distinguishes the present Sino-US tensions from Soviet–US tensions during the Cold War.[7] As Noah Feldman presciently observes, we are now entering a new global era of a 'cool war', where cooperation and conflict must simultaneously coexist.[8]

There are, of course, good reasons for critics to feel wary about how US engagement policy with China has panned out over the past half century. But when critics complain that almost no political changes have occurred in the Chinese regime, they overlook the fact that the Chinese bureaucracy has undergone seismic institutional reforms. Chinese antitrust enforcement is the ideal setting for us to see these institutional changes and how they have affected policy outcomes. From the very outset, advanced antitrust regimes like the United States and the European Union have offered generous legal

[5] Janos Kornai, *Economists Share Blame for China's Monstrous Turn*, FIN. TIMES (10 July 2019).
[6] Ana Swanson, *A New Red Scare Is Reshaping Washington*, N.Y. TIMES (20 July 2019).
[7] Odd Arne Westad, *The Sources of Chinese Conduct*, FOREIGN AFFAIRS (Sep 2019).
[8] *See generally* NOAH FELDMAN, COOL WAR: THE UNITED STATES, CHINA AND THE FUTURE OF GLOBAL COMPETITION (2015).

assistance to help China adopt a modern antitrust law and boost its enforcement capacity. Through numerous training sessions, conferences, and academic exchanges, American and European officials vied to export their model of antitrust enforcement to China. To their disappointment, China may have emulated its laws from these advanced regimes, but it has not plainly followed the Western approach in its enforcement. As elaborated in Chapter 1, much of the administrative enforcement of the AML has been driven by bureaucratic politics, particularly institutional factors such as bureaucratic missions, cultures, and structures. This is particularly evident in the enforcement pattern of the NDRC, whose predecessor was the central planning commission responsible for orchestrating, coordinating, and directing economic activities in the country. Institutions have memories, and therefore changes occur gradually, if at all. For this reason, it is not surprising that the NDRC viewed antitrust as an opportunity to achieve its own bureaucratic mission to control and stabilize prices.

Yet the Chinese state is hardly a monolith. To the contrary, a key defining feature of the Chinese bureaucracy is that power is highly fragmented. As described in Chapter 1, Chinese merger control is a consensus-building process involving the antitrust authority, sector regulators, industrial policy planners, and occasionally the local governments. The interaction between the different bureaucratic players resulted in serious disagreements, especially when it came down to the regulation of large SOEs, as discussed in both Chapters 2 and 3. And despite the commonly held perception that all Chinese SOEs are managed under one single roof, they actually belong to different levels of the governments in different regions with competing and divergent interests, as shown in Chapters 3 and 4. Since each bureaucratic department represents different interest groups and each have their own agenda and mission, they all compete fiercely to expand and advance their own turf.

This constant struggle for power among Chinese government departments was most evident in the latest government reorganization in 2018. The NDRC lost its authority over AML enforcement and saw its administrative power curtailed in a number of regulatory spheres, while the State Administration for Industry and Commerce (SAIC) carved out greater power for itself and prevailed in the overarching revamp. As the Ministry of State Administration and Market Supervision (SAMR), the central ministry housing the new antitrust bureau, is responsible for overseeing and regulating market activities, it is expected to adopt a more legal-oriented approach towards law enforcement. This bodes well for future enforcement of the AML. This sweeping government overhaul, with far reaching implications for Chinese antitrust enforcement, was ultimately propelled by market forces that succeeded the country's engagements with the West. Without the need to deepen China's market reform further there would not be a demand for a more efficient and powerful market regulator like the SAMR in the present day. It is thus a serious mistake to conclude that the engagement policy with China has been a total failure. The Chinese reforms have not been carried out as effectively nor as quickly as some critics would have liked. Nonetheless, earlier engagements with China have proved beneficial for its institutional reform. All too often, Western critics have the tendency to overgeneralize and conveniently ignore this fact.

Aside from the strategy of disengaging and containing China, are there any feasible solutions to diffuse the conflict between China and Western liberal democracies? I hope this book provides evidence that a peaceful resolution remains possible. The answer, counterintuitively, lies in the use of hostages. The hostages here are not chained men or women but rather businesses such as the multinationals topping the Fortune Global 500 List. They are not just leading household names in America and Europe but also massive Chinese SOEs with high market capitalizations. After earning enormous profits in the Chinese market, the bargaining power of foreign firms has gradually declined over the years. China's antitrust enforcement provides an excellent opportunity to scrutinize the hardships foreign companies face as they adapt to an increasingly hostile regulatory environment in China. Foreign companies have, inadvertently, become 'hostages' of the Chinese government. But globalization is not a one-way street, and Chinese companies, venturing overseas, have also been held hostage by Western regulators. These Chinese behemoths, developed and nurtured in a state-led economy, lack the independent decision-making power of those operating in free market economies. Hence, the lingering thought in the back of every foreign policy-maker's mind is that all Chinese firms, regardless of formal ownership, are ultimately controlled by the Chinese Communist Party. As such, Chinese companies have been especially vulnerable to Western regulatory attacks; the antitrust challenges I discussed in this book are some of their latest struggles in acclimatizing to Western regulatory compliance.

No-one wants to be held hostage, of course. Hostages, however, have played a vital role in peace-making for centuries. In the absence of centralized law enforcement mechanisms, ancient powers, warlords, and gangsters frequently took hostages to ensure cooperation.[9] From the Egyptian Pharaohs who abducted the heirs to the throne of the areas they conquered, to Julius Caesar who seized a massive number of hostages from defeated tribes, to the Italian Mafia

---

[9] THOMAS SCHELLING, THE STRATEGY OF CONFLICT 20 (1980).

that has swapped family members during negotiations, the practice of hostage-taking to make peace continues to be a frequent practice to this day.[10] Giving hostages signals the willingness to commit to a promise while simultaneously curbing opportunism, given that the life of the hostage is at stake.[11] Indeed, when the Chinese government tried to circumvent international trade rules by leveraging its administrative discretion to put pressure on foreign firms to lower their prices and impose technology transfer, it received great backlash from Washington. The trade war launched by the Trump Administration is a reminder to the Chinese government that deviating from global trade rules and norms carries great risks, even if executed under the pretence of administrative law enforcement.

Meanwhile, Chinese state-backed firms, ranging from sovereign wealth funds such as China Investment Corporation to leading telecom makers like Huawei, need to adapt to the foreign rules and regulations as they venture overseas. On their path to becoming global industry leaders, these Chinese companies have come to realize that one of the biggest impediments they face is their Chinese identity. Although these national champions hold good prospects of thriving in foreign markets, they must accept that a degree of their success depends on the evolving political landscape and the shifting relationship between China and Western countries. TikTok, a widely popular social media app owned by ByteDance, a Chinese company, is the latest company caught in the middle of escalating Sino-US tensions. Soon after President Trump's vocal threat to ban TikTok and other Chinese social media apps on national security grounds, Chinese technology entrepreneurs began lobbying the Chinese government to remove the great firewalls of Internet control in China. As James Liang, the founder of Ctrip argues, this bold move would improve China's global image and delegitimatize the US restrictions on Chinese social media firms.[12] Viewed in this light, China's greater integration with the global economy could become an endogenous force prompting China to reform and change.

Of course, the Chinese government is unlikely to tear down the great firewall overnight, but for Chinese tech giants to be welcomed overseas the Chinese government needs to do more at home by levelling the playing field

---

[10] Lasse Biornstad, *Why Did the Vikings Take Hostage?* (10 Nov. 2016), https://sciencenorway.no/forskningno-norway-society--culture/why-did-the-vikings-take-hostages/1439493; *see also* William Langewiesche, *The Camorra Never Sleeps*, VANITY FAIR (10 Apr. 2012).

[11] Beth V. Yarbrough & Robert M. Yarbrough, *Reciprocity, Bilateralism, Economic 'Hostage,' Self-Enforcing Agreements in International Trade*, 30 INT'L STUD. Q. 7, 10 (1986).

[12] Ironically, James Liang's article, which was posted on Sino Finance on 2 August 2020, was removed only two hours after it was posted.

between domestic and foreign firms operating in the country. In 2019, China passed a Foreign Investment Law aimed at improving the legal protection for foreign investors in China. Simply improving the laws on paper, however, is not enough. China has made remarkable law-making progress and Chinese laws have grown considerably more sophisticated over the years, but even with these laudable legislative achievements Chinese law enforcement still lags behind. The recent administrative law reform is a case in point. The amendment of the Administrative Litigation Law in 2015 has made it significantly easier for plaintiffs to appeal administrative decisions, with Chinese courts experiencing a surge of administrative appeals. But despite these encouraging improvements, few corresponding changes have been observed in antitrust enforcement. Businesses are still very reluctant to sue for fear of agency reprisal and the potential reputational sanction that might be inflicted by the administration. The amendments to the administrative law therefore have little relevance to many businesses as they do not really bargain in the shadow of the law. A more ambitious institutional reform is thus needed to inject more transparency into the administrative approval process, while ensuring there is due process in decision-making. In addition, the curbing of agency discretion is essential to prevent agency retaliation, and strict measures must be imposed to bar antitrust agencies from strategically using media disclosure to shame firms under investigation. As I illustrate in this book, public shaming has become a powerful deterrent on firms, making them subservient to government agencies.

The substantial exchange of hostages between the East and the West, which has the prospect of facilitating positive changes in the Chinese regime, should therefore give us hope for peace. It is precisely for this reason that I advocate greater economic integration. Economic interdependence raises the costs of conflict and increases the incentives for countries to cooperate.[13] Indeed, a preponderance of economic evidence has shown that trade can reduce conflict among countries.[14] Thus, the expansion of Chinese firms into foreign markets should not be seen as something to be blocked but should be welcomed as an important step towards a more prosperous and peaceful relationship between China and the rest of the world.[15] Conversely, if Chinese firms are discouraged

---

[13] CHARLES DE SECONDAT MONTESQUIEU, THE SPIRIT OF LAWS (TRANSLATED FROM FRENCH BY THOMAS NUGENT) (2011); Solomon William Polachek, *Conflict and Trade*, 24 J. CONFLICT RESOLUTION 55, 56 (1980).

[14] Edward D. Mansfield & Brian M. Pollins, *The Study of Interdependence and Conflict: Recent Advances, Open Questions, and Directions for Future Research*, 45 J. CONFLICT RESOLUTION 834 (2001).

[15] RICHARD A. POSNER, ECONOMIC ANALYSIS OF LAW 1001 (9th ed. 2014)

from entering or even cut off from Western markets, as some politicians are calling for these days, then foreign governments will hold less leverage over China. In fact, the Western policy of decoupling the Chinese economy from Western economies, while a seemingly straightforward response to rising political tensions, is eroding trust and making conflict more likely.[16] In recent years, Western hostilities directed towards China and Chinese firms have triggered strong nationalistic sentiments in China, making it difficult for a substantial minority of Chinese policy-makers to push for reforms that would allow for greater democracy and freedom at home.[17] Worryingly, policies of disengagement and containment will turn China into a more isolated, self-reliant, and inward-looking country, further heightening the risk of a full-blown war.

Certainly, my proposal to foster economic interdependence does not imply a laissez-faire approach. It is perfectly understandable that host countries want to stay vigilant about Chinese influence.[18] Thus, a pragmatic and flexible legal framework must be put in place to allow the host countries to retain significant regulatory leverage over Chinese firms, while avoiding too much red tape and undue regulatory burden on businesses. This is not an easy balance to strike but it is also the new normal that today's foreign policy-makers should be prepared for given China's rise. Antitrust lawyers and academics should also abandon the utopian ideal that antitrust law analysis is completely immune from political influence. It cannot be. As clearly illustrated by the EU's latest proposal to tackle foreign state subsidies, the fine lines between competition law, trade law, and national security are becoming increasingly blurred. In a similar vein, the US Supreme Court's decision to accord high deference to the Executive in the Vitamin C case means that politics will inevitably play a role in affecting future judicial decision-making in export cartel cases.

For sure, some external pressure on China to reduce state interference in the economy is beneficial. However, there is a danger that the current Western trend of politicizing antitrust enforcement, if carried too far, can evolve into a double-standard used against Chinese firms. The appearance of this hypocrisy would then severely undercut the ability of EU and US enforcers to convince their Chinese counterparts that antitrust analysis should be grounded in legal

---

[16] Angela Huyue Zhang, *The U.S.–China Trade Negotiation: A Contract Theory Perspective*, 51 GEO. J. INT'L L. 809, 864 (2020).

[17] Cui Lei, *Will China Return to Isolation?* THE DIPLOMAT (23 Nov. 2018); *see also* Westad, *supra* note 7. This is also consistent with my observation based on the interaction with Chinese regulators and judges.

[18] Larry Diamond & Orville Schell (eds.), *China's Influence & American Interests, Promoting Constructive Vigilance*, HOOVER INSTITUTE PRESS PUBLICATION NO. 702 (2019).

and economic analysis, free of political considerations. The trend may even backfire if China retaliates against foreign firms.

Such an outcome would be quite ironic. With the SAMR assuming a leadership role over the new antitrust bureau, Chinese antitrust enforcement is expected to become more legalized and professional. Yet as China is moving towards the law, the rest of the world seems to be moving away from it. As the Trump Administration continues to launch aggressive legal assaults on Chinese technology companies, China has fallen back on its vast market access by wielding its antitrust law against US technology giants. The emerging transatlantic consensus against China and the ensuing nationalist fury are drowning the voices of progressive Chinese reformists advocating for a freer and more equitable China. In fact, Western efforts to contain China will have the unintended consequences of regressing Chinese legal reforms to the detriment of foreign firms operating in China.

Afterword

We live five minutes away from the Hong Kong campus of the University of Chicago. With the closure of all playgrounds, our kids had nowhere to play and so we decided to visit the campus. Situated on Victoria Road against the background of the picturesque coastline, the campus building blends in seamlessly with the surrounding green hills and calm sea. As our kids were chasing each other around the giant university logo, it suddenly occurred to me that they may not be able to set foot on the main Chicago campus, where their parents spent the best years of their lives studying together.

Neither my husband nor I are Chinese Communist Party members and the Trump Administration has yet to adopt the proposal barring Party members from entering the country, but if the proposal becomes law, how would America verify our political affiliation? What sort of proof would we need to proffer to demonstrate this? Will we be held up and interrogated by border agents? These very thoughts send a chill down my spine.

We have always wanted our kids to study in America one day. However, if Sino-US tensions continue to deteriorate, will our children have trouble obtaining a visa to study in America? Six months ago, this thought would have never crossed my mind, but as the two countries are closing each other's consulates, I am no longer sure what the future holds. And even if our kids are able to study there, will they be safe? I have been watching with trepidation as a large number of Chinese students and scholars were charged with espionage in the United States, with President Trump allegedly saying 'almost every student that comes over to this country is a spy'.[1] And how will rising geopolitical tensions affect the way our children are treated there? Friends living in America have often described how American attitudes towards China have shifted since we last lived there. And soon, as a result of sweeping executive orders and the widened attack on Chinese technology companies, we may no longer be able to see our friends' moments shared via WeChat, the instant messaging app that Trump has banned in America along with TikTok.

---

[1] Annie Karni, *Trump Rants Behind Closed Doors with CEOs*, POLITICO (8 Aug. 2020).

My husband and I studied in America during the mid-2000s, a time when globalization was at its peak, and the United States and China were on a honeymoon. China had just joined the World Trade Organization a few years earlier, and there were high hopes that after China opened up its market, it would soon 'join the club of nations well along the road to democracy'.[2] The American people we met treated us with great hospitality and respect. I studied under some of the brightest intellectuals in the country and, after graduating from the law school, I practised law with a white-shoe firm in New York, working with some of the smartest lawyers in town. There was never once any doubt in my mind that I would not be fully accepted into American society.

It saddens me to see how Sino-US relations are heading towards divorce as tensions continue to escalate on a host of issues ranging from the trade imbalance between the two countries to passing the buck on the COVID-19 pandemic and the passage of the Hong Kong National Security Law. As an avid reader of both US and Chinese newspapers, I find their polar opposite stances quite unsettling. Neither side is listening to the other, and neither side is being heard.

Is it possible to salvage what is left of the Sino-US marriage? I firmly believe so, if the two sides are willing to gain a deeper appreciation of their differences and commonalities. As elaborated in this book, the sources of Chinese exceptionalism are deep-seated in the distinctness of Chinese institutions, which often reflect the weaknesses and inherent contradictions of the Chinese regime. Although Chinese institutions have been moving in the right direction towards more openness and transparency, changes occur very slowly. The institutional inertia that surfaced after the series of reform has largely contributed to discontent and anxiety over the way China regulates and is regulated. Yet these institutional problems have little to do with Chinese communist ideology. It is thus a serious mistake to perceive China as an existential threat that wants to overtake the West and completely subvert their existing governance framework. Above all, the current Sino-US strategic rivalry fundamentally lacks aspects of a pervading ideological conflict analogous to the Cold War.[3]

Moreover, given how deeply China is embedded in the global supply chain, any attempt to completely disentangle the US economy from China would seem unimaginable. It may also backfire. As I have repeatedly emphasized here, the Chinese state is hardly monolithic, and policy-making is often a

---

[2] Bob Davis, *When the World Opened the Gates of China*, WALL ST. J. (27 July 2018).
[3] Odd Arne Westad, *The Sources of Chinese Conduct: Are Washington and Beijing Fighting A New Cold War?* FOREIGN AFFAIRS (Sep./Oct. 2019).

pluralistic process involving government departments with overlapping and divergent missions. Furthermore, growing US hostilities against China and Chinese companies are stirring nationalistic fever, giving hardline officials an upper hand, as evident in China's increasingly aggressive 'wolf warrior' foreign policy.[4] This will have the unintended consequences of undermining efforts of the more progressive bureaucratic departments and unwinding some of China's promising institutional reforms. Indubitably, the rising Sino-US geopolitical tensions have resulted in profound mistrust between the two countries. But I remain hopeful that future cooperation remains possible, as long as China and the United States stay patient and far-sighted and continue to maintain significant leverage against each other. The Sino-US marriage does not necessarily need to have a tragic ending.

August 2020
Hong Kong

---

[4] Bilahari Kausikan, *China's Zealous 'Wolf Warrior' Diplomacy Highlights Both Beijing's Power and Insecurity*, SOUTH CHINA MORNING POST (4 June 2020).

Index

For the benefit of digital users, indexed terms that span two pages (e.g., 52–53) may, on occasion, appear on only one of those pages.